They Came Searching

How Blacks Sought the Promised Land in Tulsa

Eddie Faye Gates

3392

EAKIN PRESS ★ Austin, Texas

FIRST EDITION
Second Imprint
Copyright © 1997
By Eddie Faye Gates

Published in the United States of America
By Eakin Press
An Imprint of Sunbelt Media, Inc.
P.O. Drawer 90159 ★ Austin, TX 78709-0159

2   3   4   5   6   7   8   9

ISBN 1-57168-145-0

Gates, Eddie Faye.
    They came searching : how Blacks sought the promised land in Tulsa / by Eddie Faye Gates.
        p.   cm.
    Includes bibliographical references and index.
    ISBN 1-57168-145-0 (alk. paper)
    1. Afro-American pioneers -- Oklahoma -- Tulsa-- Interviews. 2. Afro-Americans-- Oklahoma -- Tulsa -- History -- 20th century -- Anecdotes. 3. Afro-Americans -- Oklahoma -- Tulsa -- biography -- Anecdotes. 4. Frontier and pioneer life -- Anecdotes.   I. Title.
    F704.T92G37   1997
    976.6'8600496073--dc21   96-48625
                                                                    CIP

Also by the Author:
    Miz Lucy's Cookies: And Other Links in My Black Family Support System (a cultural autobiography), Tulsa, OK: Coman and Associates, 1996.

    Cover photograph of Robert Fairchild by M. Teresa Valero, Applied Assistant Professor of Art, Professor of Graphic Design, and Professor of Photography, the University of Tulsa.

Oct. 2, 1998

Best wishes Weldon and Jean Saylor. (Great speaking at Kirk of the Hills Tonight!).

Eddie Faye Gates

To every black person who has ever been name-called, put down, and discriminated against — and that is most of us! — May you continue to get up, shake off the dust, and "keep on keeping on" until you find your Promised Land!

About the Author

Eddie Faye Gates is a former high school history teacher, public school administrator, and curriculum writer. She is currently an education consultant. An oral history project of her Edison High School students in Tulsa was designated an Oklahoma Diamond Jubilee Project in 1981. Videotapes made by Mrs. Gates in 1991 during her study of the Holocaust in Poland and Israel were used by the Tulsa Public Schools system to produce a ten-tape series entitled "Holocaust Education for Middle and High School Students."

Mrs. Gates attended Tuskegee Institute in Alabama for three years, and is a magna cum laude graduate of the University of North Dakota, where she received a B.S. degree in composite social science in 1968. She graduated with honors from the University of Tulsa, with a master's degree in history, in 1974. She studied the Holocaust in Poland and Israel during the summer of 1991.

Cover Design by

Norman Gates, Jr., Dallas, Texas. Mr. Gates studied art at Tulsa Junior College, the University of Tulsa, and North Texas State University. He won the Doel Reed Art award for a pen and pencil drawing that was exhibited at Tulsa Junior College and the Alexandre Hogue Award for a drawing that was exhibited at the University of Tulsa. He was the recipient of an Alumni Art Trust Scholarship at the University of Tulsa.

About the Photographer

M. Teresa Valero, Applied Assistant Professor of Art, Professor of Graphic Design, and Professor of Photography at the University of Tulsa, is a native of Venezuela. She graduated from the University of Kansas with a bachelor of fine arts in graphic design and art history, and later received a master's degree in art history.

Mrs. Valero has worked most of her life as a photographer and graphic designer. For three years, she collaborated with a poet on a Whittier neighborhood project in Tulsa, entitled "Families, Streets, and Dreams."

Contents

Chapter 5 The Promised Land at Last

Foreword

Eddie Faye Gates is an internationally recognized educator and she has used her talents and skills to create this moving literary project of Tulsa, Oklahoma's black settlers. *"Resiliency"* comes alive as the photos and their related stories take us back to our contemporary Elders and their visions for us. Their sensitive yet probing interviews provide the contemporary voice for this historical journey.

Hopefully, you will be challenged to give place to your own personal history makers. Make room in your life for their stories. Each succeeding generation needs the fuel provided by recalling, in words and images, the stories of their resiliency. The future of a people is intricately linked to the *memory* of their past.

Clifton L. Taulbert, Author
Once Upon a Time When We Were Colored **and**
The Last Train North.

Preface

I have always loved history. Among my earliest memories is this image of me sitting cross-legged on the scrubbed plank floor of some sharecropper's house listening to one of my relatives talk about the history of our family. My paternal grandparents, Joseph and Rhoda Wesley Petit, told me all the eyepopping details of how they came to Indian Territory in 1904 with twelve other black families by covered wagon from Lott, Texas, a little farming village near Marlin, where descendants of former slaves worked the Brazos River bottom lands just like the slaves had done in earlier years. My other grandparents, James Matthew and Retter Hardeman Minter, had an equally fascinating tale to tell about how they came to Oklahoma in 1918 by train from Como, Texas, a little all-black farm settlement near Sulphur Springs, where their ancestors had been slaves working Brazos River bottom plantations. Grandpa Minter had a greater incentive to leave Texas than my paternal ancestors; he had witnessed the lynching of his best friend. It happened this way. My grandfather and his friend had done nothing wrong. It seems that a group of Ku Klux Klansmen, upset about some event involving some other blacks, went out to find "a Nigger to string up!" Grandpa Minter and his friend just happened to be in the wrong place at the wrong time. Luckily for Grandpa Minter, the Klansmen didn't see him, so he quietly hid in some thickets (through which he could see the mob hanging his best friend). As long as he lived, he could never purge that image from his memory. Neither could he remain in a state that did such things as that. So he went home, gathered his meager savings, belongings, and family and went down to the Sulphur Springs, Texas train station and purchased tickets to the "Promised Land" in Oklahoma. (My mother, Vivian Minter, was six years old at the time and caused quite a commotion by getting lost in the train station! While frantic Minter relatives searched for her, she was being comforted by a sympathetic white family who had found her weeping and inconsolable. When Grandpa Minter saw her, he swept her up into his strong black arms and whisked her away from Texas whites and onto the train bound for Oklahoma. He never set foot in Texas again, not even for noted Minter family reunions. Mother, now 84 years old, says "that memory of Papa sweeping me up into his arms that day is the happiest memory of my life!")

Other relatives assuaged my cravings for historical knowledge including my favorite uncle, John Spencer Petit, with his colorful stories about Oklahoma cattle trails and cowboys, living and dead outlaws (he actually viewed the bodies of some of them and described in explicit details the gunshot wounds and the tagged toes of the "brought down" outlaws), tornadoes and dust bowls, happy times (feasts and festivals on Oklahoma prairies), and sad times including the infamous Tulsa Race Riot of 1921.

With all of this historical background under my belt, and my insatiable desire for more historical knowledge, I decided to do further research and write a book about Tulsa's early black pioneers which included some of my relatives like my great aunt, Cynthia Petit Bankhead, who was the only woman on the planning committee for the 1925 National Negro Business League meeting which was held in Tulsa August 20, 1925 just four years after the race riot. I have a long photograph, which I purchased at the Admiral flea market in Tulsa, hanging on the wall in my living room which shows those attending that meeting.

And so I did just that. I researched in libraries, museums, government archives, Indian council houses, city halls, abstract offices, and countless other places in and out of the state, and did further interviews with black pioneers and with white eyewitnesses and survivors. Then came the hard part — sifting the chaff from the wheat from all of this research and writing a compelling, historically accurate account of the experiences of Tulsa's early black pioneers. It has been a long and loving literary journey.

PURPOSE AND SCOPE OF THE BOOK

And it shall come to pass afterward, that I will pour out my spir-
it upon all flesh; and your sons shall prophecy, your old men shall
dream dreams, your young men shall see visions.

Joel 2:28

From pre-statehood days to the present, people have come to Tulsa seeking a better way of life. With its mineral-rich lands as a compelling magnet, people of all races, colors, creeds, and nationalities came here from all over the United States and from overseas to "make their fame and fortune."

Early black pioneers who came from all over the Deep South and from other regions of the United States had a vision, a vision that life would be better here for them and their families than it had been in their oppressive, often bitterly cruel, previous home lands. Though not able to participate fully — politically, economically, and socially — in their new home land, many blacks did manage, despite rigid segregation and both overt and covert discrimination, to carve out colorful, meaningful, productive, and rewarding lives in their new "Promised Land" — Tulsa.

This book tells in their own words and images, the aims, hopes, and ambitions of early black pioneers and of the pitfalls that they faced, including the terrible 1921 Tulsa Race Riot, and of their tenacity and persistence which enabled them to regroup and build again from the ashes of defeat. They will offer sage advice which — if taken — will ensure the continuation of their dream, a dream for a better life for all black people in Tulsa.

The black pioneers, and the white eyewitnesses and/or children witnesses of the Tulsa Race Riot of 1921, have been and continue to be some of the most sought after subjects in Tulsa. Their accounts of Tulsa's history-in-the-making, and especially of the Tulsa Race Riot make them "community treasures," natural repositories of a wide range of valuable information to writers, historians, journalists, photographers, and others.

Mary Elizabeth Jones Parrish, a black professional journalist, was the first to write about the Tulsa Race Riot of 1921. Her little book, *The Event of the Tulsa Disaster*, 1921, includes poignant testimonies of riot survivors who fled the Greenwood area when it was under siege May 31-June 1, 1921. She and her little daughter Florence Mary barely escaped with their lives when they finally joined the frightened, running crowds that fled down Greenwood Avenue with bullets zinging all around them. Her book is quoted by Scott Ellsworth, the white historian who wrote the definitive account of the Tulsa riot.

Ruth Sigler Avery was a child when the Tulsa Race Riot of 1921 broke out. She committed the brutal images of that event to her memory and to paper. Her intensive research for decades is perhaps the most thorough of any of the riot writers and historians. At the University of Tulsa she knew more about the race riot than her professors and they admired and respected her for that. It was Ruth Avery who befriended a young doctoral student, Scott Ellsworth, in the 1970s and gave him a list of names of black riot survivors, some of them featured in this book. Ellsworth went on to write the definitive book on the Tulsa riot — *Death in The Promised Land*. And Tulsans are thrilled that after seven decades of research and writing, Ruth Avery has her manuscript ready for publication! David Boren, University of Oklahoma president and former U.S. Senator from Oklahoma, who was one of the dignitaries at the 75th Anniversary Commemorative Ceremony held at Mount Zion Baptist Church just off Greenwood on June 1, 1996, has taken a personal interest in the Avery book. An OU publishing review team will look at the Avery manuscript. Tulsans can hardly wait to see the fruit of Mrs. Avery's long, extensive research about the Tulsa Race Riot of 1921.

Others who have felt the call to "do something" regarding the Tulsa Race Riot of 1921 are whites such as General Ed Wheeler whose riot research is legendary, and Beryl Ford who has perhaps the largest collection of riot memorabilia in Oklahoma, Ron Wallace, a black historian, who wrote a book called *The Truth about Black Wall Street*, Dorothy Dewitty, a black retired educator and second black councilor in the city of Tulsa who wrote about Tulsa's black history, State Representative Don Ross, award-winning photojournalist Don Thompson, young black Tulsa film producer Mitchell Lane, British documentary film producer Rob Rohrer, award-winning documentary film producer Mike Wilkerson of Tulsa, a host of others too numerous to mention, and me. The research of Don Ross, a black who represents Tulsa's predominantly black community in North Tulsa, resulted in *The*

Ruins to Renaissance photo exhibit on permanent display at the Greenwood Cultural Center in North Tulsa. An identical exhibit tours nationally and internationally. *The Black Settlers: The Search for the Promised Land in Tulsa* photo exhibit of Don Thompson (with captions and biographical text by this author) is on permanent display at the University Center at Tulsa, also located on Greenwood Avenue in North Tulsa.

In 1990 Mitchell Lane produced a documentary film about the Tulsa Race Riot of 1921, entitled *Little Africa on Fire*. In his research, he uncovered the name of an eyewitness to the Dick Rowland/Drexel Building elevator incident and located the man who was ten years old in 1921. This man's testimony differed from that of other eyewitness testimonies in that the man said that Rowland was the elevator operator and that Sarah Page was a messenger girl for Western Union. He also said that it was common knowledge that white girls had relationships with some of the black men who worked in the downtown "white area," and he said that was the case with Rowland and Page. Some other subjects, beginning with the Mary Louise Jones Parrish testimonies in 1921, and continuing through the recent testimonies gathered by current researchers such as Ruth Sigler Avery and this author, said the same thing about a Rowland/Page romantic relationship. Some even said that the couple went to Kansas City and got married. Rob Rohrer, an independent documentary film producer from Liverpool, England, came across the Atlantic Ocean to interview Tulsa Race Riot survivors and eyewitnesses. Mike Wilkerson, documentary film producer from Tulsa, noted for his award-winning documentaries shown on the Arts & Entertainment television channel (including films about Lizzie Borden, the girl scouts murders in Locust Grove, Oklahoma, and Judge Parker, the hanging judge), interviewed many of the persons featured in this book. And in the future there will be still others — those who will get their pens, pencils, computers and cameras ready for yet another interview with these pioneers who have an insight into Tulsa history like no other people. Oral history has "come into its own." Stephen Spielberg, whose film, *Schindler's List*, was so widely acclaimed, has put all of his other film-making projects on hold until he finishes interviewing Holocaust survivors. He feels such an urgency to complete this, as the survivors are getting on in age and some are passing on before their stories can be told. There is even more urgency to record the memories of the Tulsa Race Riot survivors and eyewitnesses because they are two decades older than Holocaust survivors. So I, Eddie Faye Gates, join those researchers and writers who love oral history and this book tells of my experiences with the wonderful people who shared their pioneer experiences and their riot memories with me.

Some of these pioneers bask in their "community treasure" status; others are reluctant participants but they cooperate with a never-ending stream of questioners in the interest of history.

Acknowledgments

Any book that is published involves the commitment and efforts of many people, but a book such as this is especially a collective effort. This book is in reality authored by all of the pioneers who were interviewed for this project, by descendants of those pioneers who are no longer alive who generously shared information and materials about their beloved ancestors, and by many others who gave countless information and memorabilia to me (such as the purple, suede 1924 Booker T. Washington High School diploma of Dr. Lloyd Hume Williams given to me by Dr. Lloyd Hume Williams, Jr.), and to others who helped in ways too numerous to mention.

Three helpers stand out because of their extraordinary efforts on my behalf: Mrs. Jeanne Goodwin, Mr. Robert Fairchild, and Mr. Clarence Love. Jeanne Goodwin, with her "schoolmarm knowledge" of Tulsa's history, her mother's wit and common sense, her delightful, wry sense of humor, and her contacts with Tulsa's black community via her family's *Oklahoma Eagle* newspaper, her church, and her organizations, has been of invaluable help. When I could not find an address or phone number, I would call Mrs. Goodwin with my frantic requests. Within thirty minutes or so, she would call, rattling off the missing information about the people "I just had to interview!" She and I talked almost daily — not just how-do-you-do, "girly" chats, but serious talks about history and people. For instance, long before an Oklahoma Historical Society oral history expert and I revised my questionnaire, Jeanne Goodwin had suggested the very changes that the expert suggested! She was also very successful in cajoling reluctant interviewees to participate. It was the women who were most reluctant; they worried about their hair, their dresses, and their "declining good looks" as they phrased it. Mrs. Goodwin soothed them, calmed their fears, and convinced them to share their histories with me. An added bonus was having contact with Mrs. Goodwin's large, extended family. A family reunion brought relatives from all over the U.S. and Canada to Tulsa in July 1994. I was honored to be chosen as one of the tour guides for the two chartered busloads of Goodwins that visited the Ida Dennie Willis Museum of Dolls, Toys, and Miniatures in Tulsa. Mrs. Goodwin's daughter, Jeanne Arrandondo of Houston, a fellow University of Tulsa alumni, visited my home and looked at some of the videotapes of the black pioneers, including the one of her feisty little mother.

When neither Mrs. Goodwin nor I could locate some hard-to-find prospective interviewee, I turned to ninety-two-year-old Robert Fairchild who has the "bloodhound sense" of an FBI agent. I first met Mr. Fairchild when we both worked on the Smithsonian Institution Project "Climbing Jacob's Ladder," an exhibit about black churches in which some of Tulsa's oldest black churches were featured. I was a planning committee member and Mr. Fairchild was an interviewee.

When I was stuck on locating a prospective interviewee, Mr. Fairchild did some sleuthing. He already knew where some of the people lived that I needed to locate, and through his sleuthing, he found all the others. Not only did he find them, he rode with me when I hand-delivered questionnaires and interviewed the little old pioneers. He was a God-send. He opened doors for me that I, a member of the "younger generation," could not have opened myself. These prospective interviewees, Mr. Fairchild, and I had some great talks during introductory visits, and the follow-up interviews. I am also grateful that Mr. Fairchild was with me to protect me from dogs. Some of those little old people had some mighty big, aggressive dogs! Overcoming my fear of dogs is another problem that I am working on.

Another "oldtimer" that I called upon frequently (I had more interviews with him than with any other participant) was Clarence Love. Not only is he a walking encyclopedia about music, he also knows the history of Tulsa as well as anyone, and better than most.

I am also particularly grateful to 82-year-old Dr. Charles Bate, one of the forty-five pioneers in this book, who gave me an auto-graphed copy of his meticulously researched book, *It's Been a Long Time, And We've Come A Long Way*, which chronicles the history of medical care for black Tulsans from pre-statehood to the present, and to Robert N. Hower, former KTUL television (Tulsa) news anchor, who shared heretofore unknown and unpublished materials left to him by his grandfather, Maurice Willows, who was sent by the American Red Cross on June 1, 1921, to "minister of the needs of poor, hapless, homeless negroes" who were victims of the Tulsa Race Riot of 1921. This was the first time in the history of the Red Cross that the agency had aided victims of "non-natural disasters." Black survivors of the Race Riot heaped praise upon the quiet, unassuming Mr. Willows and even named Tulsa's first black hospital after him. Some of the survivors are still alive and one, Mrs. Tennessee Perryman (also one of the pioneers in this book) was one of the first black nurses to be trained in the Willows hospital.

Robert Littlejohn, a University of Tulsa-trained geologist, and genealogy buff, and Curtis Lawson, an attorney and former black Oklahoma House of Representatives member, are presently doing research to write a book about Indian settlement in the Americas. They are especially interested in Creek Indians since they have ancestors who were of that tribe. Mr. Littlejohn has traced his lineage back to a Scottish trader named McIntosh who intermarried with the Creek Indian clans of Georgia and founded the famed (and sometimes infamous) McIntosh line of Creeks which, through intermarriage, spread to the Grayson (Grierson), Hawkins, Marshall, Barnett, McGillvary, Hodge, and Perryman clans of Creeks, all significant figures in the settlement of Tulsa. What is not generally known is that many of Tulsa's founding Creek families were black and many allotments that were sold to make room for downtown Tulsa building projects and for outlying expansion into the Utica Square, Bixby, and Coweta areas were owned (and sold) by black Creeks. Without the sharing of previously unpublished information about the intricate relationship between native Creek Indians, white traders and settlers, mixed blood Creeks, and black Creek tribal members, the Perryman-connected pioneer vignettes in this book (Tennessee Perryman and DeEtta Perryman Gray) would not have been complete. I am extremely grateful to Mr. Littlejohn and Mr. Lawson for unselfishly sharing some of their hard-earned research with me so that the true Indian and black history could begin to be told. From their research materials, they plan to write a book about their families' settlement in Oklahoma. They believe that they have uncovered information that will show that they are not descendants of African slaves brought to the Americas by European slave traders, but of Africans who explored and settled in the Americas, before the exploration age of the Europeans. They believe the peoples that the European explorers called Indians were (and are) descendants of early Africans. They believe that is the only explanation for the identical characteristics of mounds in Africa and of mounds in the world. Tulsans anxiously await the book of Mr. Littlejohn and Mr. Lawson.

There were other people who helped by providing me with information or contacts while I was writing this book. I am deeply indebted to them. They are:

State Representative Don Ross
State Senator Maxine Horner
James O. Goodwin, Attorney at Law and Publisher of *The Oklahoma Eagle* newspaper, Tulsa
Dr. Thomas Buckley, Dean of History, The University of Tulsa
Dr. Robert Nelson, Coordinator of Research and Testing, Tulsa Public Schools
Michael McMahon, Director, Media Department, Tulsa Public Schools
Leon Rollerson, Media Department, Tulsa Public Schools; Owner/Producer, Rollerson Broadcasting, Tulsa

Others who offered artistic, literary, or technical advice to me periodically were Charles White, Ruth Sigler Avery, John Pribram, all of Tulsa, Nancy Hope Sober of Ponca City, Dr. Ronald Hall of St. Paul Minnesota, Vladka Meed of New York City, and Dr. Richard Majors, University of Wisconsin professor who was then on leave to the Urban Institute in Washington, D.C.

For excellent media coverage, city-wide, I thank *The Oklahoma Eagle* and *The Tulsa World*, Leon Rollerson of Cable channel 41, and the local Tulsa television stations KJRH Channel 2, KOTV Channel 6, KTUL Channel 8, and The Oklahoma Educational Television Authority's KOED Channel 11, Tulsa (which broadcasts out of Oklahoma City), and my favorite radio station KRMG, Tulsa. John Erling, popular KRMG personality, is one of three people in Tulsa that I know who attended my alma mater, the University of North Dakota. Michael Taylor, a former Tulsan, and a talk show host on KPFK Radio in Los Angeles, California, did an excellent show about the research for this book and about information uncovered about the Tulsa Race Riot of 1921. (Mr. Taylor was found tragically murdered in Los Angeles in 1996.) A Los Angeles documentary film producer, Muffett Kaufman, heard the program and called me about making a film about the race riot!

Dr. Charles Christopher and his wife Dr. Anita Christopher were always on call when I needed my glasses tightened so I wouldn't tug constantly at them when I was interviewing pioneers. Alta Mae Davis, Norma Dennie Leshie, Donald Stephens, and Alonzo Batson also helped me to get nervous interviewees ready for interviewing. The women were always the ones who needed "settling down"; the men just sat down and started talking.

Also special thanks to the owners of Wilson's Family Store on East Apache Street in North Tulsa, Ebony Expressions store in the Gilcrease Hills Shopping Center, and to Kathy Wiley and Sharon Ntow. All of them help us African-Americans to purchase the fashions and other memorabilia that link us to The Motherland Africa. Kathy can transform fabrics into African works of art! Sharon, who is a native of Ghana, helps her African-American sisters in their bonding-with-Africa quests. She keeps us "authentic," that is as "authentic" as one can be on this side of the Atlantic Ocean.

My good buddies Dyanne Mason, LaVerne Hill, Helen Jones, Bobbie Johnson, and Ida Dennie Willis, all well-known, professional Tulsa women, were always available when I needed help, or when I just needed a listening ear.

Thanks to those in Oklahoma City who were so helpful during the research for this book — Rodger Harris and Dr. Bob Blackburn of the Oklahoma Historical Society, Betty Price of the State Arts Council, Donkor Khalid of the Multicultural Department of the State Department of Education, Paulette Black of the Arts in Education Department of the State Department of Education, and Robert Allen of the Oklahoma Educational Television Authority. Also Kay Bond and the rest of the staff at the Cherokee Strip Museum in Perry, Oklahoma.

After the extensive interviews with black pioneers of Tulsa, I felt the need for balance, a need for the input of white Tulsans who had knowledge of the Tulsa Race Riot of 1921. An appeal went out in the *Tulsa World* and the response was overwhelming. Rodney Echohawk, a reporter for the *Sand Springs Leader* newspaper, called and was most helpful. He has long been interested in the riot and has done feature articles in his newspaper about the event. He also has an extensive file of collected materials about the late oil millionaire Charles Page who is known as "the father of Sand Springs." Mr. Echohawk, a Creek Indian and relative of noted artist Brummett Echohawk, offered me access to any of his files. He also gave me some vital contacts for this project including his mother, Rachel Echohawk Pingry who as a young widow at 30 once stayed in the Charles Page Widow's Home in Sand Springs. In addition to her first-hand knowledge of Mr. Page, she has vivid memories from her childhood about her father's stories about the riot. I was also led to contact Opal Clark, an elderly woman who grew up in the Charles Page orphanage. From her memories, and materials, she wrote a book (published by Coman and Associates, Tulsa, Oklahoma, the same publisher that published my autobiography) about her life and about Mr. Charles Page whom she greatly admired. Her book is now in its 8th printing. But the best contacts of all that I made via Mr. Echohawk were the ones with the actual descendants of Charles Page — George Campbell, a 92-year-old retired attorney and nephew of the late Mr. Page. Mr. Campbell was a wrestler at Oklahoma A & M College in Stillwater (now Oklahoma State University) in the old days and helped the school win a national championship. Mr. Campbell lives in a nursing home and was not up to an interview. I did interview his delightful daughter, Lotsee Campbell Spradling, who lives on a huge ranch, "The Flying G," five miles west of Sand Springs. She gave me explicit directions on how to find and recognize the ranch (a huge red bull statue beckons visitors). She also gave me one of the best interviews given during my research.

Rocky Frisco, a Tulsa musician, whose band J.J. Cale once played a British Broadcasting Company broadcast, gave me vital information about the role of airplane pilots during the Tulsa Race Riot of 1921. His father was a pilot, and a racist who spoke to his son about the influence of the film *The Birth of a Nation* upon him and upon Tulsa mobsters. He said that before his father died, he repented and was sorry for his former racist views and actions during the riot. I wasn't aware that the Ku Klux Klan had so heavily infiltrated the music industry at that time.

Three other eyewitnesses to the Tulsa Race Riot of 1921, when they were children, shared their memories with me. H.A. Johnson was a fifteen-year-old when the riot broke out. He lived on Pine Street and says that he and another boy stood all day and watched the mob activities on June 1, 1921. They actually witnessed shootings and they watched the terrified blacks fleeing the riot area. Mr. Johnson worked forty-six years at Sun Oil Company in Tulsa and now lives in an apartment in Skiatook, Oklahoma.

Robert Hull, Jr. was the son of a Christian Science practitioner who hid her black maid during the riot. She also hid relatives and friends of the maid who sought a safe haven in the midst of the inferno.

Dovie Tucker was a 17-year-old girl when the riot broke out. Her parents ran a general store/post office/blacksmith shop near the riot area. Mrs. Tucker observed the frenzies of the riot and she never forgot the sight of those fleeing blacks.

Beverly Culmer's father, C. R. Stanley, was a baker and was one of the Tulsa mobsters, but just for one day. He later regretted that he became caught up in the mob fever and rode with the Klan that day, June 1, 1921. His daughter says that he was so ashamed and so appalled because of his actions that day. He said that "I just got caught up in the mob fever. I will regret that until my dying day!'

Betty Eldridge lived on Archer Street in 1921. She gave vivid details of four men taking part in the riot in a touring car — her grandfather and three uncles.

Mrs. Jean Houston's late husband was later a photographer for Channel 6, CBS television, Tulsa. He left her an extensive file of riot-related photographs which Mrs. Houston generously shared with me.

Other whites who responded gave extensive interviews which are featured in chapter 6 of the book.

Norman Gates, Sr., is the best proofreader that I know. His methodical engineering mind, and his slow, careful approach to proofing, perfectly balanced my bullet-speed editing which often caused me to overlook something.

Norman Gates, Jr., is one of the most talented artists that I have ever known. At age five his artistic talents began to emerge and he gets better every day. He was able to take his mother's grandiose pie-in-the-sky ideas and create book covers that said exactly what she wanted to say!

Pace Printing store in downtown Tulsa provided valuable services to me when I wanted them done "yesterday." Thanks to them, and also to Ed Eakin and Virginia Messer at Eakin Press.

Grateful acknowledgment is made for permission to publish the copyrighted works of participating authors, newspapers, magazines, electronic materials, etc. Every reasonable effort has been made to trace the ownership of all materials included in this book. Any error that may have occurred is inadvertent and will be corrected in subsequent editions provided notification is sent to the publisher.

Introduction

The black pioneers featured in this project were like all other human beings who have walked this earth. They had feelings and basic physical, psychological, and spiritual needs which they sought to fulfill. They adapted to their environment, circumvented obstacles, and utilizing everything in their physical and mental environments, they survived; some even prospered.

That they were human should never have been an issue, but it was. What made it an issue was their biological differences (skin color, eye color, hair texture) from the people who had wrestled control of world power between the fourteenth and nineteenth centuries — white people of Europe and the Americas. Oh what a difference those extra drops of melanin in the skin of black folks made (and still makes)!

It was not until July 1950 that a group of science experts from all over the world met at the United Nations Educational, Social, and Cultural Organization (UNESCO) in Paris, France and adopted a definitive statement on race. The lengthy document, replete with scientific jargon, can be succinctly summarized by the following simple statements:

1. All men (Note: this is a generic term for mankind and includes women) belong to the same species - Homo Sapiens.

2. Human races, at the present time, are classified by most anthropologists into three major divisions — the Mongoloid division, the Negroid division, and the Caucasoid division.
3. All men (mankind) are probably derived from the same common stock.
4. Differences between different groups of mankind are due to evolutionary factors such as isolation, hybridization, and natural selection.
5. Groups with varying degrees of differentiation have been classified in different ways for different purposes.
6. The likenesses among men (mankind) are far greater than their differences.
7. The different races are capable of interbreeding with one another, and can interchange blood, organs, etc.
8. Isolating barriers, physical and environmental, plus cultural and social ones, kept human populations more or less separated and as a result, they exhibit certain physical differences.
9. Unfortunately, most people use the term "race" in non-scientific ways. Many national, religious, geographic, linguistic, or cultural groups have been erroneously identified as races of people.
10. Whatever classification the anthropologist makes of man, he never includes mental characteristics for it is generally recognized that intelligence tests do not in themselves enable scientists to differentiate safely between what is due to innate capacity and what is the result of environmental influences, training, and education.
11. There is no definite evidence that there exists inborn differences in temperament in the various human populations. As for personality and character, these may be considered raceless. In every human group a rich variety of personality and character types will be found, and there is no reason for believing that any human group is richer than any other in these respects.
12. It must be asserted with the utmost emphasis that equality as an ethical principle in no way depends upon the assertion that human beings are in fact equal in endowment. Obviously individuals in all ethnic groups vary greatly among themselves in endowment.

The scientists at UNESCO in Paris in 1950 concluded with a summary that basically said that biological studies lend support to the ethic of universal brotherhood; for man is born with drives toward co-operation, and unless these drives are satisfied, men and nations, alike, fall ill. Man is born a social being who can reach his fullest development only through interaction with his fellows. The denial, at any point, of this social bond between men and other men brings with it disintegration. In this sense, every man is his brother's keeper. For every man is a piece of the continent, a part of the main, because he is involved in mankind.

It is ironic that something so simple as a biological mechanism for the adjustment of human beings to their environment (which is what "race" is) should have become such a complex issue, often with life and death consequences. But that is exactly what happened in human history. Skin color, eye color, and hair texture that once helped people to survive in tropical Africa became entangled in all kinds of psychological and sociological baggage which detracted from and diluted what observers like Alexis de Tocqueville and Gunnar Myrdal called "a near-perfect representative form of government," our very own American democracy.

Though the scientific facts stated above were always true, it was a long time before many Caucasians could accept them; some still don't. Sometimes emotions block rationality and reason. It was during World War II that many white soldiers proved for themselves the scientific fact that all human blood was the same. Faced with the prospect of bleeding to death or receiving "Negro blood," they opted for the latter. One Southern soldier, appearing in the Tony Brown Journal program, "When The Eagle Flies," rejoiced over having had red blood of a black soldier pumped into his veins as he lay dying on a European battlefield. He was not only grateful that his life had been saved; he was grateful for having overcome the ignorance of racism.

Misunderstandings and misinformation about race, ethnicity, and culture have resulted in fractured, insecure, and troubling periods in American history that appear and reappear persistently and methodically. Here are a few definitions to help clear the air and lift the fog of confusion:

Race - biological characteristics — skin color, eye color, hair texture — by which one is born into one of the three major scientific divisions of mankind.

Culture - a system of acquired knowledge and beliefs that people use to interpret their experiences and generate and define social behavior.

Ethnic group - people identified by common race, religion, language, culture, etc. (Poles, Irish, Germans, Jews, etc.).

Ethnic pride - positive feelings about one's own group or culture, characterized by wholesome activities such as St. Patrick's Day celebrations, German Oktoberfest events, African-American Kwanzaa celebrations, etc.

Ethnocentrism - belief in the superiority of one's own culture characterized by negative speech and actions toward other groups.

Assimilation - giving up or compromising one's own culture in order to be accepted, or to become a part of the dominant culture in one's society.

Cultural plurality - numerous cultural groups with distinct individual cultures peacefully coexisting with each other, all sharing the same basic, over-all opinions about religion, government, education, values, etc. while respecting, and even appreciating, the rich varied individual cultures in the society. (Note: The federal government of the United States, when dealing with its diverse populations, uses the term "the federal five" — European-Americans, Native Americans, African-Americans, Asian Americans, and Hispanic Americans).

Life would have been different for the black Tulsa pioneers, and their ancestors before them, if the principles of universal brotherhood had been accepted by all mankind; but they weren't and oh what a difference that made! Erroneous beliefs about race, coupled with greed and avarice, led to the largest enslavement of human beings in history. The rippling effects are still being felt to this day, both in a stripped and debilitated Africa, and in a fractured America that still has to come to grips with the issue of race.

African Heritage

Oral Traditions, Family Values, Religion, Culture

*I*n addition to sharing the biological characteristics of race (all black pioneers featured in this book had at least one progenitor of African descent; some of them had only African ancestors, but others also had slave master blood running through their veins), most of the African ancestors of the Tulsa black pioneers shared a common cultural experience — a painful wrenching from their homeland in Africa and a no-return voyage across the deep waters of the Atlantic Ocean on a slave ship.

Africa, the second largest continent in the world, was not always viewed as a dark and heathen continent whose peoples were useful only as slaves. In fact, if one examines an historical timeline, it can be readily seen that until the 1400's Africa and its peoples were perceived of as human beings just like the rest of the human beings inhabiting the planet earth then, and they coexisted, peaceably for the most part, participating in lively trade (gold, salt, and ivory) and exchanging ideas with Europeans, Asians, and other Africans along the Indian Ocean route, donkey caravan routes, the Guinea Forest route, trans-Sahara route, and the Mediterranean and Red Sea trade routes. No inferences of inherent inferiority prevailed then; in fact, the peoples with whom Africans traded and interacted with wrote complimentary accounts of their endeavors with the Africans.

Having an abundance of highly desired natural resources — gold, salt, and ivory— resulted in Africa developing empires comparable or superior to those in Europe, Asia, and the rest of the known world then.

There are many references to Africa in the Holy Bible. In Genesis it is stated that all people in the world today are descendants of Noah's three sons — Shem, Ham, and Japheth. Ham's family is supposed to have moved westward into Africa and ancient maps of Africa called the continent "the land of Ham." Early Bible books refer to Egypt as a mighty empire in the northeast section of the African continent. The Pharaohs of Egypt were African conquerors and their great stone pyramids, built by slave labor, remained for thousands of years as the largest buildings ever raised by man. They were one of the seven wonders of the ancient world.

Ethiopia is mentioned frequently in the Bible — its rivers, its people, and its trade. It was then called Nubia, and was part of what is now Egypt and the Sudan. The Hebrews called it the land of Cush because Cush, the son of Ham, settled there. Queen Sheba journeyed all the way to Jerusalem to visit King Solomon (a child born nine months later was the ancestor of the Ethiopian royal family. Haile Selasse, the Conquering Lion of Judah, from this royal dynasty, was deposed in 1975).

Other Bible persons who had experiences in or with Africa were Abraham (who sheltered there from a severe drought) and Joseph who sojourned to Egypt. Palestine, or Canaan, was economically dependent on Egypt during the time of Abraham, Jacob, and Joseph. The great biblical teacher Moses was born and educated in Africa. Joseph, husband of Mary, fled to Egypt with the baby Jesus. At the crucifixion of Jesus, Simon of Cyrene, (present Libya) was sympathetic to the mocked-and-scorned Jesus and was forced by Roman soldiers to carry the cross. An Ethiopian eunuch was converted to Christianity by Philip.

The early African kingdom, Egypt, was superior in culture, art, architecture, science, and knowledge at this time.

The main products of ancient and medieval Africa were ivory, gold, and salt. The earliest records of international trade with Africa is an Egyptian hieroglyphic of the era of Queen Hatsheput's reign in 1477 B.C., showing the return of Egyptian merchants from the land of Punt, now known as Ethiopia.

Later Africa's more exotic exports — its animals — captured the attention of its trading partners. A Chinese emperor was so enthralled with a giraffe from Africa that he sent a special expedition back to Africa just to take more giraffes to China!

When the early European, Arab, and Oriental merchants and traders first explored Africa they found spacious, orderly cities and cultures that were similar, in some ways, to their own cultures of the same time period. They found royalty living in more elegant dwelling places than their subjects, just as in their lands. Examples were the Oba (King) of Benin in Nigeria, or the King of Dahomey,much later, in the nineteenth century, Queen Zhinga of Nigeria, the counterpart of England's Queen Victoria.

The fact that, prior to the 1960's, not much was known in the Western world about African civilizations is due to bias on the part of Western writers. What the Western world called "World History" was but an extension of the study of Europe or the New World (of European colonization) with focus on antiquity in terms of Greece and Rome. It has been said that history is "the lie agreed upon." The "lie agreed upon" by Western leaders perpetuated the myth of African inferiority and European superiority for much too long!

British historians are credited with "opening up" World History to include all continents and all peoples of the world. Basil Davidson is perhaps the foremost British expert on Africa today. His extensive research is heralded by scholars and students alike on all continents. One-third of the information for his books was based on African records; the rest is from European, Asiatic, and American chronicles. His works, those of his fellow British, and those of scholars and authors on other continents, as well as the perspective of time, have allowed some of the myths about Africa to die, have allowed some wounds to heal, and have opened up the way for further setting the record straight regarding Africa and its peoples.

In the 1960's and 1970's, American historians and authors wrote extensively on the hot topic of Africa after the civil rights movement of the '60's gave credibility and validity to Africa. The civil rights movement had generated much interest in Africa, in slavery, and in the after-effects of slavery. All kinds of writers got on the "bandwagon of African validation." A plethora of books, electronic media presentations, guest lectures, travels to the African "motherland," etc. prevailed in America, and the rest of the world. Some of the literary and electronic works were excellent such as

Alex Haley's phenomenal book, *Roots*, published in 1971, which put the finishing touches, in a charming, readable manner, to African history and culture. Others were just awful and should never have seen the light of day, and they wouldn't have had it not been for the "Africa euphoria" permeating the country at that time. Nevertheless,a moveable feast of information about Africa exists today. No longer is there any excuse for anyone, anywhere, to remain ignorant about Africa or about peoples of African descent!

The recent research about Africa and its peoples has led to much new information about a long-neglected region and people.

Historical research and archeological explorations in Africa by European and American scholars and anthropologists uncovered a gold mine of information about Africa, information sorely needed to set the record straight concerning the "Dark Continent." These learned people found that the term The Sudan, meaning "the country of the Black People," was used by the Arabs to refer to the great belt of savannah stretching across Africa from the Atlantic Ocean to the Red Sea. North of it lies the Sahara Desert, south of it the tropical forest. In the west the Niger River flows through the Sudan. It was in this region that large, well-organized, predominantly black states, called empires, were established during the period known to Europeans as the Middle Ages. These empires were significant in a commercial sense because of their great markets where goods were exchanged; they were also significant because from the eleventh century onwards, until the slave trade permeated Africa, the towns of the Western Sudan were the main centers of learning and science at the time.

Among the great kingdoms (empires) in West Africa were Timbuktu, Ghana, Mali, Songhai and Benin. Artifacts from the Nok, Benin, and Hausa cultures in Nigeria, memorabilia from Ghana, and from other cultures in ancient West Africa are on display in museums in the world's largest and most renowned cities.

In Inland Africa was the Congo Forest Region. Despite isolation, pestilence (mosquito, termite, and tse-tse fly), human life and conditions had not stood still in the region. Scientists found that the whole continent of Africa, with the exception of the Bushmen, had passed from the Stone Age to the Iron Age at about the same time as the Europeans. (A few tribes, like the one studied recently by National Geographic in the Philippines, and a few other examples in the world, have still not made the transition). The Bantu tribes, ruled over by the King of Congo, knew how to work metals including iron and copper, and were potters, and skilled weavers. They were friendly to traders and missionaries and were often spoken of by Europeans as being the most intelligent of the African peoples.

In East Africa were the thriving, bustling Swahili empires of Naga, Cush (Kush), Meroe, Axum, Punt (Ethiopia), Malindi, Mombasa, Kilwa, Mozambique, and Sofala.

The Great Mosque Ruins of Kilwa, built in the twelfth century, in East Africa, and The Great Zimbabwe Ruins in South Africa were so superbly built, without any mortar, that at first Europeans refused to believe that they had been built by Africans. Today, there is archeological and anthropological proof that they were indeed built by Africans!

Africans had their respected, beloved, and sometimes feared leaders just as Europe did. There was King Ezana of Axum (now Ethiopia), a descendant of King Solomon of Israel and the Queen of Sheba, who converted to Christianity in 333 A.D., making the Abyssinian Kingdom of Ethiopia the world's oldest Christian nation. Mansa Musa, King of Mali in the 1300's, was considered the wealthiest man in the world at that time with salt the source of his kingdom's wealth. On a pilgrimage to the sacred Islamic city of Mecca, he and his entourage changed the economy of all the nations they crossed. Sunni Ali and Askia Mohammed were rulers of Songhai, while Dom Alfonso I was King of the Kongo. Dom Alfonso, who became a "blood brother" of the Portuguese monarch, was praised by the Europeans for having such a progressive, efficient form of administration in his nation. Tenkhamenin, King of Ghana, had one of the largest standing armies of his time in 1067. He could raise an army of 200,000 warriors. William of Normandy conquered England in 1066 with 20,000 troops.

In conclusion, the decline of Africa, and the "mythification" of Africa as a dark continent of noble, cannibalistic savages came with the advent of the European slave trade. Before that, Africa, Europe, and Asia had a long history of mutually satisfying trade in which all the peoples were treated with respect.

While little was known about the interior of Africa since most trade was done in coastal regions, there was no supposed natural inferiority regarding Africans and no theories about the inherent failure of the continent to develop and mature; those theories were developed to explain and justify the European-developed slave trade which disrupted the normal routine of Africa.

When human populations, consisting mainly of the "cream of the crop" of human populations — the strongest, healthiest men and women of child-bearing age — were taken out of Africa, from the fifteenth century through the nineteenth century, and when the continent was left to be exploited of its bountiful natural resources of gold, ivory, and diamonds by Europeans to enrich their countries, a formula for the failure of Africa was created, and the rippling effects are still being felt on that continent to this day. Likewise, the rippling effects of the institution of slavery are still felt by peoples of African descent on the continents where they live today, mostly in North and South America.

It can never be known exactly what route African civilization would have taken, or to what levels it would have risen, had not the European/American slave trade impacted the history of the continent. But even a child, with but a rudimental understanding of the concept of cause and effect, could make some logical assumptions. It is obvious that Africa and its peoples would have been better off had its prime resources — its strongest, most able-bodied men and women, and its rich mineral resources — been available to industrialize and make affluent its peoples rather than Europeans and Americans.

African history might not have exactly paralleled Europe's or America's. Even with similar human and natural resources, nations often develop differently due to religious, social, and cultural differences. It is known that the Africans had a world view that differed significantly from the European world view. They were more inward peoples, less inclined to travel and colonization (though there are records of some exceptions); they were also oral people who focused less on written records. They were also very religious peoples — animists, Moslems, Christians, and others — who placed great emphasis on sharing the natural world and natural order with all living creatures as well as with the ancestral dead. But, given the fact of the early examples of African civilization which paralleled or exceeded European civilization before the European slave trade era, it can be assumed that the line of civilization and culture would have continued.

So this was the heritage that the black pioneers in Tulsa had inherited from their African ancestors. That these captured and enslaved ancestors were able to hold onto some vestiges of their previous culture, under extreme hardship including the pain of death, and to pass that culture on to their progeny is a tribute to the indomitability of the human spirit. This dogged determination helped the ancestors of today's African-Americans to survive the strange, new world of slavery in an alien, hostile, and strange land. Later, this legacy also helped early black Tulsa pioneers survive in equally strange and hostile places.

The American Experience

Slavery, The Civil War, and Reconstruction

The Portuguese explorer who plucked the first slave from Africa's west coast in the 1400's didn't realize that he was making world history; but that is exactly what he did! From that single event, a form of commercial slavery would later develop, a slavery unparalleled in human history.

The first handful of hapless Africans whose paths crossed European explorers in Africa at this time were viewed as mere exotic trophies, not unlike the giraffes and other exotic African animals taken back to Europe in earlier eras. Captured African slaves, taken to Europe, became household novelties — "exotic" servants in the homes of affluent Europeans. Later, 1441 to be exact, the European slave trade system began. In that year, a Portuguese captain took aboard his ship twelve Africans whom he had captured along the coast of Mauritania. These slaves were taken to the Portuguese capital of Lisbon not as exotic trophies, but as products to be sold for cash. Within twenty years as many as 800 slaves a year were brought from Africa to Portugal.

The profound need for field labor in the Americas (the attempt to enslave the Native Americans there had dismally failed) led to the creation of the European/American slave trade, a massive economic enterprise that changed the course of world history. Before it was brought to an end almost four hundred years later, this slave trade system had ripped millions of Africans from families and villages and had wreaked havoc, cruelty, and suffering upon those captured peoples wherever they were taken. On the other side of the coin, this slave trade system allowed the European nations to plunder an Africa weakened by this unnatural, massive slave trade system and to enrich, industrialize, and "civilize" their imperial kingdoms.

This was not the first example of slavery, nor were Africans the first peoples ever to be enslaved. According to anthropologists and historians, slavery has existed since the beginning of mankind and was practiced in Biblical days, and in early Greek, Roman, and Arab history. Africans also sold slaves, themselves, before the creation of the European/American slave trade. These earlier forms of slavery were, however, totally different from the commercialized, race-based, closed system of the European/American model.

In ancient civilizations, conquering armies used to routinely kill defeated enemy soldiers and all males in conquered villages (keeping the women as concubines). Enslaving conquered males, instead of murdering them, was often a welcomed alternative; thus, this early form of slavery was actually considered a civilizing influence in society.

Early Greek and Roman slavery was non-racial, was usually the result of military conquest, and was an "Open" slave system where there were ways that slaves could gain freedom — through marriage, religious conversion, service in the military, through monetary purchase, etc. Greek slaves were usually treated with dignity and respect, many of them serving as teachers. In fact, the Greek word for educator is "pedagogue" which originally meant "slave." Slaves who had fought for the Roman Empire were routinely granted full citizenship and became useful, productive citizens in the empire.

It was the Arabs, moving in from North Africa, who organized the slave trade on a commercial basis. They were also the last to give it up, Saudi Arabia not doing so legally until 1962. Arab slavery began as earlier forms of slavery had — as a result of military conquest; later, Arabs took slaves at random on their caravan routes through Africa. Even so, Arab slavery differed greatly from European/American slavery. It was also an "Open" slave system. Most Arab slaves were used in households where they were treated well by their masters. In fact, many converted to the Islamic religion and became "brothers with their masters," in the same religious faith. Historians agree that the cruelty and harshness found between slaves and masters in the Americas rarely existed in the Arab world, or in any of the other places where slavery was practiced in earlier times.

One of the most mystifying aspects of European/American slavery is the role of African leaders, in the process. Some apologists have used this as a basis for exoneration of European slave traders. But according to leading scholars such as Basil Davidson, the renowned British historian, and perhaps the foremost expert on ancient, medieval, and modern Africa, it is a misconception that African chiefs sold their own people into slavery. Rarely did that happen. Like leaders in other time periods, and even to the present, African chieftains had a double standard for the treatment of its respected and valued populations and its undesirable populations. It was these less desirables — captured enemies "prisoners," malcreants, etc. in the society — who were sold into slavery. Davidson cited five basic reasons for African participation in the slave trade:

1. **Military Necessity:** African chiefs traded with Europeans at first with a variety of commodities — ivory, gold, copper, cloth, etc. and a minimal number of slaves. The main good that African chiefs desired in exchange were guns which were needed for protection from neighboring, hostile tribes;

2. **Fear:** There was fear that one's own tribe would be used by European slavers if the chiefs did not provide slaves from their "undesirable" population pool. Thus chiefs did willingly sell war captives, convicts, and others not considered a part of the tribal group. On the other hand, they fought desperately to keep their own from becoming slaves and pleaded with European monarchs for the return of respected members of their tribes who had been "mistakenly" taken. Chronicles of such pleas are available today such as the poignant plea of Dom Alfonso, King of the Congo, to a Portuguese monarch. Sometimes in an effort to prevent their own tribe from being enslaved, African tribes raided "enemy" territories and their hapless victims became the slaves of the Americans;

3. **African Misconception of European Slavery:** It has already been mentioned that Africans practiced slavery, but accord-

ing to historians it was not the equivalent of European slavery. It was not chattel slavery in which the human slave was regarded as property without any rights. According to leading historians, African slavery was more a form of serfdom. Thus, Africans holding such serfdom beliefs had less compunction about selling slaves to the Europeans;

4. **Greed:** Some African chiefs succumbed to the lure of easy booty, and indiscriminately sold slaves in exchange for guns, liquor, and cheap baubles;

5. **Hopeless Entanglement:** Many African chiefs who participated willingly in the early slave trade balked when slavery began to get out of hand and to dominate European/African trade relationships. But they were so hopelessly entangled by then that they could do nothing against an industrially-superior continent made so ironically by slave labor.

One reason that the European/American slave trade was able to last so long according to historians was the lack of world support for Africa, and the absence of world censure against Europe and the Americas. There were various psychological, sociological, and economic causes for this mindset of the era. Africa was a non-Christian continent and its inhabitants physically strong, and noticeably different racially, which would make the mechanics of holding slaves simpler; also, slavery was a lucrative economic endeavor. Thus Europeans and Americans reconciled their spiritual values and political principles so that they could justify the institution of human slavery, and the system flourished.

According to leading historians and scholars such as Phillip Curtin, Basil Davidson, Edward R. Kolevzon, and others, one cannot underestimate the role of African slave labor in promoting the wealth, affluence, and industrialization of Europe and the Americas.

What started out in West Africa as "novelty slaving" in the 1400's soon turned into the lucrative, four-hundred year European/American slave trade. The first African captives were from nearby coastal regions of Africa, where so many slaves were captured that the region, once known as the Gold Coast, was renamed the Slave Coast. The Slave Coast and the ports from which human cargoes sailed for an infinitude of slavedom were called "slave factories" because there seemed an endless supply of slaves

out of Africa. Slave pens, coexisting side by side, held slaves captured by the British, Dutch, French, and Portuguese until the
slavers had enough cargo for the Atlantic trip. Germans, Italians,
and other Europeans, less colonial-minded and/or less successful
than the colonials listed above, got in on the tail end of colonialism.
They played a lesser role in the colonial carving up of Africa.

Later, during the seventeenth century, when the demand for
slaves grew at a rapid rate, as England, France, and Holland started
colonies in the Americas, slavers began to go into the heartland of
Africa for slaves. Historians estimate that millions of captives died as
they marched, often in chains, from the heartland of Africa to the
coastal factories. Those who survived the long treks across the rugged
African terrain were housed in the slave pens of the various European
slave traders until they could be packed onto slave vessels for the no-
return Atlantic voyage. Millions more died of hunger and disease as
they crossed the Atlantic in overcrowded slave ships.

Much has been written about Goree Island's House of Slaves
in Senegal, West Africa. In the seventeenth century, a Dutch explorer had named the island, located at the westernmost tip of Africa,
Goree Island. It was the closest and most vital slave trade depot to
America, and it was the last view of home for half of the African
slaves shipped across the Atlantic between the fourteenth and nineteenth centuries.

The pinkish looking stone building known as the Slave House
is noted for its "Door of No Return." At the end of a dark stone
corridor in the house is a rectangular hole through which the blazing light of the sun is reflected from the Atlantic Ocean. Slave ships
would pull up to that door and captured Africans would be pushed
through that hole onto the ships for their last voyage. The sight of
that hole evoked terror, and according to some records, the most
unnatural, disturbing, agonizing human wails ever made by man and
heard by man!

Today, some African-Americans, viewing this umbilical connection to their past, are said to have been overcome by intense,
profound grief and sadness at the sight of that rectangular door. For
those wishing the exact location of Goree Island, it is cradled in the
lee of Cape Verdi Peninsula, three kilometers — about two miles —
from Senegal's coastside capital, Dakar, which has been sometimes
called "Paris of West Africa." That title is also claimed by the Ivory
Coast's city of Abidjan. The old Goree Slave House is now a rose-

colored, stone museum with a courtyard abloom with bougainvillea and other tropical flowers. But, like Nazi concentration camps in Europe, that Slave House cannot be sanitized or beautified enough to remove the horror of its past.

Between the fifteenth and nineteenth centuries, the African continent earned the nickname "Black Mother" because of its seemingly inexhaustible supply of humanity exported to work the mines and plantations of the western hemisphere. Nobody will ever know the exact number of slaves transported to the Americas (and to other parts of the world — Europe, India, and even China). Estimates have varied from between fifteen million and fifty million as the grand total of human cargoes while others have stated that the total was even higher.

There were two methods for packing the slave ships, the "loose" method in which fewer slaves were packed on board and where there could be better nutrition, hygiene, and sanitation with a resulting lower mortality rate during the voyage, or "tight" packing which was just the opposite and whose results were also exactly the opposite. Slavers who practiced the "tight" method of shipping unceremoniously dumped the bodies of slaves into the chilled waters of the Atlantic Ocean every few days or so.

Some slave ships were very detailed and orderly with separate cells for men, married, childbearing women, and special cells for virgins, for children, for recalcitrants and unruly slaves. A few slaves — including mothers who jumped overboard into the cold Atlantic waters with their children rather than be slaves — committed suicide rather than complete the no-return voyage to America, but most captives survived the voyage and landed at seaports in the Americas for their new lives in a strange and alien land. (Sometimes, there was a stop in Liverpool, England before the final voyage to America).

Some slaves, destined for the United States, were first "seasoned", or "broken in", in the West Indies. The "Triangle Slave Trade," that is, the trading of African slaves for Latin American rum to be exchanged for more slaves in Africa, proved a very lucrative commercial endeavor for Europeans. It was one more link in the lucrative commercial institution of human slavery.

The first glimpse of the new world for enslaved Africans was of the coastal cities in which they landed — Boston, Philadelphia, and New York in the earlier days of slavery, and of New Orleans, and Charleston, in the later slave era. The indignity of the auction block, where they suffered dehumanizing searches of their teeth, tendons, muscles, and any other body parts that would-be masters wanted to examine, awaited them — and then to the fate that Europeans and Americans had outlined for them — the Southern plantations to toil as unpaid servants in a growing and prosperous land!

There are numerous resources about the slave trade and about plantation life in the United States, some focusing on the political or economic aspects of slavery, and others stressing the social and human factors of slavery. One of the best which balances all of those factors is Dr. Kenneth Stampp's *The Peculiar Institution*. Dr. Stampp, University of Wisconsin-trained, and a history professor at the University of California, Berkeley, 1946-1965, visiting professor at Oxford University 1961-1962, and at Harvard in 1955, wrote the definitive book on slave life in the United States. Slavery was indeed a peculiar institution, for it clearly conflicted with the high spiritual and democratic principles upon which the American nation had been founded. And it caused a kind of self-delusion in the nation in which pseudo psychological and sociological "theories" were developed to explain away the inconsistencies and to justify the unjust institution of human slavery.

Dr. Stampp, who finished his distinguished career as a Harvard professor, tells the story of slaves, collectively, yet his chronicles of the daily lives of slaves — the sound of the clanging bell at sunrise, to the slaves' "tired and fitful slumber" when they fell into makeshift beds and pallets in dirt-floored cabins often after midnight after they had fed and tended to their own children and families — make the reader feel a oneness with each individual slave and share his or her painful plight.

Even under the trying system of slavery, slaves managed to carve out a "subculture" and most of them adapted to the system at least in a surface way, and survived. Some learned to read and write, and became skilled craftsmen, inventors, etc. But most just lived the subsistence life of a slave. Slave narratives, and accounts by descendants of slaves, help to personalize the institution of slavery.

When it became impossible for the northern states of the United States and the southern states of the nation to co-exist, despite a series of compromises regarding the painfully divisive issue of slavery, the Civil War occurred. The years 1861-1865 represent one of the most tragic periods in U. S. history, during which brother was pitted against brother, and physical and mental destruction, unparalleled in the history of the American people, devastated both the North and the South.

Blacks fought in this war just as they had fought in all of America's previous conflicts, and just as they have continued to do so to the present time. Though black male slaves were left to tend the plantations while white men went off to fight for their way of life, many of them left and joined up with Union troops to help fight for their own liberation. Some were cited for their bravery; others were captured by infuriated Southerners and given terrible retribution for their "betrayal of their masters." One such incidence involved Confederate Gen. Nathan Bedford Forrest who later founded the Ku Klux Klan. He summarily executed a group of captured black soldiers during the Civil War.

EMANCIPATION: It is ironic that there has been such emphasis placed on President Abraham Lincoln's Emancipation Proclamation of January 1863 since it did not free a single slave! It ordered those holding slaves to free them, but since the Confederate states where the slaves were being held had seceded from the Union, the document was not binding on them and in effect did not free a single slave. Still it was a good public relations item. Psychologically it did the slaves some good — it gave them hope or rather it did those things for those slaves who learned about it. The ancestors of some of the black settlers in this book living in Texas didn't get the news until June 1865. That gives black people a celebration day. To this day Juneteenth celebrates the day that Texans learned about emancipation. Although emancipation didn't free anyone, still the principle of it is worthy of celebration. Present day Juneteenth celebrations, such as Tulsa's popular Juneteenth celebrations annually on Greenwood Avenue, are rooted in that first celebration held in Texas.

RECONSTRUCTION: There are two schools of thought regarding Reconstruction:
  1. That it was a period of undue, unjust and punitive hardship upon the South which resulted in:

a. Whites being severely punished with malice by the North for having broken away from the Union.
b. A period of pampered, preferential treatment for undeserving blacks which resulted in their premature inclusion into the political, economic, and social strata of southern society.
c. An erosion upheaval, and destruction of a noble "Southern way of life."
2. That it was a period at first that marked a watershed in American history, when it appeared that America would, at last, live up to its professed high spiritual ideals and democratic principles and become a nation of equality, justice, and freedom for all of its citizens. It was a period marked by:
a. Transition from rhetoric to reality for black people marked by government policies which began the implementation of political, economic, and social inclusion for black citizens.
b. Unparalleled progress for black people during which significant educational and political gains were made, including blacks serving in high political positions in local, state, and national governments.
c. The eventual abandonment of black people in 1877 into the hands of their former enslavers.
d. The return of harsh, punitive Southern white rule to the South during which black people were returned to virtual slavery via illegal and extra-legal means — Jim Crow Laws, "gentleman's agreements," and "spiritual and physical terror" at the hands of the Ku Klux Klan;
e. The beginning of a century of benign neglect at best, and cruel, condoned abandonment at worst by the United States in regards to its black citizens.

During and after the Civil War, there were great losses on both sides. But there are some clear successes after the war that must be recognized and acknowledged. Slavery was abolished (13th Amendment); citizenship and equal protection under the law were established (14th Amendment); and political representation for all citizens guaranteed (15th Amendment). Other vital platforms in the mosaic of American democracy were established also. Black Tulsa pioneers believe that the second view of Reconstruction, listed above, is the most accurate. Black people in America saw the initial gains that their people had made during the Reconstruction Era, 1865-1877, vanish when the U.S. government struck a deal in the 1876 "Contested Election" (between Samuel Tilden and Rutherford B. Hayes). In exchange for Southern support, government troops were withdrawn from the South and full control of the South returned to Southerners. The hopes of blacks for full political, economic, and social assimilation into the American democracy were harshly dashed. There ensued nearly a century of second class citizenship for blacks. It would not be until the 1960's that the United States seriously addressed the issue of equality for all American citizens.

In the interim, the ancestors of the Tulsa black pioneers resigned themselves to more hard times. With the unfulfilled promises of Reconstruction ringing in their ears, they buckled down for the long haul to freedom and a better way of life. They felt the tremendous loss of the coveted forty acres and a mule — promised, but never delivered. That is why there is a movement in the United States today for black reparation payments similar to the payments that the U.S. government made to Native Americans and to the Japanese for injustices committed against them.

And so, after Reconstruction had failed them, the grandparents and the parents of the Tulsa pioneers featured in this book set out to find The Promised Land. It obviously was not in the Deep South where they had witnessed such colossal levels of political, economic, and social oppression including systematic, and increasingly routine lynchings!

The cruelest blow, perhaps, was the failure of the newly freed blacks to share in the government's subsidization of westward expansion at that time. Many of today's "fiscal conservatives" in government who decry "the modern welfare state with its endless entitlements" live safely and securely on economic dowries first procured by their ancestors because of early post-Reconstruction westward expansion policies of the U.S. government! Many a bootstrap for economic advancement was created for whites then. But not for most African-Americans! Their ancestors were systematically, and deliberately, left out (with a few exceptions). Lacking bootstraps with which to pull themselves up, and even lacking boots, they left the Deep South where promises had been broken and their dreams had become nightmares. The forty acres and a mule that they were promised never came. And so they left, by wagon trains (like the Petit and Chatman relatives of Tomissa Chatman, featured in this book), by horseback, by train, by automobile (in various stages of disrepair), and by foot. They migrated in search of a Promised Land.

It is ironic that as newly freed blacks made the transition from slavery to freedom, they made some of the same mistakes that their enslavers had made. For instance in creating their subcultures, they adopted one of the main characteristics of the dominant, white culture — a caste system based upon skin color, and hair length and texture. Just as those biological characteristics had determined which black people would work in the "Big House" and which would work in the fields, so in freedom caste was used to delegate roles in the black culture.

W.E.B. DuBois, in his classic book *The Souls of Black Folk*, describes the wrenching conflict in the souls of black Americans as they struggle to reconcile their two cultures, their two selves — their black selves, their American selves — in an often hostile land. But these ancestors of ours did just that, and their offspring, the pioneers in this book, did adapt, did reconcile, and did survive! Using mother wit, wisdom, cunning cleverness, and even humor, they overcame terrible odds and lived, some of them even prospering, in a less-than-hospitable land.

Wayne Faubion, Ponca City, former cowboy, Big V Ranch west of the 101 Ranch

Cowboy Hill Burial Grounds, Ponca City, OK.

Grave of Bulldogging black cowboy Bill Pickett in the segregated graveyard, Ponca City, OK

Windmill, Oklahoma

Oil well, Oklahoma

Philip Rhees, age 8, with Pete the Greaser, Drumright, OK, 1921. Drumright was largest oil field in the world at that time. Pete is shown with the horse-drawn oil-residue spreader, which had an oil-sprinkling device in back, to sprinkle the oil residue which couldn't be refined for sale. The mixture waterproofed the oil field roads.

Ponca City, Oklahoma pioneers Gerald and Nancy Hope Sober

Post-Reconstruction/ Freedman Era

Wanderings, Migrations, Settlements

O ne of the most unsettling periods in American history, especially for black people, was the post-Reconstruction period after the federal troops pulled out of the South in 1877 and Reconstruction officially ended.

White Southerners, still chafing over their loss of the Civil War, and their "noble way of life," took back control of the South with a vengeance; black people bore the brunt of their anger. It would be a dark period in United States history, with many a blot on the spiritual and democratic principles upon which the nation was founded. For nearly a hundred years, black people in America would undergo bondage for a second time. It was during this period, or immediately following it, that most of the black pioneers of Tulsa embarked for "The Promised Land." Their meanderings took them over tortuous roads and streams and many of them wound up in Oklahoma which was being widely advertised then as a heaven on earth. A variety of advertising, including David Payne's pamphlets,which were even posted in federal buildings in Washington, D.C., whetted the appetite of searchers.

These black pioneers were not the first Americans, nor the first people, to seek a Promised Land. From the beginning of history, people have searched for better land and for a better way of life.

In biblical days Moses searched, and from the top of Mount Nebo in the land of Edom in Southern Jordan. He caught a glimpse of the Promised Land for his people. Other Hebrew children, and countless mortal beings since, have also diligently searched for promised lands.

Other searchers for "a good life for their people" were already in the region now known as Oklahoma when some of the parents and grandparents of the black pioneers featured in this book came. The Indians (now called Native Americans) had been here longest. The plains tribes had been here millennia before the first European explorers came in the 1500s. The Five Civilized Tribes (so-called because their culture was most like the "civilized" European culture) had been here since the 1820s and 1830s, when some came voluntarily because they sensed the eventual takeover of the South by European Americans and others came by forced removals. A few of the black Tulsa pioneers' grandparents came on the forced marches. But most came during the unsettled period after the end of Reconstruction. Other nomadic tribes, plains tribes, had been in the region even longer.

White settlers were already here: The first Europeans to set foot on what is now Oklahoma soil were the explorers who came from Europe in the fifteenth, sixteenth, and seventeenth centuries in ever increasing numbers to explore the Americas. Black men were on those early voyages too. Diego el Negro was a crewman on Columbus' final voyage, 1502-1504. Nuflo de Olano was one of thirty blacks with Vasco Nunez de Balboa when he reached the Pacific Ocean and Ferdinando de Soto is known to have brought blacks to the Mississippi River. In 1520 Spanish conquistador Hernando Cortez had about 300 blacks in his company when he explored the area now known as Mexico, one of whom planted the first wheat in the new world. Blacks were also part of expeditions in South America. Estevanico (Little Stephen), a black with the Spanish expedition that found the Seven Cities of Cibola, is believed to have been the first black to set foot in Oklahoma. He was later killed by Zuni Indians.

Later European American settlers in the region were the cattlemen who came during the brief, brisk cattle boom when Oklahoma's proximity to cattle towns in Texas and Kansas made the territory's lands, trails, and creeks prime property as drovers pushed their herds across the Goodnight-Loving Trail, the

Chisholm Trail, and other cattle trails across the territory. It has been estimated that between 1866 and 1886, five million cattle were driven from Texas to cattle towns in Kansas!

Next came the oil men in the early 1900s, the adventurous, wheeler-and-dealer entrepreneurs who became Oklahoma's new royalty — people, mostly from the eastern United States, people whose names would soon be household words in Oklahoma — Harry Ford Sinclair, James A. Chapman, J. Paul Getty, Robert F. Galbreath, Josh Cosden, Charles Page, William G. Skelly, Billy Roeser, brothers Frank and Waite Phillips, E.W. Marland, and Thomas Gilcrease, Earl Harwell, Joseph A. LaFortune, Dewey Bartlett, Sr., James M. Gillette, Robert M.McFarlin, and others. Some of the names would become household words in the nation. When the city couldn't supply the needs of these rich oil men, they built their own banks and bridges, hotels and restaurants, and, of course, their elegant showcase mansions. These men were like little boys with new toys and tried to outdo each other, especially in building their homes. Tulsa is blessed to have such a wonderful collection of these elegant dwellings, some of which are on the National Register of Historic Homes.

When Edwin Drake brought in the first oil well in Titusville, Pennsylvania on August 27, 1859, he started a craze. Soon it seemed that "every man and his brother" wanted to make a fortune in oil — which they called black gold, crude. It wasn't always that way. The first dabblers in oil soaked up the golden globules from standing waters with blankets, squeezed the oil out by hand, bottled it and sold it as elixirs (medicine)! But the liquid gold that came in after the 1860s was used for another purpose — fuel/energy, and it ushered in a new era in American history.

People first began dabbling in oil in Oklahoma in the 1870s, but the first commercial oil well in Oklahoma was drilled in 1897 in Bartlesville, Oklahoma (a town named for oil man Jacob Bartles). That enterprise is now Phillips Petroleum Company.

On June 24, 1901, oil was discovered at Red Fork, four miles west of Tulsa. The "Sue Bland," named after the part-Creek Indian wife of one of the owners, Dr. J.C.W. Bland (the other partner was Dr. Fred Clinton), was the first real gusher drilled in Oklahoma. *The Kansas City Star* and other national newspapers wrote about it, calling it a "real gusher" coming from a depth of 534 feet and spouting its liquid gold fifteen feet over the top of the oil derrick!

Naturally, this kind of media attention grabbed the nation and soon Oklahoma was overrun by oil speculators, other speculators, gamblers, promoters, lawyers, hucksters, and fortune tellers. By the way, legend has it that the Sue Bland proved to be a flop, producing only two barrels of oil during its four-day existence, only two measly barrels after that magnificent fifteen-foot gushing beginning!

What really put Tulsa on the map, oil wise, was the Glenn Pool oil explorations, just outside Tulsa. Ohio-born Robert F. Galbreath brought in the "Ida Glenn" well on November 22, 1905; he later brought in 121 more wells, only one of them being a dry well, and Tulsa's legacy as "Oil Capital of the World" was ensured.

Some of America's wealthiest men didn't actually come to Oklahoma, but they invested in Oklahoma's oil industry. Andrew Mellon, the Pittsburgh tycoon, invested $7 million in Glenn Pool, beginning the Gulf Oil Company. Not all of the investors made fortunes; some made fortune after fortune, and lost all like Josh Cosden, who lost two oil fortunes, and Billy Roeser, who lost a $50 million fortune — every single penny, plus his big mansion and all the fancy things he had bought with oil. Even those who lost their fortunes did not seem to regret their "oil experience." It was an exciting era for those dream-makers, those adventurous risk takers, those ambitious nomads of the past. Their discoveries changed Oklahoma's history. Oil would become the state's single most important resource for decades to come.

The railroad men came right on the heels of the oilmen, building the rails to carry out the liquid gold being siphoned from the bowels of the earth. Soon the plaintive wails of train whistles from competing railroads could be heard as the convoys rolled down the tracks of the respective railroads — Atchison, Topeka, and the Santa Fe; The Katy; and the Midland Valley. In 1939, the three stations combined to occupy one building, a beautiful art deco building at First and Boston which was called The Union Depot. The depot was closed in 1967. Due to intense citizen efforts, the building was saved from demolition to make way for "urban progress." Today it is an inheritance from the past that Tulsans savor; it also houses the offices of the Wiltel Company.

Interspersed with all these populations, from the beginning, were farmers, and others all seeking their Promised Lands — gypsies, and a variety of religious peoples seeking prosperity and a place to practice their religion in peace. (Jews established strong roots in early Oklahoma and today Oklahoma City and Tulsa have sizeable and prosperous Jewish communities.)

All these diverse peoples and cultures did coexist in the rough-and-tumble Indian Territory and Oklahoma Territory, not always peaceably however. Sovereign Indian nations took care of law and order in their domain (hanging trees are part of the "archives" in cities in Oklahoma that served as tribal capitals in the old days) and Judge Isaac Parker dispensed frontier justice at a federal level from his Fort Smith, Arkansas court, where many an Oklahoma outlaw had his day in court, and his night in a lonely cemetery. Many others simply took the law into their own hands and to this day "the gun barrel mentality" is alive and well in Oklahoma!

When the black pioneers' parents came to this region in the late 1800s and early 1900s, there were more white farmers in the region than ever before. Having worn out or seriously diminished the growing power of the soil in the original Atlantic states, the Ohio Valley, and the Midwestern states, European American farmers had now pushed into Indian Territory and Oklahoma Territory, which would be called the state of Oklahoma after "marriage" in 1907.

All the settlers in Oklahoma had many questions when they set about making Oklahoma their Promised Land. Where would they stay, what would they eat, and who would be their neighbors? Would they be safe in this "wild and wooly" western frontier region? Using mother wit, all the lessons they could pull from the recesses of their minds, and by trial and error, they found the answers to all those questions. They lived in hastily thrown together shelters; they ate what they could trap and forage. They befriended others and the "frontier spirit" or "the prairie mentality" of live-and-let live flourished in the region. A poignant example of this was the practice of leaving little prairie string dolls in trees for future little migrating children to play with. Legend has it that when families came across the prairie by wagon train there was little room for children's toys. Mothers saved all their yarn and string scraps and made small dolls for their children to play with. At each stop, a string angel was left in a tree to safely guide the next wagon train and to provide a toy for a tired little traveler in search of the Promised Land. (Note: Prairie string dolls may be purchased at the Pawnee Bill Museum in Pawnee, Oklahoma. My little string doll is on display at the Ida Dennie Willis Museum in Tulsa).

It is a miracle that the parents and grandparents of Tulsa's black pioneers had been able to keep some of the remnants of their African heritage — the folklore, rituals, food patterns, fashion, hairstyles, etc. — given the punishment they received for such "blatant insubordination" as clinging to, and practicing, their "heathen" culture. But they did! And with that knowledge, together with what they had learned running the plantations of the South, they were able to put down roots in Oklahoma.

From their storehouse of information, held mostly in the minds of the people since many had not had the luxury of formal education and could not read and write, they were able to survive. Their first dwellings were temporary — quilts spread under wagons, quilts thrown over saplings and trees, nearby caves, and abandoned dwellings, in various stages of disrepair, relics left behind by former searchers who had gone on to new Promised Lands.

Their first permanent dwellings were mainly farms and the houses reflected either their economic status (usually extreme poverty) and the natural environment (rock, sod, lumber — whichever was available). From their plantation days, they had learned about the environment, about nature and climate. They knew which side of the land to build the house to provide the most comfort during the changing seasons (bedrooms were located on the southwest side of the house to take advantage of prevailing winds to lessen the effects of Oklahoma's scorching summers, and to provide protection from its cold north winter winds). They knew to locate their barns far enough from the house (to the east or northeast) to keep the pungent animal odors away, but near enough for the farmer to get his gun to protect his animals and property; their outhouses were located far enough (to the east and northeast, like the barns, but closer to the house for those nocturnal visits) in order to curtail odors and to avoid contamination of their water wells.

They knew which breed of hogs would provide the most meat and lard for the family (Poland China, Duroc, Yorkshire) and which chickens would provide the most eggs (Leghorns), which would provide the most meat for the stewing pot (Domineckers, Buff Orphingtons, Rhode Island Reds), and which chickens were the most maternal and aggressive, and most likely to survive predator attacks (Leghorns, Banties). Some of the pioneer wives loved raising exotic chickens — fuzzy-feathered chickens with naked red bottoms, and chickens known for their colorful combs, plumes, and feathers. They knew that guinea fowls made good "watch dogs," and were noted for their snake control and tick control abilities. Also black people loved the dark, succulent meat of the guinea fowl. (Someone ought to do a study on why blacks prefer the dark meat of fowl over the white. Without black clients, fast-food chicken places would have a glut of dark meat to dispose of!) These pioneers also knew that raising geese was a good option, for not only did they provide eggs and meat, but feathers for pillows and mattresses.

The pioneers knew which breed of cow would produce the most milk (Holsteins, Guernseys), which would produce the most butter (Jerseys), and which would produce the most beef for the table (Herefords, Angus) for those rare occasions when a beef would be slaughtered for family consumption, and to share with neighbors.

They knew that mules were more "user-friendly and cost-productive" than horses, and so began the tradition of black farmers and their sturdy mules. But if a farmer just had to have a horse or two, he preferred the large, Morgan, work-horse type of horse. Black farmers also liked the looks of the American Saddlebreed, the Appaloosa, and various quarterhorse breeds, though rarely could any of them afford such-animals.

Pioneers also had an assortment of other "utilitarian" animals on their farms such as goats and sheep. They also had a regular run of nondescript cats and dogs of assorted sizes and breeds. Some of these animals were useful and earned their keep; others were totally useless but gained a permanent home due to the softheartedness of pioneer wives and children.

Pioneers knew what crops to plant and where to plant them for maximum productivity and efficiency. The women knew what flowers and shrubs to plant, for beauty and for pest control, and what vegetables to grow in their gardens.

Most of the black pioneers featured in this book did not move directly to Tulsa. First, their families had settled in various, isolated rural regions of Oklahoma, or in small farm hamlets such as Tullahasse, Beggs, and Wetumka, or in slightly larger towns such as

Muskogee and Okmulgee, not too far from Tulsa, or in areas a good bit further to the north such as Perry and Pawnee. Some Oklahoma towns such as Henryetta were so unfriendly to blacks that they had "Sunset Laws," which meant that a black had better not let the sun set on him in that town! Some blacks, in an effort to offset such policy, founded their own towns — at one time at least fifty-eight all-black towns flourished in Oklahoma, such as Liberty, Langston, Red Bird, Gibson Station, Tullahassee, Chase, Marshalltown, Ferguson, Lincoln City, Wellston Colony, Boley, Grayson, Boynton, Summit, Redland, Moffet, Wybark, Taft, Foreman, Bookertee, Clearview, Rentiesville, Vernon, North Fork Colored, Lewisville, Canadian Colored, Lima, Bailey, and Tatum.

When these early black pioneers tired of farming and small-town life, they left to come to that magnet for black people in northeastern Oklahoma — Tallasi, Tullahassee, Tallahassee (Creek Indian for "Old Town"), Tulsey, Tush Hog Town, T-Town, or as it is known now, Tulsa! Here, in their own words, are their stories of their search for the Promised Land in Tulsa.

4

In Their Own Words

Tulsa Black Pioneers
Tell Their Story

ALICE ANDREWS
b. May 23, 1902, Shellville, Texas

I am grateful to God that I am able to get around, take care of myself, be active in Morning Star Baptist Church in North Tulsa, and be active in my housing complex. With the help of my "little buddies," I can do anything that I want to! "Little Buddy" (a small, generic walker) takes me all over my little apartment and allows me to do my own cooking and cleaning; with "Big Buddy" (a larger walker), I can get to my garden (a small terrace outside her high-rise North Tulsa Senior Citizens apartment overlooking downtown Tulsa), and with "Best Buddy" (a wheelchair), I am able to go on the weekly bus tour from the complex to a major mall in south or east Tulsa.

I am grateful to God that I still have my good memory. How I remember those good old Greenwood days. Greenwood was something else! We had clothing stores, shoe stores, hotels, and all kinds of businesses on Greenwood then. Oh, black Tulsa always had an abundance of hotels. First, there was O.W. Gurley's hotel and then A. Huff's hotel, and the Phillips, Titus, Morgan, Carr, and Sanders families which had hotels. There was the Stradford Hotel at 301

Alice Andrews

North Greenwood. From Archer to Cameron Streets, in the Greenwood area, we had beautiful hotels then like the Strassner which was a three-story hotel that reached from Cameron Street to the alley where Vernon AME Church is now. Mrs. Warren also had a beautiful three-story hotel, and Hotel Small was a big, roomy three-story hotel. We had ladies dress shops, hat shops, and shoe shops. For a wider variety of dresses, we went to Second Street in downtown Tulsa to Cohn's, a Jewish store.

Blacks had some nice houses, too. John Emerson was the first black man in Tulsa to build small, practical houses for black people off Apache and Zion streets. It was sort of like a first housing project in North Tulsa. Then the Mann brothers built an addition where Highway 75 is today. Some of those houses still remain. I wish you could see them. They are very nice little houses. You know what is important about the success of John Emerson? He only completed the third grade, but he was an excellent builder! Tell that to the young people. They need to learn to have faith in themselves. They must learn to respect their talents and cultivate and use them; then they can be successful just like John Emerson was!

The one thing that black people didn't have in Tulsa then was public transportation. Before Simon Berry introduced public transportation to North Tulsa in the 1920s, there was no pavement any further than Greenwood Avenue. The only transportation that blacks had was the old Sand Springs streetcar which went down the Santa Fe Railroad tracks and the Midland Railroad tracks. When we got off at the Greenwood stop, we had to walk down the railroad tracks to keep out of the mud. Simon Berry brought transportation to North Tulsa with his little jitney which cost only five cents. Then he bought a second jitney. White people eventually got a hold of Berry's transportation system, but black people were always grateful to Simon for being the first to add North Tulsa routes to the public transportation system of Tulsa. To us, Mr. Berry was a hero. Later, he was framed and sent to prison, but to us he was always a hero. He kept us black people from having to keep walking down railroad tracks to keep out of the mud!

The worst thing that happened to black people in Tulsa's history was that awful race riot in 1921. I knew Dick Rowland well; I had known his daddy, who everyone called "Dad" Rowland before Dick was born. Dick was the boy who accidentally bumped into or stepped on the foot of a white girl in an elevator. When whites got through "blowing up" that incident, they had made it into a sex attack in the elevator! About Dad Rowland, he owned a lot of property in North Tulsa — a little shop of some kind on the corner of Greenwood and Cameron, and where his shop stopped on Greenwood, and all the way to Cameron Street, a whole block of little shotgun rent houses. My sister-in-law (Ed Lacy's mother) lived in one of those rent houses. I used to babysit Ed and his brother in one of those little houses. They were such sweet and obedient children. Dad Rowland had other property besides these properties in the Greenwood area, too. So that Dick Rowland was a well-off boy. He didn't have to work if he didn't want too. But he did work, as a bootblack. Anyway that's what I know about the Rowlands.

That riot was a terrible thing. At the time, I lived with my mother in a little house on the corner of Norfolk and Oklahoma Streets, not too far from the Greenwood and Pine area, but far enough away that we were not in danger of being burnt out. I was asleep the night of May 31st, but my mother witnessed the riot and the riot aftermath. She said she sat at her living room window all night watching the people running down the Santa Fe Railroad tracks, just running and running trying to get away from the horrors of the riot. There were no paved roads in North Tulsa then. That is why the women and children were running down the railroad tracks, so they could keep out of the mud. The women were still in their nightgowns and they were holding their children's hands and just dragging them along. The children were crying. We later learned that the men had been rounded up and taken to the Convention Center, the Fairgrounds, the 11th Street and Skelly Drive area (now the University of Tulsa stadium area), Booker Washington High School, churches, and other places for "safekeeping." What that actually did was to leave the Greenwood area defenseless. What made it even worse was that the Home Guard troops that were sent in sided with the whites. That is what allowed things to get out of hand so quick. Mobs just went on the rampage with no restrictions put on them by white authorities. They looted and burned straight down Greenwood, all the way to Pine. But they did not cross over to the Lansing side. Before they could do that, a second militia group came (the Oklahoma National Guard sent by the governor of Oklahoma). That group took control of the crowds, but not before mobs had completely destroyed

Greenwood! The next morning when I woke up to go to work, my mother told me about the riot. I looked out the window and was startled. It looked like the world was on fire!

We need to teach our young people to think more about others. Tell them to always do right by others and live an honest, clean life. Do things for others, like Simon Berry did. Don't just think of self all the time. If a person follows these rules, he or she will have a long, harmonious, peaceful life.

REV. ALFRED BARNETT
b. February 2, 1923, Tullahassee, Oklahoma

When I was a young man, I worked in some of Tulsa's finest hotels and restaurants where some of the best customers were the oil men. I waited on Frank and Waite Phillips, Bill Skelly, Robert LaFortune, John Mabee, and many other wealthy oil men. Mrs. R. L. Davison, chairman of Women's Volunteer Services in Tulsa in the 1930s, was responsible for arranging a lot of the luncheon/programs in downtown Tulsa which brought in many oil men. There was always a lot of excitement among the waiters and waitresses, busboys, and dishwashers when one of those programs was coming up. Those programs gave us an opportunity to meet and serve, and hear from some of Tulsa's finest leaders. I remember when I worked as a busboy at the Tulsa Chamber of Commerce in the 1930s, there was a forum every Thursday. When the oil men came in to eat, everybody would be looking at them. They were special people. I especially remember one meeting. The workers all came in and turned in their money, but they were short of their goal. John Mabee got up and sung a song, *Don't Fence Me In*, and then he donated the amount of money it needed to "go over the top." I always respected Mr. Mabee for doing that for the city.

Today, I don't wait on oil millionaires any more. I minister to the sick and needy, the elderly black, and poor in nursing homes in North Tulsa. I share the Bible with them and I bring them something that money can't buy — communication from the outside world. My routine is always the same — a short prayer, a song, a scriptural selection, and a short sermon. I share the books that are the plainest and most inspirational to me — Matthew, Mark, Luke, and John; sometimes I deliver sermons from the Old Testament, especially from Genesis and books that tell the story of Abraham, Moses, and Joshua.

Some people appreciate my coming and some don't. Those who don't care for me think I'm not a fancy enough preacher, or else they are still loyal to their own ministers. Two of the people that I ministered to when I first got the call from God to begin my ministry, I will always remember — Opal Dargan and Henry C. Whitlow. Both of them were outstanding people in the community, well-thought of people. But they were both so loving and kind to me. They gratefully received my message and welcomed me into their homes.

When I give my services in the nursing homes, some people listen quietly, and some not so quietly. But I love them all and I do notice improvement in the physical and mental condition of the patients after I start ministering to them. There is no place on earth that I would rather be than to be sharing the word of God with people in nursing homes.

DR. CHARLES JAMES BATE
b. January 1, 1914, Castalian, Tennessee

We must never forget the past. We must especially tell the story of what black doctors went through in the past to pave the way for the present generation of doctors and caregivers. Oh my, we had a rough time! Young doctors today have everything handed to them on a silver platter — scholarships, free books, fancy internships, and when they start to practice, they get subsidized and they get big, fancy cars. It was different in the old days. The boys in my class worked in all kinds of places, and at all kinds of jobs trying to scrape up tuition which was $40 to $50 a year. That doesn't sound like much now, but then it was awful hard to come by. We worked on farms, in wheat fields, cotton fields, tobacco fields, on boats, railroad tracks, and Pullman cars — just any place that would hire strong, young men. We scrimped and saved our money. Sometimes we wouldn't get a haircut for three or four months.

When we got ready to intern, there were very few places for young black doctors. Washington, D.C., Nashville, Tennessee, New Orleans, Louisiana, and St. Louis, Missouri took a few. Intern pay

Dr. Charles Bate

ranged from $5 a month in some places to a maximum of $15 a month in "good places." Today, interns start off at about $25,000 a year.

When we did start our own practice in the black community, it was heartbreaking to see the conditions then. I sometimes pray to forget some of the things I saw. For instance, due to segregation laws, blacks could not be admitted to white hospitals then. Before there was a black hospital in Tulsa, most black women delivered their babies at home with midwives in attendance. Or some of them sent for a white doctor who didn't mind treating 'Colored' folks in their own homes. Black people who needed operations were especially susceptible; they were operated on in their own homes in unsterile, inadequate surroundings. Then they were left to recuperate in the midst of noisy families. It is no wonder that so many of them hemorrhaged and died!

It is interesting how Tulsa's white hospitals first 'opened up' to blacks long before civil rights acts mandated it. Rich white oil men and other businessmen were often very fond of their black servants and when the servants became ill, they would often just show up at Hillcrest Hospital (then known as Morningside Hospital) at 11th and Utica Streets, or at St. John's Catholic Hospital up on 21st and Utica with their ailing black servants. These hospitals had been built with Masonic money and contributions from wealthy oil men and wealthy businessmen. So, even though the state of Oklahoma was entrenched in segregation, white doctors couldn't ignore the demands of these wealthy white benefactors. In the 1920s, Hillcrest set up an area on the first floor, in the north wing, where black servants could be treated, but after a short period of recuperation in 'colored rooms' in the basement, they were sent home to recover.

One incident that occurred in Hillcrest Hospital caused me to hold a grudge against a white doctor for many years. It involved a childbirth case and a black woman. A very obese black woman showed up at Hillcrest in great distress. The attending physician examined her and determined that she needed an operation immediately for a large ovarian tumor; the 'tumor' turned out to be a healthy, black baby! The perplexed white doctor didn't know what to do with the baby; the mother was put in the 'colored ward' in the basement, but he couldn't put a screaming baby in there with recuperating adults. So the good doctor put the baby in a broom closet! That really bothered me and I did hold a grudge against that doctor.

But one day when he and I were talking, he told me that the incident, as I had heard, was true. He said he was ashamed to be a part of a system that would treat another human being that way, but he said that he had no choice. At that time, he simply could not have put that little black baby in the nursery with white babies in Oklahoma. I thought about it and I knew that he was telling the truth. So my grudge against him just dissolved and we became close friends. Oh, we had some rough times then. Black people didn't have the opportunities then that they have now, and they didn't get proper credit for their inventions and creativity. Why they discovered things in the medical profession, and in all other segments of society, for which white people got the credit! I could write a book about it. In fact, I did write a book about the medical profession. Don't let people forget what we black Americans have been through. All Americans need to know this history — black, white, young, old, rich, poor — everybody. Young blacks today are ignorant of their rich cultural heritage, and white youth are arrogant because they don't know the heritage of black people. They think that everything was invented by white people. Yes, there is a great need for setting the record straight in the U.S. Don't let people ever forget what we as black people went through. It was especially difficult in the medical profession and we must never forget the rocky road that others went over in the past to make the path smoother for all of us today.

HUBERT BRYANT
b. January 4, 1931, Tulsa, Oklahoma

My class, the class of 1956, was the largest law school class in the history of Howard University. We began with sixty-five students, but sadly only thirty-four of us graduated; we lost quite a few to death and to other circumstances. As young law students, we were exposed to some of the greatest constitutional minds of our time. We were able to sit and listen to what lawyers call 'dry runs' — the speeches and arguments being practiced and rehearsed to be given before the courts. We heard some of the finest black legal minds rehearsing arguments to present before the United States Supreme Court. We were so impressed by their procedures, their mannerisms, and modes. That is what encouraged quite a few of us

Judge Hubert Bryant

to become involved in the NAACP and The Legal Defense Fund when we left law school.

History will corroborate that Howard University had some of the finest law professors in the nation. We had the best teachers possible including James M. Nabrit, Jr., one of the most outstanding constitutional law professors in the nation (he later became president of Howard University), Spottswood W. Robinson III who is now on the U.S. Court of Appeals, Frank D. Reeves, Jack Greenburg, author of a book about black lawyers, Louis Redding, George E.C. Hayes (who later became a Washington, D.C. commissioner), U. Simpson Tate, and, of course, Thurgood Marshall. Assistants to these great professors were rising young lawyers such as Robert Carter, who was Thurgood Marshall's assistant, and Wiley Branton of Little Rock, Arkansas.

It was because of great lawyers such as these that I became so interested in the NAACP. I was privileged to assist the national NAACP in the 1987 lawsuit against the city of Tulsa which resulted in Tulsa changing the commission form of government that we had all those years to the mayor/council form of government.

But before that, I had the great honor of working with Tulsans during the civil rights movement of the 1950s and 1960s. Tulsa has had a long and varied history in the field of law and civil rights. The city always had a number of people who never hesitated to step forward, to put their bodies on the line, when the time came to break down racial barriers. Quite a number were young people who became involved with the NAACP and with the CORE organization (Congress of Racial Equality). They were very vocal and very active. They wanted to challenge segregation everywhere. They participated in sit-ins to try to integrate restaurants, theaters, parks, and other public accommodations. They were fine young people and many of them are prominent, active Tulsa citizens today. But I still remember them as those young men and women who put themselves on the line to bring about justice and equality when it wasn't popular to do so and when it could be downright dangerous. They just wore out Piccadilly's Restaurant, they had so many sit-ins there! There was Bobby Eaton, Billy Rountree, Alice Cornelious, Mable Rice, Shirlee Johnson, and Don Ross. They were brave young warriors then.

Those sit-ins posed a dilemma for me, however. It just so happened that I was the city prosecutor at the time. I had to represent the city of Tulsa when those young people got arrested on trespassing charges, as the city called it. Yet I sympathized with them. They understood and we never lost our friendship; and we are fast friends today. They knew I was just doing my job. Still I worried about them and their safety. Once, in a conversation with the Tulsa Police Chief, I warned that I never wanted to see a mark on any one of those kids, ever! And I never did. Tulsa policemen didn't want an image like that of Deep South policemen; they never roughed up our protestors. But I still worried about the youth when they were in jail. Once, while I was pondering the situation and looking for answers, I found a solution in the most unlikely place — in a rare and seldom used City of Tulsa ordinance. It allowed youth to be released into the custody of a lawyer. Sometimes, a black lawyer would sign for "custody" of 50 to 60 of our jailed youth protestors at a time. We had a good laugh over that law passed for some other purpose than for promoting black civil rights! Those were some difficult days, but we did what we had to do. Through our efforts, segregation barriers came down and Tulsa became a better city.

ALPHA CALHOUN
b. September 17, 1912, Eufaula, Oklahoma

ALVAH LOYCE DYER
b. August 3, 1918, Muskogee, Oklahoma

Our political process is far from perfect, but, like Winston Churchill once said about democracy, 'It is the worst kind of government possible, except for all the rest!' That is why I take the right-to-vote so seriously. It is not only a privilege, it is our duty. In the past, black people had great faith in the power of the ballot box. Right after the Civil War, they were elated and many of them expected immediate, full political, economic, and social equality. But, of course, that was unrealistic and was impossible to achieve instantly. Still, we've made progress. Just look at the rising number of blacks who are being elected to office in local, state, and national elections today! We've come a long way since that period right after the Civil War and before Reconstruction ended when blacks were so elated and uplifted because of the election of people of their

Alpha Calhoun

Alvah Loyce Dyer

race to powerful positions, including federal congressional posts, only to have their hopes dashed by white resistance and, especially, by nearly a century of Ku Klux Klan violence and intimidation which resulted in the mass disenfranchisement of black people in the U.S. Thank God those days are over. We must never let people forget how hard our people had to fight for the right to vote. Black people ought to fill the precincts on voting days.

— Alvah Loyce Dyer

We must not forget our history and we must do a better job of convincing our young people of the need for participation in the voting process. Young people need to know about the importance of voting. We must never let them forget the people — black, white, red — who fought and died for the rights which they (youth) take for granted. They think that schools have always been integrated and of course they can't remember a time when public facilities weren't open to them. Teachers and families must work together to educate these youngsters about the struggles that our people went through to get to this stage of history. They need to learn about the Dred Scott Decision, the Plessy v. Ferguson Supreme Court Decision, Brown v. Board of Education, Topeka case, the Civil Rights Act of 1964, the Voting Rights Act of 1965, and all the other acts and court decisions that have helped our people move up a little bit higher toward equality. Don't let them forget the martyrs like Andrew Goodman, Michael Schwerner, and James Chaney, three young civil rights workers who were murdered by Klansmen and buried in a dam in Mississippi in 1964.

You can never start too soon to instill spiritual values and democratic principles in young people. You must begin, even when they are just babies, to teach youngsters to respect each other and to obey rules. I get practice in that every day helping my wife, Doretha, in her Day Care Center, Al-Dot. It is a joy to be working with those children. I hope that when they grow up, they will love and appreciate our American democracy. I hope that they will take the right to vote seriously and that they will always be at the polls on election day!

— Alpha Calhoun

ELIZABETH CHAPPELLE
b. January 2, 1921, Wagoner, Oklahoma

I am an original Okie. I was born in Wagoner, Oklahoma. When I graduated from high school, I went to Langston University where I received a degree in Home Economics. I came home to teach in Red Bird and Wagoner. Then I went back to college and got a master's degree in education from the University of Tulsa. I also did further study at the University of Omaha and the University of Oklahoma.

In addition to my teaching, I helped my husband raise the children, twins T. Oscar, Jr. and Flora, and our son Carlos. The children were always my first priority, but I also helped my husband at Morning Star Baptist Church. One of the happiest church duties I ever had was to prepare dinner for Dr. Martin Luther King, Jr. when my husband brought him to Tulsa to speak at the church. Oh I fixed my Sunday-best dinner that day! I prepared my usual "feast food" or Sunday dinner — chicken, roast, potatoes, greens, salad, cornbread, apple pie, coconut cake, tea and coffee. Martin just relished that meal! He was such a nice young man, a very down-to-earth person. He was so friendly, yet serious about what he had to do. I will never forget that nice day when he came to dinner at our house.

I also helped Thomas to run the two nursing homes that he bought — Chamor Nursing Home and Rest Haven Nursing Home. That was sure a lot of work. That's why he sold them. He said when he was gone he didn't want me tied down to running those nursing homes and running myself ragged.

I did civic and community work, too, but I always preferred to keep quiet about it. I was a preacher's daughter and in those days the women stayed out of the limelight and helped the man who was head of the household. That was especially true if the husband and father was a preacher. When I was growing up, I always said I would never marry a preacher! But of course I did, and we had forty-four wonderful years of marriage together.

My mother and grandmother had the philosophy that if you were blessed in life, you owed a lot back to God. Well I was certainly blessed, so I did my best to repay God. I gave a lot of "Women's Day" speeches at various churches, but mostly I followed my mother and grandmother's advice. I did things not for recognition, but to repay God for all his blessings. The children

Elizabeth Cooley Chappelle and Rev. T. Oscar Chappelle

have been my biggest blessing. I am so proud of them. Thomas, II is carrying on his father's ministry at Morning Star and Carlos is a lawyer. Sadly, Flora died when she was a young woman, leaving four children. Those children are now grown and "doing us proud." One grandchild graduated from a university this May, while another grandson graduated from Fisk University in Tennessee and has entered Meharry Medical School. When those grandkids graduate, I go to their graduations no matter where they are. Oh yes, I have been bountifully blessed!

TOMISSA NORVELL ADAMS CHATMAN
b. April 13, 1912, Beggs, Oklahoma

I have had so many disappointments and hardships in my life, but with God's help, I have survived. I guess you could say that the worst disappointment in my early life was when my father and my grandfather had their Indian lands in Oklahoma taken away from them by greedy white people. The Adams families of Beggs, Oklahoma were descendants of Creek Indians and blacks who had come to Indian Territory during forced marches in the early 1800s. Our family had an allotment of land in the Beggs area and oil was found on the land. In 1899, my father, grandfather, and some other black Indians in the area went down to the Creek Indian capital in Okmulgee to get their leases approved. We children were so happy. We thought we were going to be rich! But the plan fell through; the leases were never approved and eventually our land with its rich oil fields was taken away from us. So we never became rich like the whites did. So there went my chance to become a rich "oil woman" like the Rockefeller, Sinclair, Skelly, Getty, and other "oil women" in America!

The next sad thing that happened to me was that my only child, a son whom I named George but who was always called 'Bill,' was born deaf and mute as it was called. In those days, handicapped children were kept in institutions where they were cared for and taught by professionals. I think it is better today when all children, even the severely handicapped, are kept at home and loved and nurtured by their own parents. But that is not the way it was in the old days so I missed a lot of the hands-on raising of my own child

Tomissa Norvell Adams Chatman

because he was institutionalized by the state at the Deaf, Blind, and Orphans Institution for Coloreds at Taft, Oklahoma. When Bill did come home for visits, he had a great time, especially when the eight cousins from the Ferman Petit family were around. His eyes just lit up when he was around those children. It seems like he just "drank up" every move they made so he could remember it when he went back to Taft. Those little Petit children thought Bill was a lucky little boy because, as an only child, he had plenty of toys and new clothes all the time. But I would have gladly given up all material things if only my child could have had the ability to hear and speak!

Everything was not always sadness though. I remember happy times in my childhood. I remember that my mother, who was part Indian, part Mexican, and part black, was an excellent cook. We got the best foods from all three cultures! My Daddy's favorite eating was when Mother combined black and Indian dishes. From her Indian heritage, she had learned to make softkee (ground corn), eechie (a beverage), grape dumplings, wild onions with scrambled eggs, fried rabbit and fried squirrel. From the blacks in the family, she had learned all about 'Soul Food.' But her favorite food was Mexican food which my Daddy didn't like. So when Mother had a craving for Mexican food, she would go to the home of some of her Mexican friends and get her fill of Mexican food! Mother was always doing something with food — preparing it for future *'lean days.'* She would slice pumpkins, put a string through each slice, and hang the slices on the clothes line to dry in the hot summer sun. She would slice bushels of peaches and apples and have my brothers spread them on top of the roof of the house to dry. Those dry foods, together with fruits, vegetables, soup mixtures, and a little meat, which she would preserve (called canning) in jars would tide us over during the winter months.

The happiest memories that I have are of my late husband, Ralph Chatman. We were married for over fifty years. I first saw Ralph when I was twenty three years old and he was twenty six. I was walking to the store in Beggs from our rural home and Ralph drove by on the old highway 75. He was driving the yellow 1921 Buick of his aunt, Cynthia Petit Bankhead, a Tulsa school teacher and community leader. Behind the car was a trailer in which was a piano that he was moving from Okmulgee to Tulsa. Ralph knew my brothers, and he had seen me from a distance, but he had never met me formally. After that, we began to court and six months later we were married. We moved to a farm in Pumpkin Center, Oklahoma. Later, we moved to Tulsa and lived at 311 East Davenport Street in one of his Aunt Cynthia's rent houses. We bought this home, our final home, at 619 E. Young Street. When we bought the house, we didn't know that up the street, closer to North Cincinnati, was the house that used to belong to Charles "Pretty Boy" Floyd during the 1930s. Someone is always at that house, taking pictures and talking to neighbors about whether they ever saw 'Pretty Boy.'

I do miss the old days. It seems like people were more thoughful toward each other then. Husbands, like my Ralph, seemed to have been more protective and more gentle with their wives. And mothers seemed to be more nurturing toward their children. I wish that people could be more tender and kind with each other today. I wish it wasn't necessary for mothers to have to work while their children are young so their families can have a second income. I believe if mothers could stay home and nurture and train their children while they are young, society would not have all these bad problems that we have today.

Oh yes, I did get a second chance at motherhood. In 1956 we heard about a two-month-old black baby boy Freddie, who had nowhere to live. So Ralph and I took him in and he never left us! In 1973, we heard about a little black girl, La Toya, who was two months old. We took her in and she never left either. Freddie's two children and La Toya's four are the grandchildren that we never had from our Bill. Bill died in 1975 at age 43 from complications from diabetes and heart problems. I thank God for sending me two more children and six grandchildren to love.

LT. COL. MAJOR CLARK, Ret.
b. December 7, 1917, Headland, Alabama

It was a hard life for black people in Alabama after the Civil War, and especially after Reconstruction ended in 1877. My ancestors lived on the land and did the best that they could with what they had. When my father married my mother in 1905 in Headland, Alabama, his father gave him forty acres of land. By 1914 economic conditions in the South were getting worse and my father found it harder and harder to make a living tilling his worn out land and

Capt. Major Clark, Leghorn, Italy 1946

Lt. Col. Major Clark, 1960, retirement from the U.S. Army

to cope with boll weevils, floods, declining cotton prices, and the exploitation of whites. So he went to work in Newark, New Jersey leaving his family behind in Alabama. When he returned to Alabama, things got even worse. With his 'northern money' all used up, he borrowed $542.72 to tide the family over, mortgaging his forty acres of farm land as well as his entire crop of cotton, corn, cottonseed, fodder, cane, peas, potatoes, turpentine and other produce to be raised during the years 1919-1922; all rents coming to him from 1919-1922; two mules, each twelve years old, and one two-horse wagon and harness.

When he couldn't come up with the mortgage payments, Dad had to sell the farm to satisfy the debt and that is when we moved to Oklahoma.

We had heard that Oklahoma was 'the land of opportunity.' But we found that basically Oklahoma was just about the same as the South with Jim Crow laws requiring segregation of public education, transportation, and other public places. But one thing was definitely better here — the schools for blacks. Even though they were segregated and not equal to white schools, they were infinitely better than schools in the Deep South. I excelled in school, mastering with ease all the subject matter presented to me by my teachers. But when I graduated from high school, my parents didn't have the money to send me to college.

Since I didn't have money to go to college, I continued my 'teenaged' jobs — picking cotton, cutting yards, etc. Because of my reputation as an outstanding achiever and as a trustworthy person, members of the white power structure competed for my services as a part-time worker around their homes and businesses. One of my mowing jobs was directly across the street from the National Guard Armory which housed the equipment and guns of Battery E, 160th Field Artillery, Oklahoma National Guard. I got a glimpse of the troops twice a year when they were either leaving for or returning from summer camp. I just fell in love with the military. I noticed that there were no blacks in the unit, but I had built up a healthy self-esteem through my work with whites, and I knew in my heart that I could be as good a field artilleryman as any of the members of that unit if given the opportunity. In 1940 I enlisted in the U.S. Army and was assigned to the 349th Field Artillery Regiment at Ft. Sill, Oklahoma.

I had the opportunity to observe the U.S. military from three unique vantage points: (1) As an enlisted man in segregated units with black enlisted men and all-white officers (1940-1942); (2) As an officer in segregated units with black enlisted men and white and black officers (1942-1944); (3) As an officer in completely segregated units with black enlisted men and all-black officers (1944-1945).

The specific areas where I served were as follows:

The 597th Field Artillery Battalion, 1942-1945, in Leghorn, Italy;

The 350th and 686th Field Artillery Battalions in Germany, 1946-1947;

The 3rd Korean Army Division, Senior Artillery Advisor, 1951-1952;

595th Field Artillery Battalion, Ft. Sill, Oklahoma, 1952-1953, Battalion Executive Officer;

69th Anti-aircraft Artillery Battalion, New York City, 1954-1955.

When I retired from the military in 1960, I just couldn't make a complete break. In 1962, I was hired by McDonnell-Douglas, Tulsa, an aerospace firm, beginning as a non-supervisory employee, but moving up to a supervisory position within a year. In 1967, I was Configuration and Data Manager for the Apollo Range-Instrumented Aircraft Program. This was the program which modified a communication platform for communication with the Apollo astronauts.

I have never regretted my choice of a career. But it would have been so much easier and so much better if there had not been so much racism then. Racism was prevalent in the military at that time and race, not efficiency, was the basis for rank, assignments, and awards. That is why that now, since I have retired, I am devoting my life to setting the record straight about the role of blacks in the military in the U.S., about misconceptions concerning the Buffalo Soldiers, and to ensuring that deserving black soldiers get the medals, though decades late, that were due them years ago, medals that they earned on bloody battlefields in Europe and in the Pacific making 'the world safe for democracy.'

It is a shame that black soldiers did not get the recognition that was due them. Some of the actions of blacks on the battlefield were just outstanding and had they been white, they would have received the nation's highest medal at once! Two classic examples are Lt. John Fox and Sgt. Ruben Rivers, a native Oklahoman, who died on battlefields in Europe while performing extraordinarily heroic deeds! There are a lot of people working today to try to rectify the injustices done to blacks in the military. Rep. Charles Rangel of Michigan, Sgt. Rivers' white commanding officer, U.S. Senator James Inhofe, and various other military officials, including me, are actively involved in this effort. In February 1995 I wrote a letter to President Bill Clinton regarding this issue. I will not rest until I finish writing my book about the significant role of blacks in the U.S. military, and until black soldiers, some killed on the battlefield under the most heroic conditions, and others dead of old age, get the recognition and respect from their country that was due long ago, but which was denied due to racism. Rivers' commanding officer said he would not stop until Rivers got his just reward; he felt God was keeping him alive for that purpose. I feel the same way!

LaVERNE COOKSEY DAVIS
b. May 24, 1904, Royce City, Texas

We left Texas and moved to Oklahoma in 1916 settling in Pawnee. Three years later, we moved to Tulsa. We left Texas because conditions were just terrible for black farmers like my Dad. We heard that things were better in Oklahoma, especially in Tulsa which was a booming oil town then. We heard that there were many good jobs for black folks in Oklahoma, what with all those oil people coming in from the north and from the east. But I didn't find Tulsa to be much different from Texas. In Texas my first job when I was eleven or twelve years old was washing dishes for a white lady in exchange for piano lessons. In Tulsa the only job that I could find was being a maid for a white doctor in South Tulsa. After the Tulsa Race Riot of 1921, I left Tulsa. I just couldn't face the prospects of spending my life being a maid.

Oh, that riot was such a terrible thing. It left its mark on me; I just can't ever forget it. When the riot started, it was in the wee hours of the morning. I had gone to bed and after midnight, I got a telephone call from the doctor who was still downtown. I wondered why he was calling me at that late hour. He told me not to go into

LaVerne Davis

Little Africa. That is what white people called North Tulsa in those days. I thought that was strange for him to tell me that. I wouldn't have been going into North Tulsa at that late hour anyway. Well later on the doctor called me again, and this time he was more urgent in telling me not to go into Little Africa. He said 'Hell has broken out in Little Africa. Don't go down there!'

I was safe in my maid's quarters in South Tulsa, but many of my friends in the Greenwood area had their homes burned to the ground. Before their homes were burned, some of the people were taken out of their beds. They went to detention centers in their pajamas and housecoats because the police wouldn't give them time to dress. I was so disturbed. I didn't know where my friends had been taken. Later I found out that most of them had been taken to the Convention Center. Five or six days after the riot blacks could get passes from the militia to go down into the Greenwood area to try to find friends and relatives. That riot was a tragic thing and it has stayed on my mind all these years.

Although I was safe in South Tulsa in my maid's quarters, I could see that red blaze, and since my boss had warned me, I knew that that blazing fire was destroying the beloved Greenwood community. When I did get down to Greenwood after the riot, I was so hurt by what I saw. To wake up and see nothing but ashes and buildings burnt to the ground, I couldn't keep the tears from falling.

After the riot the job situation in Tulsa didn't get any better. The only jobs available to blacks were either in the service industries — in hotels, restaurants, lounges, etc., or as maids and housemen in south and west Tulsa mansions of oil millionaires. That's why I left Tulsa. I first went to Pittsburgh, Pennsylvania where I worked seven years in the millinery business. Then I moved to Kansas City, Missouri and improved myself by going to nursing school and becoming a Licensed Practical Nurse. I enjoyed my career in nursing, but I returned to Tulsa in the 1970s to be near my sister, Katherine Butler. I worked thirteen years for the Tulsa Red Cross and retired in 1984.

I have seen a lot of changes in my lifetime. One thing that I wish is that people would listen more to what elderly people tell them. These people have lived longer, they have seen so much, and they can give so much good advice if only people would listen to them! Americans need to learn to respect older people more, and to respect people who are wise even if they are not formally educated.

Too often they listen only to the educated, to the 'high leaders.' Uneducated people are not 'ignorant.' Many of them are good, wise, intelligent people who just may not have had the opportunity to get a formal education. We could learn a lot from them if only we would learn to listen. I've read that in other cultures, there is great respect for the elderly; unfortunately, that is not true in the United States. Here, they are often viewed as just a burden on society. That need not be the case. I'd like to tell people, especially young people, to get back to being more loving, caring people. Then we would have a more loving and caring nation like we used to have. Families were more together then and they reached out and helped others in the community. We cared about each other. We were raised to treat others as we would want others to treat us, barring none. We were taught to work for the betterment of all people, barring none!

ALFRED STANLEY DENNIE
b. September 27, 1903, Arcadia, Oklahoma

I'll never forget that day we went from our little hometown of Welleston, near Arcadia, to Oklahoma City to celebrate Oklahoma's statehood. The streets in Oklahoma City were just full of people, yelling and screaming like wild banshees! The circus came down the railroad tracks and musical sounds were coming from everywhere. There were the exciting sounds of the calliopes, and carousels playing music for the merry-go-rounds, itinerant street musicians playing, music drifting out of saloons, and rousing, stirring gospel music floating out of tent churches. Oh what an exciting day that was! I shall never forget it. That was one of the happiest days of my life.

One of the saddest days of my life was when my father put me in an orphanage in Kansas City, Missouri when I was eleven years old. When my parents divorced in 1912, I was sent from Oklahoma to live with my Dad in Kansas City where he was a taxicab driver. The younger children remained with my mother. When it became impossible for my Dad to care for me and drive his cab at all hours of the day and night, he reluctantly put me in the Guardian Angel Orphanage, a Catholic orphanage. At first I was sad but then I grew to love that orphanage and those nuns. Those were the sweetest

Alfred S. Dennie at his induction into the Oklahoma Jazz Hall of Fame.

Alfred Stanley Dennie (of Tulsa) with the JAP Allen Band, Kansas City, MO., 1928

The Alfred S. Dennie Family, Tulsa, 1966. L to R: Rear: George Luther Dennie, Edna Works, Norma Leshie, Howard Dennie, Ida Willis, Lawrence Dennie. Front: Seated: L to R Alfred S. Dennie, Ruth Ann Morris Dennie.

nuns. They taught us kids how to sew, mend, bake bread, clean floors immaculately — how to be ourselves, how to survive! And they didn't proselytize either. They knew that some of us weren't Catholic, so they let us be. It was at that orphanage that I was introduced to classical history, literature, Latin and the arts. When I was a grown man with a family of my own, I always put aside some money to purchase classic books and music for my children. The nuns opened up the world to me. That year I spent at the orphanage was a good year. In fact, it was one of the best years of my life!

I had some good years in music, too. Jazz music was in its heyday then. Not only is Jazz music of historical significance, it is an exciting form of music that requires great discipline, hard work, and creativity. Jazz was a way to keep people out of trouble, to keep them happy. It took their minds off their problems. I knew and played over 600 songs. I knew them all and could play them all. I could show off that music! Because of my reputation, music houses would give me music free because they knew I would play it. I got free musical scores from all the major music publishing houses.

I played with a lot of great musicians, but my all-time favorite was Duke Ellington. Duke was a fine, kind man. Sometimes I would rent a big house for my band and Duke would come; sometimes Duke would rent the house and I would come and bring my band. That's the way it was in those days. Even famous musicians like Duke, Count Basie, Lionel Hampton, and Cab Calloway couldn't stay in white hotels in the South and Southwest. So we took care of ourselves. We either stayed with friends (the Goodwin family was always befriending visiting bands) or we stayed in black hotels like the Hotel Small in Tulsa. Or we rented a big house, like I said earlier, where lots of bands could stay together while performing in the area.

Oh I loved that music. Music was just in my blood. Musical talent just runs in my family. I grew up hearing about the musical talents of my relatives. My aunt Jeraldine received a degree in music from the University of Kansas in Lawrence which was financed by Harriet Beecher Stowe and the New England Immigrant Aid Society; Aunt Carrie was a Coloratura soprano who toured with the famous Fisk Jubilee Singers after her graduation from Oberlin College in Ohio; An uncle, Frank Dennie, sang and played guitar with the George Morrison Band in Denver in 1912; and another one of my uncles, Richard Dennie, played piano professionally in the Old West. So music was just in me. It just had to come out!

ROBERT FAIRCHILD
b. April 25, 1904, Hot Springs, Arkansas

Whatever I have accomplished in life, I credit to God and to my mother. It was my mother who taught me to love God. When I was a little boy, she would read Bible stories to us children. She had a big Bible and she would read about Daniel in the lion's den, the three Hebrew children, and David and Goliath and other such stories. I thought they were the most fascinating stories that I had ever heard! From my youth, I have loved God and have been active in the church. I joined Vernon AME church when I was nine years old and I have held every position possible except that of pastor!

My other passion, besides religion, has always been education. For some unknown reason, I always had a desire for learning. I never understood why, I just felt compelled to learn. When I graduated from Booker Washington High School, I decided I was going to go to the University of Nebraska like my friend Lloyd Hume Williams. At first, I wanted to be a lawyer, but my mother talked me out of that. She said 'No, don't be a lawyer. They tell lies.' So I decided to major in business instead. But, Lordy, before I got enrolled in college I had a rough time. Let me tell you I had a very rough time. You see, my hard-earned savings from my after-school and summer jobs that I had entrusted in the care of a teacher that I was staying with were stolen from me by the teacher! (I was staying with the teacher because my stepfather had thrown me out of the house). That deceitful man told me that the amount of my savings equalled exactly the cost of my room and board. I was so despondent I nearly died. But where there is a will, there is a way. A good lady, the mother-in-law of Professor Seymour Williams, befriended me. She diligently saved my earnings the summer after I graduated but she did more than just save my money for me. She taught me so many things.

At first, when I went to live with the Williams family, she resented me. But finally, she discovered that I had something good in me. One day she just threw her arms around me and began to teach me. She didn't have much formal education, but oh what

Robert Fairchild

mother wit she had! She taught me the importance of taking a bath, of sleeping in pajamas rather than in my underwear, of getting an education. We became close friends. When I left for the university, she said 'Bob, whatever you do, don't you leave. You stay there!' And I did. When I left the train station for college, my mother saw me off. Her final words to me were 'Bob, I don't have any money to give you, but when you get to Nebraska, stay on your knees to God and if you do, you will make it.' I took her advice. I literally 'lived on my knees' during those college years.

But before I went off to college, I lived through one of the worst experiences of my life — The Tulsa Race Riot of 1921. The riot got started over a false accusation against Dick Rowland, a nineteen-year-old bootblack who worked in downtown Tulsa. I knew Dick when he was a star football player at Booker Washington High School. He had a reputation of being 'a good-looking ladies' man.' I worked downtown as a shoeshine boy so I was very familiar with that building where the elevator incident happened. The restroom on the fourth floor of the Drexel Building was the only one in downtown Tulsa that Negroes could use. That elevator often stopped uneven. I believe that is what happened the day that Dick stumbled into the seventeen-year-old elevator operator Sarah Page who I heard was a business college student. But after the rumors spread that Dick had assaulted the girl, things got ugly in Tulsa. That *Tulsa Tribune* article (May 31, 1921) talking about lynching a Nigger stirred up things even more. The night the riot started my Booker Washington classmates and I were rehearsing at the Dixie Theater on Greenwood Avenue for our high school graduation. Someone came and told the instructor to let us go because there was going to be trouble on Greenwood. So he dismissed us about 8:30 P.M. I came out onto Greenwood and it was packed with people. Some of the men had been drinking and were cursing and shooting their guns into the air. One man said 'Don't be wasting your bullets like that! You might need them later.' And they did. They kept talking about what they were gonna do. So they went on downtown to the court house about 9:00 P.M. There were lots of white people there. They were mostly unarmed. A white man, about sixty-five or seventy years old, tried to take a gun from a Negro. He said 'Nigger, what are you doing with that gun?' The

Negro man replied, 'I'm gonna use it if I have to!' In the struggle, a shot was fired and the riot was on.

Later, I did go on home. Things kept getting worse. All you could see and smell was smoke and fire; and you could hear those gunshots going off. I was so scared. I said 'Mama, we had better get out before they get to our house. Mama, let's get outta here; they're gonna kill us!' I was so scared.

After the riot was over, Greenwood looked like a war zone. It was just totally destroyed. People were just milling around in the streets looking dazed. My family was lucky. We were one of the few families whose home was not destroyed, and we had no deaths in our family. Oh Lord, that was such a terrible time. And so unnecessary. Mankind just needs to learn to live together in peace. When they learn that lesson, there won't be any more riots and wars.

Well, I did go on to college. Those were some hard days, those four years at the University of Nebraska. Like I said, I stayed on my knees, praying to God a lot, but I made it! I held all kinds of jobs to pay my college expenses. I had to do it all by myself (with God's help). I worked shining shoes, barbering, waiting tables and janitoring in the Sigma Nu Fraternity House, and as a waiter in a dining car on the Great Northern Railroad's St. Paul, Minnesota route. The best jobs that I had were the Frat House job and the dining car job. Mr. and Mrs. Pace, who were the chef and waitress at the Frat House, gave me all the leftover food which I shared with all the other hungry Negro students on campus. That food was a Godsend. I earned $700 working one summer on the railroad job.

It was a long, arduous journey but on June 6, 1931, I graduated from the University of Nebraska which was ranked sixth in the nation in terms of academic standards. I was one of six blacks out of a class of 965. I wept with joy when I got that degree and I promised God I would spend my life helping youth so they wouldn't have it as rough as I had had it. And I have kept that promise.

CHATMAN FERGUSON
b. April 22, 1899, Cheneyville, Louisiana

When I answered an ad to work at Douglas Aircraft in Tulsa, I was so happy. I was always quick to learn and I was mechanically minded. I could have done anything at that company, but all they would let us black men do was dust and janitor. So I quit. That's when I went to work as a Pullman porter. That Pullman job was one of the happiest events in my life. My favorite train station was Grand Central Station in New York City. But the first time I went into Grand Central Station, I got lost. When my train stopped at the station for a short layover, I went out a door to take a look at grand old New York City. When I got ready to go back in, I never could find that door that I had come out of. By the time I worked my way back into the station through some other door, I had missed my train!

I'll never forget my first visit to the Hotel Theresa in Harlem in the 1930s. We Pullman porters liked to stay there when we had a couple of days layover. That was the largest, finest black hotel in the United States then, but it had no hot water! I just couldn't figure that out. If it had such fancy curtains, towels, and furniture, why didn't it have hot water? In the 1960s Fidel Castro of Cuba once stayed at the Hotel Theresa. He brought his own live chickens with his entourage. At that time, the hotel did have hot water and even provided boiling water for Castro's chickens. The Cubans killed, scalded, plucked, and cooked their own chickens right there in the hotel! There was a lot of activity at the hotel that day.

I always wanted to be a postman. When I took the Pullman job, it was only to be a temporary job. I told my wife that if the post office in Tulsa responded to my application in 1934, she was to drop everything and mail all the postal materials to me at once! When the post office did respond to my application, she did just that. I left the Pullman job and got right on back to Tulsa. After an interview, I was hired and became the second black postman in Tulsa. My supervisor wasn't too happy about that and my first day on the job, he tried to set me up for failure. He knew that I couldn't drive, that I had never been behind the wheel of a vehicle. Yet he assigned me the job of delivering Special Delivery Mail. So I just prayed to God about my situation. I said 'God, I ain't never had a gearshift in my hand before. It is a totally foreign object to me. But I want this job;

Chatman Ferguson

I need this job. So you show me how to drive this van and I will do it.' I wasn't afraid. I knew it was right for me to have that job. I knew I was in my right place and that God wouldn't let me down. And he didn't. God told me how to do everything except how to back up! So I just put the van in first gear and kept it in that gear all day. I was careful to park where I wouldn't have to back up. I made it just fine. It was really God that maneuvered that van all day. I thanked God for taking care of me. I didn't appreciate what that supervisor had done. That was the way some whites were in the old days; it seems like they took delight in setting up black men for failure. But I would never accept that. I knew that I had the same intelligence as any other man, and that if I was given a chance, I could learn anything that anyone else could learn. I just never let race be a cause for me to fail.

ERNIE FIELDS, SR.
b. August 28, 1904, Nacogdoches, Texas

Ernie Fields, the last of six children born to former escaped slave Reverend Thomas Jefferson Fields and his wife Mary Jane, came kicking and screaming into an imperfect world on August 28, 1904 in Nacogdoches, Texas. But Fields never let poverty, racism, injustice, or any other imperfect factor limit him or curb his enthusiasm, optimism, and compelling drive to have his life "mean something." Trials and tribulations in a harsh, unjust world were but stepping stones for the indomitable Ernie Fields!

Ernie Fields never knew his father, for shortly after Fields was born, his father, Thomas Jefferson Fields, was killed by a stray bullet on a street in Taft Indian Territory where the Fields family had moved. Times were hard for Ernie's plucky, widowed mother and the devoted youngest son in the family helped out as much as he could. While in high school, he held several jobs including one at a shoeshine parlor in Muskogee.

It was in Muskogee that Fields first became enthralled with music. Mr. Fields credits Walter Thomas, a young Muskogee man, with influencing him to become a professional musician.

Upon graduation from high school in the little all-black town of

Ernie Fields' "Best Swing Band in America," 1940's. Ernie — 3rd from right, holding trombone.

Taft, Oklahoma in 1922, Ernie Fields, Sr. went to far-away Tuskegee Institute in Alabama to learn a trade (applied electricity) so he could earn his livelihood in the future. When Ernie Fields first tried to get into the Tuskegee Institute band, he was turned down for two reasons: (1) He couldn't play an instrument and (2) He didn't have the money to buy an instrument so he could learn how to play one. He remedied the situation by buying a used trombone that a needy student offered to sell for $6.00. The destitute student settled for the $3.00 offered by Ernie Fields. The rest is history! Fields did learn to play and to earn spending money for his present needs, and because he just plain loved it, he formed a college band and played gigs in Tuskegee and surrounding little Macon County towns. It is ironic that his "real" job, as an electrician, was not the major source of his livelihood. It was his hobby, his avocation — music — that became the driving beat of his life and earned him fame and fortune.

Though he worked for a time after graduation as an electrician for Tate Electric Company on Greenwood Avenue in Tulsa, soon he was doing so many musical engagements that he gave up electrician's work to become a full-time musician. (He didn't like hooking up electric wires in hot attics during Oklahoma's brutally hot summers either.) By the 1940s and 1950s, Fields had made a name for himself. In a December 1941 Chicago Defender *newspaper poll of Best Bands and Musicians in the U.S., Ernie Fields ranked 8th out of 26, ranking behind only the older, more established bands of Count Basie, Jimmie Lunceford, Duke Ellington, Lionel Hampton, Cab Calloway, Erskine Hawkins, and Louis Armstrong, in that order. His band, "America's Sweetest Swing Band," was catapulted into national prominence when it placed high in* Cash Box Magazine's *1959 poll for Best Pop Orchestra in the U.S., and when Fields and the band subsequently made a guest appearance on the Dick Clark show. From then on the band, one of the top ten bands in the U.S., was booked solid all across the U.S. playing on military bases, major college campuses, and in the finest clubs, ballrooms, and theaters from coast to coast.*

Record sales for the Ernie Fields Band, on the Rendevoux and the Okeh labels, boomed with hit after hit. But it was the band's mega-hit, "T-Town Blues," and "In The Mood," a phenomenal million-seller, that rocketed the band to musical eternity. It was only fitting and proper that Oklahoma should give Ernie Fields, Sr. its ultimate music honor. In 1990 he was inducted into the Oklahoma Jazz Hall of Fame

at the same time that former Oklahoma Citian Jay McShann, a pro-
tege of Alfred Dennie, was inducted. The Fields musical legacy is being
carried on by Fields' son, Ernie Fields, Jr., who is a popular music pro-
ducer in Los Angeles.

The world is a better place because of the vision, brashness, and
perseverance of Ernie Fields who was one of "the best" and who gave
Americans the kind of music that they wanted to hear. Today, Ernie
Fields' records, tapes, and CDs are collectors' items. They bring back
poignant memories of an era that America will never forget! In his own
words, Ernie Fields says the following about his legendary career.

— Eddie Faye Gates

I always did like music. When I was a student at Tuskegee
Institute in Alabama, I played in the college band. Then I formed a
little band of my own for two reasons — I was just crazy about
music and the money sure came in handy. Soon, I had so many gigs
in Alabama, and even across the state line in Georgia, that I could
hardly keep up with them.

When I graduated and came back to Tulsa, I worked for a while
in my field of applied electricity, but when that began to get in the
way of my music, I gave it up and devoted myself entirely to my
music. I have never regretted it.

Oh those music days were some good days. I played with the
best of the musicians — Duke Ellington, Count Basie, Cab
Calloway, and many others whose names became household words.
I think that Duke Ellington was the most outstanding of all the
musicians that I met, but Count Basie was my favorite. Duke was
nice, too, but Count and I were as close as two crossed fingers.
There was another great musician who did not get the recognition
that I think he deserved, Roy Milton. He was a superb musician —
so natural, so easy! Jimmy Rushing was good too.

I was happy that people liked my band's music. I am proud that
we were able to give the people the kind of music that they wanted.
It was just wonderful to be rewarded for doing something that was
so pleasurable for us to do. I thank God for giving me my musical
talents. I am glad that I was able to share that talent with the world.
When our band's songs became hits, we were just happy and elated.
All of us, it was a team effort. When our record, *T-Town Blues*, won
so many awards and became such a big hit, it surprised us. I got a

lot of recognition and praise for that record, but it was more than just my creation. It was more than me who composed that song. A lot of us worked on it. We didn't expect it to take off like it did. But we sure did like it!

Looking back, I am glad to have been a part of the music world during the Jazz and Big Band era. I think that some of the best music ever produced in America came during that time period. Of course all musicians naturally like their own kind of music best. There is always some bias and a certain amount of generation gap. I remember when Duke, Count, and I used to sit around discussing the changing musical trends. Once we were talking and a 'modern'-song came on the radio. Count Basie said 'What is that? What kind of music is that? They call that music!' He didn't like it at all. None of us did. We had no idea that Be-Bop and all that 'New Wave' and modern stuff would catch on. But it did. I still think the old Big Band and Jazz music was better. We were the best!

DR. JOHN HOPE FRANKLIN
b. January 2, 1915, Rentiesville, Oklahoma

Dr. John Hope Franklin has certainly earned the "home and hearth" period in his life which he now enjoys in his Durham, North Carolina hometown. His rich legacy lives on. His impeccably researched, readable, definitive writings on slavery, the Civil War, Reconstruction, and civil rights history continue to enrich the lives of scholars, writers, and the general reading public.

Dr. Franklin received an A.B. degree from Fisk University, an M. A. degree from Harvard, and a Doctor of Philosophy degree from Harvard University. He has received numerous awards including the Guggenheim Fellow, the Clarence Holtz Literary Prize, the Bunn Award, the Cleanth Brooks Medal, the John Caldwell Medal, the Fellowship of Southern Writers, the Encyclopaedia Britannica Gold Medal Award, the John Hope Franklin Publication Prize of American Studies Association, and the Oklahoma Book Award. He has also received numerous honorary degrees from various universities. Dr. Franklin taught at Fisk University, St. Augustine's College, Howard University, Brooklyn College, Cambridge University, the University of Chicago (1964-1982) and Duke University.

He was appointed chair of a national race advisory board by President Bill Clinton in 1997.

Dr. John Hope Franklin

All of my life I've been a serious person. I always had strong ambitions and kept on-task all the time so I could accomplish my dreams and visions. I know that coming from the kind of family that I did contributed to my thinking and behavior along those lines. My dad, Buck Colbert (B.C.) Franklin, was a strong personality, a fine lawyer and a respected member of the community in Rentiesville, Oklahoma where I was born and later in Tulsa where he relocated. There he set up a law office on Greenwood Avenue and earned the reputation as an outstanding lawyer both before and after the Tulsa Race Riot of 1921, especially after the riot. The little tent 'office' that my dad, P.P. Chappelle, and I.S. Spears set up on Greenwood after the riot devastated North Tulsa, including the law offices of these three lawyers, is legendary in Tulsa history. From that little 'office,' those wonderful lawyers 'went to bat' for black Tulsans and fought to protect their legal rights in the midst of a hostile environment — the city hall of Tulsa which should have been protecting the rights of its citizens.

My mother Mollie Parker Franklin was a wonderful person too. She was a school teacher in Rentiesville where I was born in 1915. She was such a dedicated and revered teacher. In fact, it was her dedication that caused her to remain in Rentiesville that May of 1921 when the race riot occurred in Tulsa. She was supposed to have joined my Dad in Tulsa in May, but she wouldn't leave the Rentiesville school system until she had properly concluded her work there — all the testing, grading, paper work, and clean-up work. So that is how my mother and I just barely missed being in the Tulsa Race Riot of 1921!

I have always loved history. That is why I chose it as my life career. I just feel that mankind must know the proper history of the human experience in order to understand the past and present, and to prepare for the future. I was especially interested in setting the record straight regarding the history of black people in America. So I focused on their experiences — in Africa, on plantations during slavery during the Civil War, during migrations after the Civil War, and their constant struggles for human and civil rights. My long teaching career at various universities is completed. Now I have retired from teaching and have moved on to another phase in my life. Not a day goes by that I am not asked by some person, some organization, or some cause to do something 'for the good of mankind.' I'm learning to say 'no' to most things. I just want to take care of my wife and to enjoy 'home and hearth' now.

Alice Andrews knew John Hope Franklin when he was a thirteen-year-old paper boy in Tulsa. Even then, she knew he was special. This interview with Alice Andrews took place on April 7, 1995, in Tulsa.

When I was a young newly-wed living on Easton Street in Tulsa, I became acquainted with a young boy, about thirteen years old — John Hope Franklin. He lived down the alley from us across on Frankfort Place. He was the paper boy who delivered *The Tulsa Tribune* newspaper in the evening. My house was near the end of his route and young John Hope would always come upon my porch, put my paper in my hand, and sit down on the porch and visit with me. He would just pour out his dreams for the future. Oh what a bright lad he was! We'd talk and talk and talk. Then I'd say to him, 'John, go home Honey before it gets too dark.' He would jump up and say, 'Alright, but I'll finish telling you my plans tomorrow.' And he would, too. Oh he was a little darling. He was just an excellent boy. I knew then that he was going to make something out of himself some day. And he did, too. He became a wonderful college professor and writer. Whenever he comes to Tulsa, and sees me, he just hugs me and talks about our 'porch talks' all those years ago.

That's the way it was then. Children were so respectful to their elders, and the elders were so caring and protective toward the children. We loved them all, even the ones we called 'bad' in those days. But even the 'bad' kids in those days weren't bad according to today's standards. They were just mischievous and got into the usual boyish devilment. I remember five boys who were always getting into trouble. I nicknamed them 'The Five Musketeers.' My house on Easton Street was just across the alley from Booker Washington High School. Mr. Rogers' mechanics building was right next to the alley. He was such a good teacher and did his best to keep those boys in his class. It amused me to see how he got those boys to do things. But despite his best efforts, some of the boys got into trouble, especially for slipping out of class, going down that alley, and on down to Greenwood avenue to get into devilment. Those boys I called 'The Five Musketeers' were examples of that.

They were Jimmy Wimbush, George Webb, Carl Anderson, Pleas Anderson, and Don Ross. Would you believe it! Today all of them are ministers except Don Ross! And Don is a fine, upstanding citizen. He represents North Tulsa in the state legislature in Oklahoma City. Before that, he was a journalist with *The Oklahoma Eagle* weekly newspaper published in North Tulsa. Don is writing a weekly column in the *Eagle* once again. I sure am glad. I just love his writing. I am so proud of him and of those other 'Musketeers.'

That's what I keep telling people. Never, never lose faith in any child. Don't write off any child as hopeless. We can save our children if we just take the time. Principal E. W. Woods and all those teachers in Tulsa then took time with the children, even with the ones called 'bad' or 'tough.' Parents re-inforced what the churches and schools were teaching the children, and the whole community pitched in and helped. We all helped to mold those children! Even the 'bad' ones responded. They were always polite and respectful to their elders. Underneath their mischievous behavior, they had good hearts. They were really sweet children. We reached them and molded them; we didn't let them turn into dangerous, mean, cruel criminals.

Now John Hope Franklin was a different story. He was everyone's prayer of what a child should be. He was such a sweet thing. I am so proud of him.

ERNESTINE GIBBS
b. December 15, 1902, Kansas City, Kansas

Oh how I loved Booker T. Washington High School and the wonderful teachers that we had. It is true that the school lacked a lot of things. We didn't have a cafeteria, library, auditorium, or gym. But in those days, people didn't give up and throw in the towel over little problems, or even over big problems like racism and poverty. They made do with what they had. What we had was an outstanding principal, Mr. Ellis Walker Woods, and fine teachers like Mr. West, the science teacher, good coaches, and parents who stressed education and disciplined us firmly. If anyone got in trouble at school, he or she was in double trouble at home later.

How did we make it without proper facilities and supplies? We improvised; that's what we did! No cafeteria? No sweat! We

Ernestine Gibbs

brought our lunch from home, walked home for lunch, or did without lunch. Some students sneaked down on Greenwood to 'The Beanery' but Mr. Woods really got onto you if he found out. No library? Mr. West brought his personal books from home and used an extra room to start our first Booker T. Washington Library. No auditorium? Booker T. Washington was a two story building with a basement, and a second floor which was supposed to be divided with three rooms on each side. One side was not divided and that undivided side became our auditorium or whatever else we needed it to be. We were experts at 'making do.'

Even with 'make do' facilities and cast-off supplies from white schools, Booker T. Washington students excelled. One year Jim Ellis represented the school in the city Spelling Bee. He and a white boy were in a showdown. Eventually, Jim missed a word and came in second. We were so proud of him. Another time Lillian Briggs represented the school and came in fourth. We just never let anything stop us. That included sports. The school was too poor to buy uniforms for the girls' basketball team, so we made our own 'uniforms.' We got yards of jersey cloth — a bolt of black cloth, and a bolt of orange cloth —— and made our 'Bumble Bee' uniforms. One leg of the bloomer was black and the other one was orange. We were supposed to look like orange and black bumble bees. Those were the school colors and the bumble bee was the school mascot. We were some fine looking girl Hornets in those home-made bloomers and jersey tops, if I do say so myself!

We were so proud of that school. And even though it was segregated, and unequal to white schools, we got the best education possible under those conditions. Mr. Woods inspired and motivated us all — students, teachers, parents — to do our very best. I will never forget a message he gave to the student body at an assembly in the 1920s. He said that we were as good as ninety-nine percent of all people, and better than the other one percent. We believed that and we never stopped proving that Mr. Woods was right.

In fact the night that the Tulsa Race Riot began, I was studying for my final tests at Booker Washington High School. School was going to be out in two days. Oh, what a tragedy that race riot was! It burned everything we had. We lived on King Street over in the middle of some train tracks. A man knocked on our porch and said put out the lights. There is fighting and burning on Greenwood. I went to bed. Soon a young man, a family friend, came from the hotel on Greenwood to our door. He was so scared, he could not lie down. When daylight came, the people were moving down the train tracks like ants. We joined the people. My mother, cousin, and I soon lost my brother and our friend. Everyone was going to the Golden Gate Park located on the East Side where Crawford Park is now. It was just weeds, grass, and trees then. A man came by and asked my mother to follow him. So we went on out in the woods. We met people about 12:00 o'clock noon. We lay on the ground to rest. We were near a house and the man asked for water. The white man came back with him and told us all to come into his house. It was about 4:00 o'clock P.M. then. Men came by in cars and took us to the fairgrounds. There we were given food, water, and pop.

We were given mattresses to sleep on and something to eat the next morning. The man we were with asked Mother to keep his gun. He said he was going to help bury the dead. When he came back, he got his gun and we never saw him again. A man then offered to take us home. Going through Greenwood, I thought I would never come back to Tulsa. Greenwood was a war-torn place. When we got home, we found the only things that were not burned were something like metal — pieces of stoves or beds. All the trees were burned; everything was gone! By then, trains were coming into Tulsa. We went to Sapulpa where my mother's sister and family lived. There we found my brother and friend who had swum across the Arkansas River to escape the riot.

By August of 1921 we were back in Tulsa looking for work. My mother found a place where she could live. She would do laundry and clean once a week to live in a small room and bath attached to the garage. This room was called 'the quarters.' Most white people had quarters. Soon there were houses built by Negro men in the Greenwood area. Someone would rent a house and families would rent a room. Oh, I will never forget that riot as long as I live. I can shut my eyes and still see the smoke, fire, and ashes from that awful riot. I'll never forget it. No, not ever!

JEANNE GOODWIN
b. July 6, 1903, Springfield, Illinois

Despite weathering many storms of adversity, and despite her many successes in life, Jeanne Goodwin does not see herself as unusual. She shrugs off any attempts to commend her for her adjustments to adversity and for her numerous and wonderful contributions to her family and to the entire community. But the community honors her anyway. Among her many awards and tributes are the North Tulsa Heritage Foundation Image Awards tribute and her most recent, her induction into the Tulsa Historical Society's Hall of Fame.

— Eddie Faye Gates

I'm no hero. I just did what had to be done. What doesn't kill you makes you stronger. I have always lived by my father's motto which was that if adversity struck, 'Don't get bitter, get better!' We come from strong stock. One of my uncles, Simeon Osby, fought alongside Theodore Roosevelt in the Spanish-American War. The picture of him fighting in the famous Battle of San Juan Hill was a strong motivator for us children.

Growing up in a strong orthodox Baptist family provided us children many opportunities to develop strong family values, good work habits, and discipline. Our parents were strong, loving disciplinarians. We had specific chores which taught us punctuality and persistence. We went to church to learn about faith and brotherly love and we went to school to learn knowledge of other things. Our father was very strict about the purpose of school. If one of his children misbehaved in school, he or she was sure to get a whipping at home. Actually, we were obedient children and seldom required discipline from our parents. In fact, my father never had to lay a hand on me. My father said that he sent us to school to learn knowledge, not behavior. He said that it was his job to teach us manners and good behavior. And he did. I used that same philosophy with my own eight children.

It seems like all my life I have been dealing with children, with my own eight and with the many others that I taught during my years as an elementary teacher. But before I began my long teaching career, I had several brief, wonderful career opportunities. When I finished high school in Springfield, I enrolled at Fisk

L - R James Osby, age 1, Jeanne Osby (later Goodwin), age 8, Springfield, Illinois. James was electrocuted when he was 13 when he touched a metal pole at the Osby's farm home.

L to R Thelma Harrison (first cousin of national NAACP director Walter White) and Jeanne Goodwin. The former Fisk university roommates are shown here at the Bethlehem Center of Social Work, Nashville, Tenn. where they were social workers in 1926.

University where I graduated in 1926 with a degree in sociology. From 1926 to1927, I had the privilege of working with renowned black sociologist E. Franklin Frazier at the Atlanta School of Social Work in Atlanta, Georgia. In 1927, I went to St. Louis and worked as a social worker. That year I married my husband whom I had met at Fisk. I came to Tulsa and began my teaching career in the area — first as a substitute teacher at Booker T. Washington High School, then as a teacher at two-room Alsuma School which had two teachers and later, as a teacher at Bixby's two room school which had only one teacher (me!). I did my last years of teaching in Tulsa at integrated Fulton Elementary School in South Tulsa.

I loved every minute of my teaching career. Whenever a child needed me, my own or one of those entrusted in my care in the classroom, I did what I could to meet that need. What I needed most in the classroom was adequate supplies. But most of my teaching career was during America's days of segregation and supplies for black children were extremely limited. But I did the best that I could with what I had and with what I could beg, borrow, or scrape together. I brought oatmeal boxes and other containers and made little pretend stores in the little segregated schools where I taught. How the children loved their little store! What they didn't know was that they were learning all the while they were stocking and clerking in that little 'store.' I retired from Fulton at age 65. Between all that teaching, I took six maternity leaves, a record for Oklahoma, I believe!

If you are a mother, you are always on call to help your children. I was especially concerned about getting my son Jim (Tulsa attorney James O. Goodwin) into a good college. Knowing that he was going to have to work with his mind and not with his hands (he lost his right arm in a train accident when he was eleven years old), I was determined that he was going to get the best education possible. One day while I was in the beauty parlor, I overheard some ladies talking about Tulsa oil man Joseph A. LaFortune. They mentioned that he was on the board of directors of Notre Dame University. It was during the 1950s and white universities were beginning to accept blacks then. I determined then and there that Jim was going to go to Notre Dame. I went home and fixed up a 'college prep' packet to carry over to Mr. LaFortune's house, a packet that included Jim's grades from the Cathedral Boys High

School in Springfield, Illinois, numerous references and a list of seventeen awards that Jim had won. When I got to Mr. LaFortune's house that night, wouldn't you know it, he was out! But I left the packet with the maid with strict orders that she give it to him the minute he came home THAT NIGHT! She did. Mr. LaFortune did what he could on Jim's behalf, and Jim became a student at Notre Dame where he became one of the first black graduates. This was before the days of Affirmative Action and minority scholarships. Jim got into Notre Dame on his own merit, and my husband mortgaged his insurance to pay for Jim's college expenses.

In those days our commitment to children didn't stop when the school bell rang in the evening. Teachers took children to places where they would be exposed to social and cultural opportunities that they might not otherwise have. I worked with Mrs. Lillian Perry, wife of Dr. William Perry, who founded the Tulsa branch of the Jack and Jill Club. We took children to cultural activities and to places where learning could take place in non-school settings. We took them to places such as the post office, the courthouse, banks, bakeries, and ballets. We exposed some of those children to the first cultural experiences of their lives. We also worked with the Girl Scouts and with Camp Fire Girls. (I also worked on adult issues, too, such as serving as vice-chairman of Governor George Nigh's Tulsa County Heart Association, and on his Diamond Jubilee Committee.)

That's the way it was in those days. Parents, teachers, ministers, and others in the community were there to meet the needs of the children. We didn't have a lot of material things then, neither at home nor at school. But we made do with what we had. The children were embraced in a net of intertwined, loving arms and they did what was expected of them. We need to get back to that kind of care and discipline for our children. Those lessons that my father taught us children so long ago are just as valid, and needed, today as they were then.

THELMA DeETTA PERRYMAN GRAY
b. April 17, 1918, Tulsa, Oklahoma

In the early 1900s, Daddy moved his family to Tulsa where he owned a huge spread of farm land at Mingo Creek. How we four-teen children loved that place! There were no streets, just one road to the house. It was just acres and acres of timber and farm land; we children just considered it our vast play land. I remember that creek that my brothers loved so well — it was deep with clear blue water. It was so deep that my brothers never could find the bottom of it and they were all expert swimmers. When we children weren't doing chores, we could be found in or on that creek — mostly in it. We put everything in that creek and I do mean everything — hogs, cows, horses, and baby sisters and baby brothers. One of the worst whippings that I ever got was for putting the babies in the creek with some pigs one day. Our Grandma Grayson caught us and she tore us up with a switch! But that didn't stop us from swimming in that creek. We went swimming so much that in the summer time, we didn't even bother to wear clothes. We were called 'the little naked Perryman children' because of that habit. If we looked up in time and saw someone coming down the road, we would run to the house and put on some clothes. Otherwise, we just stayed naked to be ready to jump into that creek.

Daddy tried to pass on his 'Indian ways' to us children, espe-cially to my brothers. He taught the boys how to fish. Daddy could catch fish when no one else could. Sometimes he would dynamite the fish. Then he would have a big fish fry and invite all the sur-rounding neighbors and the town folks too. He would fry the fish 'Indian style,' rigged together on some kind of wire apparatus that he made and lowered into bubbling hot hog grease heated in black, iron washpots over outdoor coals of fire.

One of Daddy's 'Indian lessons' involved piling all of us chil-dren into a wagon and taking us to some kind of 'Indian camp.' I remember that he always took along a lot of pots and pans. The girls just played and watched, but Daddy and the other Creek Indian men taught the boys how to do things — mend things, groom and harness animals, and other things that the tribe thought young men should know. I don't remember all the things that the boys were taught there, but I do remember that the Indian men were very

Black-Creek Indian Perryman family reunion in Tulsa, June, 1996, descendants of Lewis Perryman (credited with being the founder of Tulsa).

DeEtta Perryman Gray, with cane, matriarch of Tulsa's Black-Creek Indian Perryman family. Shown in the white Perryman family cemetery on Utica Avenue in South Tulsa.

somber and sincere during these skill lessons. We kids knew that this was something important. I don't think that my brothers ever forgot those 'Indian camp' lessons.

The saddest event in my life was when my Daddy got killed. My Dad was the lighter-skinned son in his family; he took mostly after the Indian side of the family. Unlike his darker-skinned brothers, he could pass for Indian and he was allowed into the white hotels. One day some white oil men, who knew about Daddy's large land-holdings, took him into the Mayo Hotel in downtown Tulsa and got him drunk. Then they talked him into signing his land over to them. When my Dad sobered up, he regretted what he had done and he sought a lawyer to help him get his land back. He couldn't find anyone in Tulsa to side with him and take his case, so he went to Oklahoma City. There he found a Jewish lawyer who sympathized with him and took the case. That lawyer said Daddy had a strong case and he worked very hard preparing for court. The day before Daddy was to testify, he was found dead. The official ruling was 'accidental death due to a hit-and-run vehicle.' But everyone knew that he had been murdered for his land. That was typical in Oklahoma at that time. Many unscrupulous white oil men and other business men tricked Indians out of their land holdings. Some married Indians and some of the spouses turned up murdered. Those were some awful days for Indians. People glorify the early oil days in Oklahoma and made heroes out of the oil men. Some of them were good, decent men who gave much back to the community such as Charles Page of Sand Springs who took care of that town like it was his own family; but some of the oil people and early business men were bad people who exploited the Indians. It was not a good period for Indians, except for a few tribes like the Osages. They benefited when oil was found on their lands in the Pawhuska area, but most Indians were exploited and some, like my Dad, lost their lives.

POCAHONTAS GREADINGTON
b. April 30, 1910, Muskogee, Oklahoma

I didn't start out to be a math teacher. I graduated from Langston University with a B.A. degree in education, but I always loved math best and took more math courses than any other courses. When I began teaching elementary education, I sometimes was

Pocahontas Greadington

assigned a 'home room' class which was the polite word for teaching everything — social studies, English, math, everything except the special subjects like music, physical education and such.

After teaching for a while, I became disturbed about the bad image that many students had about math, especially minority children. So many thought that math was hard, that it was not practical, or that it was for 'nerds.' I wanted to show them that math was practical, that it was fun, and that it was for everybody. I wanted to be able to better motivate students so that they would want to learn math, so they could see and demonstrate its practicality. So I went to graduate school at Oklahoma State University in Stillwater to earn a master's degree in mathematics. That was one of the best decisions I ever made. I had some of the finest math professors in the nation and I learned about all kinds of creative, motivational techniques, about math curriculum trends in the nation, and about the publishing field.

When I returned to Tulsa and the classroom, I was all fired up! I also had a student teacher from Oklahoma State University. That young man was a godsend. Elementary children really love having men as teachers. Just look at the movie *Kindergarten Cop* and you will see how children are drawn to the male teacher. I really used that young student teacher to show children how much fun math could be, and how wonderful it is to be able to do math.

I also got a chance to have some input into the math publishing field. The Houghton-Mifflin Publishing Company of Boston, Massachusetts was a major source of math materials in schools throughout the United States. I ordered so many of their materials, after my OSU graduate school experience, that a Houghton-Mifflin representative came from Boston to see me.

After we talked, he asked me to be on a writing team that was developing a new math textbook to be used nationwide. I accepted and it turned out to be a most rewarding experience, and I got all kinds of excellent textbooks and supplemental materials as a result. In 1969 I was asked to write a new handbook for elementary math teachers to use in Tulsa public schools.

Another thing that disturbs me is the habit of Americans to put down, to pan, to condemn American students and math and science education in this country. It is grossly unfair to compare our students with those in Europe, Japan, and other nations that have elitist systems of education that provide superior education for a small percentage of their students, but weed out and send forth the majority of their student population to be the labor force (often unskilled) of their nations. In the United States, students from all strata of society are given a good, wholesome, practical formal education. That was the intent of the founding fathers, that education in this country would be for the masses, not just for a privileged few.

We should not sell our children short. They are not math and science illiterate. They are bright and capable. They just need to be challenged more by their parents and by their teachers. Any child who can learn seventeen verses of some popular song and sing it through without missing a beat is not dumb! Why not channel that ability into useful learning? There are just too many distractions for our children today. But we can't do away with the twentieth century distractions; we have to learn to work around them.

Another thing that we need to do in this country is to stop telling minority children, especially blacks, that they can't learn math and science. While it is true that different individuals, and cultural groups, do have distinct learning styles and patterns, that does not mean that they can't learn certain subjects, or that they should be systematically excluded from certain subjects. If you look at the history of math, science, and inventions, you will find plenty of examples of blacks who were excellent in math and science and who created and invented many things that have enriched our society. All children can learn. We must motivate them better and make sure that they learn what is best for them and ultimately what is best for society.

ANITA HAIRSTON
b. November 5, 1907, Port Gibson, Mississippi

Access to education was never easy for me. In my native Port Gibson, Mississippi, public education for blacks went no further than the tenth grade. So my parents sent me to Southern Christian Institute, a private black boarding school in Edwards, Mississippi to complete my high school education. Then I enrolled at Langston University in Oklahoma. When I graduated from Langston, I moved to St. Louis, Missouri where I had to go back to college for a year because the St. Louis school system wouldn't accept some of my Langston credits. After that year of remediation, I got a teaching job in the city where I was very happy with my career. But my career was cut short because I met a young man.

Anita Hairston, first black graduate of the University of Tulsa.

I met Everette Hairston, a young dentist from Virginia, through the Disciples of Christ Church in St. Louis. Later, when he asked me to marry him, I said yes. But when he asked me to leave St. Louis and my teaching career to join him in Oklahoma where he was going to set up his practice, I was very reluctant. But I did quit my job and come to Oklahoma with him in 1946.

I joined the Tulsa branch of the NAACP and served on its education committee. I attended an NAACP meeting in Los Angeles in 1948 and when I came back to Tulsa I was on fire to do something to help my own community more, to help the city provide more opportunities for black people. I had been thinking about going to graduate school. I didn't think that it was fair that black Tulsans had to leave the city, the city where they paid taxes just like everybody else, and go out of the city, and out of the state, to pursue graduate study. So I decided that I was going to go to the University of Tulsa; but, first I would have to integrate it! I didn't think I would have much trouble. After all the U.S. Supreme Court had ordered the University of Oklahoma to admit George McLaurin and Ada Lois Sipuel. But that court ruling had no effect on the University of Tulsa. The university rejected my application for admission to school for the fall term of 1949! I just couldn't believe it. I tell you, I was mad. I was simmering.

Still simmering I confronted Dr. Harry W. Gowans, then dean of the University of Tulsa's Downtown division. This time, I met with partial success. Dr. Gowans said the University of Tulsa would provide classes for 'Colored students.' The catch was that the 'Colored' students couldn't attend classes on the campus; the university would provide the classes in George Washington Carver Junior High School in North Tulsa. I had mixed feelings. On the one hand, I was glad that I could be a University of Tulsa student at last, but I was disappointed that I couldn't go to class on the main campus. I longed to stroll that beautiful campus, to have classes in those classic buildings such as Tyrell Hall and in Kendall Hall, and to study in the magnificent McFarlin Library (named for Tulsa oil man Robert McFarlin). But that was not to be at that time.

I was asked to recruit other black teachers to study with me at Carver. Twenty signed up but they let me down. Only one black teacher from Tulsa, Algerita Jackson, and five black teachers from Wagoner joined me in my graduate studies. It wasn't all that I expected. Still I was grateful for the progress that we as blacks in

Tulsa had made. It was a first step toward integration and full equality. My grandfather always told me "One step is better than no step."

In just one year black students were allowed on the main campus. The spring of 1950 Dr. Sandor Kovacs, a University of Tulsa Sociology professor, put me in his class on the main campus. Years later Dr. Kovacs was asked why he made that decision, why he became the university official to integrate the TU campus. He said 'I just felt that she (Hairston) would get more out of her studies on the main campus. I asked my students how they felt; not one objected.' I instantly became a part of that class. The teacher was beautiful! The students were beautiful! It was a wonderful experience. Once the class went on a field trip to a house in Sand Springs (a little town just outside Tulsa). The entire class rode a bus to the home of a Sand Springs family who was host to the class. We had dinner with the family. We had the best time. Everyone was just as nice as could be.

When graduation time came in May 1952, some blacks in the community were apprehensive about me marching. They felt that there might be trouble if I marched across that stage and so they suggested that I have my diploma mailed to me. But my mind was made up. If that class of 1952 marched across that stage, I was going to march across it too. I was part of that class and they were not going to mail me anything! And so I did march across that stage.

Things have changed so much. In 1952 blacks were fearful that I would be mistreated if I marched across the stage with my class. Now the University of Tulsa couldn't be nicer to me. In 1987 I was an honored member of the class of 1952's 35th reunion. They made such a fuss over me. Now, the first thing you see when you walk into the TU Alumni Center is a picture of me in my cap and gown on that day in May 1952 when I made history. Some people call me a human rights activist; some call me a hero. I'm pleased when my friends call me those things. But I wasn't trying to be a hero. I spent my whole life just trying to make this world a little better for all people. When I see students of all colors strolling over the beautiful TU campus today, I thank God for making me the vessel that made that possible.

Fannie Ezelle Hill and Rev. Benjamin Harrison Hill.

FANNIE EZELLE HILL
b. August 8, 1904, Americus, Georgia

I have had a long and rewarding life, and I thank God for that. I was born and raised in Georgia. People ask me how I could be so loving and kind, and be from Georgia, too! Well I credit that to my loving parents. I had the most wonderful, loving parents in the world and my grandmother on my mother's side, an ex-slave, lived with us. I was taught to love everybody and not to be bitter no matter what experiences suffered. My grandmother was a slave until she was thirteen. She didn't like slavery, but she never let that experience poison her mind. She was precious and she was not bitter at all. Another thing that people do not know is that growing up in Georgia was not all prejudice, racism, and bitterness. Yes, it is true that some of the worst discrimination, prejudice, and racism ever known to mankind existed in the Deep South, but there were also examples of compromise and coexistence between the races, and sometimes downright brotherhood, fellowship, and love. My experiences with Jimmy Carter's family is an example of that.

There was such a paradox in the Deep South. Even though there was rigid segregation and often times cruelty and violence directed against black people, there were also acts of kindness and genuine friendship between people of the different races. An example of this was the friendship between my family and President Jimmy Carter's family which flourished right during this terrible period of segregation in Georgia. My brothers had played with the Carter boys when they were growing up in Plains, Georgia. The friendship between our families was solidified during a crisis which occurred in my immediate family. When I was a young wife and mother my nine-month-old son George became gravely ill and the doctor who had been summoned to treat him informed us that the baby would probably not live through the night. I was heartbroken and distraught. In fact I was mad at God and I said to God, 'If you are going to take my baby so soon, why did you send him to me in the first place!' My mother was shocked by my outburst and sent me to my room to rest and pray. But I couldn't pray, I couldn't sleep, I couldn't eat. I couldn't do anything but think about my precious baby and how I feared that he would be dead in the morning. Miss Lillian, Jimmy Carter's mother, a nurse, was aware of my baby's illness. When she finished her duties that day, she rode out to our house that evening by horseback and brought a remedy for the baby. My mother followed the directions religiously and the remedy worked! When I awoke the next morning (somehow I had fitfully slept), I was afraid to look into my baby's room because I thought he would be dead. But I was drawn to that room. I slowly crept into the room and went over to my baby's crib. He looked up at me and gave me a little grin. I grabbed him up into my arms, squeezed him tight, and wept tears of joy. That was the happiest day of my life. From that point on the Carters, the Johnson, and the Hill families were as united as blood relatives. My 'baby' is now a retired United States Air Force officer.

There is nothing I wouldn't do for the Carter family. When I learned that Jimmy was running for President, I joined his campaign trail. When he was in the White House, I accepted numerous invitations to join the family for various activities in the Capital. Yes, mutual respect, friendship, and love will always exist between our families. The bonds are strong enough to withstand any so-called human factor such as race.

Actually I found Tulsa's form of prejudice and discrimination more difficult to adjust to. When I came to Oklahoma, I had taught school for ten years in Georgia and Mississippi. My poor husband sure had a rough time adjusting to the South. You see he was born in Nova Scotia, Canada and raised in Colorado. He wasn't used to segregation. In Georgia I had to train him how to deal with segregation. He would drive up to a gas station pump and sit there expecting the service station man to put gas in his car for him just as he did for other customers. He just couldn't understand why he was being treated differently because of his color. But that was the way it was in Georgia for black people then. But in Georgia and over the deep South, there were provisions for black people, unlike in Oklahoma.

I was used to attending the best movies in beautiful movie theaters. Even though we had to sit in the balcony, we got to see the same current movies that white folks saw. In Tulsa blacks were not allowed in white theaters, not even in the balcony! North Tulsa had only two movie theaters and they showed poor quality, out of date films. When *The Ten Commandments* came to the Orpheum Theater in Tulsa, I was determined to see that film. I went down to the Orpheum every day that movie showed, but the answer was always the same, 'Now Mrs. Hill (they knew me well because of my husband's work at Vernon AME Church and as an activist in the community, and because of my own interfaith activities to promote peace and brotherhood in the community) you know we can't allow you in because of the law.' But I kept going every day just to show my indignation over Oklahoma's unfair segregation laws.

Tulsa was so segregated then. There were no stores, restaurants, movie theaters, no public accommodations opened to blacks. We used to see the white women meeting in tea rooms to discuss issues, but you wouldn't see a black face there, though black people were most often the subject of the 'issues' being discussed! Seidenbach's was one of the nicest stores in Tulsa then. Mrs. Seidenbach and I were among the first to begin the process of breaking down racial barriers in Tulsa.

The women of different races did begin to meet together in their churches and homes. I had a conversation with Mrs. Seidenbach. She was receptive to making changes in their store by hiring a black clerk, but she was fearful of what other whites would think. I told her, 'Do what you feel in your heart is right. Just follow your heart!' She did, too. She hired the first black saleswoman in a white Tulsa store. Whenever a black person would come into the store, that black clerk would be called. 'Course, Seidenbach's still had a floor on which the elevator would not stop if a black person was aboard — Tulsa was so hung up on race. I remember I once had an interfaith tea in my home and one of my dear white friends came. Her husband drove her to my house, but she said he wouldn't come in. He was afraid his white friends and neighbors would label him a 'communist.' Well I went out to the car and said to him, 'Come on in, we won't bite you!' He came in and we later became very good friends. Most people are good people and mean well. We just have to love them and help them overcome their fears so we can live together as brothers and sisters.

It is better today. Accommodations are open to all races, there is inter-racial exchange between the churches, people go to school together, go to the same hospitals, and socialize together. So we have come a long way. My generation did its best to speed up this process. In the '40s, '50s, and '60s, we called ourselves 'Salt and Pepper' groups (black and white) and we did our best to smooth the path with our religious dialogue groups. That opened up thought to an equal society. Then we proceeded on to active civil rights protests to bring 'the cause' to full fruition. Those were some exciting days — the civil rights protest with Tulsa's wonderful religious

Jobie Elizabeth Holderness

and secular elements coming together, young and old, black and white, for justice and equality in the city. My participation in the 1963 Civil Rights March on Washington was the highlight of my civil rights activism days. I will never forget that day as long as I live. Yes we have come a long way. People still think too much about race though. Like the man who had been trying to locate Vernon AME Church. He said he had been looking for the black church. I told him, 'No wonder you couldn't find it. It's not black, it's red brick!' The next day, my comment, and a photograph of me, appeared in the *Tulsa Tribune* newspaper. That is the way I feel. We need to stop being so hung up over race, over the color of someone's skin. We need to be busy about God's work. We need to just love everybody!

JOBIE ELIZABETH HOLDERNESS
b. September 27, 1900, Sulphur Springs, Texas

All my life I have loved children. It's no wonder that I chose teaching as a career. Actually, I didn't choose teaching; it chose me. It was a calling. I taught high school math at a Port Arthur, Texas high school for a short time before I moved to Tulsa. But it was in Tulsa that I found my true 'calling' — to spend my life teaching history and literature to lively, squirming, little elementary school boys and girls! That's what I did for forty-two years at Dunbar Elementary School in North Tulsa. It was a struggle teaching in all-black, segregated schools which had such limited supplies in those days. Parents had to struggle to get the paper, notebooks, pencils, pens, and textbooks that their children needed. Oh how some of them struggled! They would sacrifice anything so their children could get an education. If they had to cut back on something, they would do it so they could get those school supplies that their children needed — they would even cut back on food and clothing, if necessary. You see in those days education was highly valued. It was viewed as the main way out of poverty and racism; it was seen as the avenue for upward mobility in American society. It was the main path to the 'American Dream.'

When Tulsa public schools integrated in the 1960s, I was retired from teaching, but I went back to work as a substitute teacher. When I substituted in white schools, I couldn't believe the differences between those gleaming, teeming-with-supplies schools, and the sparsely-supplied 'Colored' schools that had been typical in the days of 'separate but equal' (vastly unequal) schools. There were so many excesses in the white schools. Their labs looked like little miniature NASA space centers. Why just in the lockers at these schools, there were more supplies than we had in our whole, segregated North Tulsa schools! The children looked like little fashion models. I remembered my early days at Dunbar when I would leave my classroom and go to the store that my husband Lynn and I operated on Greenwood Avenue, and pick up two and three pairs of shoes, and two or three coats for my little students who desperately needed them.

That store was more than just a store — it was a place where black people in the community knew they could come to for help. It was sort of a community social service agency. Of course, first of all it was a store, an old-fashioned country store that had a little bit of everything in it — all kinds of food items, underclothes, socks, stockings, gloves, dresses, pants, shirts, hats, all kinds of notions that people needed, and a little bit of every kind of junk. I remember we had a little stool for people to sit on while they were being fitted for shoes. Some people didn't come in to buy anything. They just came to visit or to get the correct time from our big, round Coca Cola clock on the wall. Others came for specific help — help in filling out forms and paperwork of all kinds, or help in getting sick people to the doctor or the hospital, whichever was needed. This was in the days before easy mass transportation, and bus routes didn't go into North Tulsa. Neither did people have private automobiles like they do now. Getting sick blacks proper medical care was no easy task. When the suffering showed up at our store, either Lynn or I would take the person to get help while the other one minded the store. If we had an influx of would-be patients, we would call one of the local, black funeral homes to send over a hearse. If they were not having a funeral that day, they would oblige. Many a sick North Tulsan showed up at a doctor's office, or at a hospital, in a somber, black hearse!

Those were some good old days. I miss the old Greenwood days. There were a lot of good things that came as a result of integration, but there were some losses, too. There are the equal opportunities for all races today, the equal access, but the black community lost some valuable things in the process. Urban renewal not only took away our property, but something else more important — our black unity, our pride, our sense of achievement and history. We need to regain that. Our youth missed that and that is why they are lost today, that is why they are in 'limbo' now. They do not have the roots, the pride, the unity that we had in those Greenwood days. I hope that we can give our youth a better sense of their history, their roots. They need to know what black North Tulsans did. They need to feel that pride, claim that success and move forward.

HUGH HOLLINS
b. November 2, 1913, Gilmore, Texas

As a young man in the little colored community of Gilmore, Texas, I was a farmer like my Daddy, my brothers, and most of the other black males in that part of Texas. And I was a pretty good farmer if I do say so myself. But it was always barbering that I loved best. When I was growing up in our little farming community, I was a leader among the poor black farm kids. For some reason, I always had the knack of talking and making others listen to me. The other boys always looked up to me and listened to me.

When I was eight years old, I talked one of my little playmates into letting me cut his hair. I charged him a nickel for doing it. I can't put into words how happy I felt when I finished that haircut and when I put that nickel in my pocket. Something just clicked in me and I felt that someday I was going to be a famous barber! I kept practicing cutting hair and I kept getting better. By the time I was twelve years old, my reputation as a hair stylist was spreading. By the time I was fourteen, I was earning good money giving 'style' haircuts to all the black boys in Gilmore. (I was also earning money helping grownups do carpentry jobs. That is why I called myself a 'Jackleg of all Trades'.)

I kept trying to learn all I could about barbering. I began to pay attention to the hair styles of whites in nearby Mineral Wells. I was curious about how they cut their straight hair. There were two colored boys in Gilmore who had what we called 'good hair' in those days, hair that was straight like white folks' hair. One was my brother who had fairly good hair; the other boy was a neighbor who

The late Naomi Hollins and Hugh Hollins, long-time Tulsa barbers

had dark skin, but he had straight hair, hair just as straight as any white person's. I begged both of them to let me experiment with their hair. I told them that I wanted to start a style in the community. And they let me cut their hair! I cut my brother's hair first. I cut his hair just like I had seen the whites cut their hair, but I added my own touch like using the razor all around, knocking the line in the back with a razor. I called it 'box cutting.' Then I cut the other boy's hair, adding my own special touches. My reputation spread and soon all the colored boys were coming to me for 'box styles.' And wouldn't you know it. Those white barbers in Mineral Wells stole my style and never gave me no credit for it. They renamed my 'box cut' 'The Longbranch.' But that Longbranch was nothing but the style I had created, and they never gave me no credit for it, no credit at all!

When I grew up, I had other jobs before I became a barber full time. First of all, I was a farmer and helped my Dad and brothers bring in many a good crop. I was also a pretty good jackleg carpenter. I went to Texarkana, Arkansas to work in a bomber plant in 1942. Then I came back to the Mineral Wells area of Texas and worked as a barber and as an inspector of cookware at the army base there. Then in 1944, I went to Oakland, California and worked at the naval yard there. I came to Oklahoma in 1946. First, I worked in Hugo and then in Oklahoma City. In Hugo, I met Alonzo Batson who had moved to Tulsa. He kept telling me what a good place Tulsa was for barbering. He wanted me to come and set up a nice barber shop in a safe place in North Tulsa. He suggested that I locate further up on Greenwood, not down on Deep Greenwood. He felt that there were too many shootings and stabbings down there, especially on Thursday nights and weekends when black people got their days off, and their wages from their South Tulsa employers and headed to Greenwood for partying. And usually during their partying, someone got shot or stabbed. I did set up my shop further on up like Alonzo had suggested and I had thirty years of happy barbering there. When Urban Renewal came through there and bought us black business people out, I had to move out to the 46th and Cincinnati area of Tulsa. It was alright out there. I had a nice little shop, but it was nothing like the shop I had on Greenwood all those years. I sure did love Greenwood in the old days.

JUANITA ALEXANDER LEWIS HOPKINS
b. July 29, 1923, Tulsa, Oklahoma

I just love history and I especially love sharing the history of Tulsa with anyone who will listen! Black Tulsans have such a rich and colorful history. It's a shame that so many people don't know it. That's why I'm always talking about it. That's why I'm always giving interviews. If just one person learns something about Tulsa and its fascinating history from what I share, then it's worth it. Some of Tulsa's history, I have learned through observation; I have learned other history by hearing about it from those who lived it (like the Tulsa Race Riot of 1921 which happened just two years before I was born) and still other history, I have read about. Oh what a history Tulsa has! When Greenwood was in its heyday there were ten black hotels in the Archer/Greenwood area, numerous drug stores, grocery stores, cleaners, shoe shops, millinery and dress shops, tailor shops, pool halls, theaters, funeral homes, doctors' and lawyers' offices, restaurants, and schools in the area. There were unskilled, semi-skilled, and professional people coexisting side by side — barbers and hairdressers, businessmen and professionals, and black policemen, including my father C.J. Alexander who was one of Tulsa's first black policemen. There were mostly good people, but there were some 'underworld' characters, too, mainly bootleggers and numbers runners. There were cultivated, sophisticated black people, there were working class, salt-of-the-earth people, and there were a few eccentrics and 'crazy' people.

One of my favorite stories was the one my mother told me about one of the richest black men in Tulsa at that time, who was also one of the city's most eccentric. He wore nothing but overalls — every day of the week nothing but overalls! And he didn't trust banks so he kept his money at home, hidden away in various sized tin cans. Once he went downtown to buy a new car. The salesman, turned off by the sight of this 'po' colored man in overalls, was quite abrupt with the man and unceremoniously and speedily tried to get rid of him. He bluntly told the unlikely looking customer that he (the salesman) couldn't extend him any credit. The overalled man replied, 'I didn't ask you for no credit' and he proceeded to withdraw wadded-up greenbacks from assorted tin cans. When he had counted out exactly the amount needed for the new car that he wanted, the poor salesman nearly died of apoplexy!

Juanita Lewis Hopkins

One of my mother's saddest stories was the one about her experiences during the 1921 race riot. The first day of the riot, my mother said that she and her good friend, Mrs. Alma Long, mother of the late, popular Tulsa activist Opal Long Dargan, went behind the white mobs that had set fires and tried to douse the flames with buckets of water. But that pitiful little 'fire brigade' was no match for the ever-increasing white mobs and soon they abandoned their hopeless efforts. The second day, things got so bad that the mothers and children fled the area. The men had already been picked up and incarcerated. That is the ones who were not already dead. My mother left carrying my six-month-old brother, C.J. Alexander, Jr., in her arms; Mrs. Long was by her side, holding six-year-old Opal by the hand. Her husband, Charles Wesley Long, had been taken to a detention camp but his wife didn't know it then. She was beside herself with worry. She kept wondering, out loud, whether he was dead or alive. Little Opal was home from school with the measles and that is how she got to be a participant in history.

After the riot Tulsa rebuilt from the ashes. In fact the North Tulsa after the riot was even more impressive than before the riot. That is when Greenwood became known as 'The Black Wall Street of America.' There are so many stories to be told about North Tulsa and its determined people — about its struggles with racism, about its creativity, adaptation, and survival. I always tried to share that with the many students that I taught. I estimate that I must have taught over 6,000 students during my career and I loved every minute of it! I am so proud of all of them. I even have walls in my home filled with paintings done by some of my students (including Paulette Black who is now the State Arts Coordinator for the State Department of Education in Oklahoma City and Alex Corbbrey who is an internationally renowned artist today). Tulsa produced so many talented and creative people. I just jump with joy when I see a television or movie credit listing a Tulsan, or when I see a beautiful painting by a Tulsan, or hear a piece of music written or performed by a Tulsan. Bob Rogers, a Booker T. Washington high school graduate, is a major New York City set designer. I often see his name in credits for spectacular set designs for media productions. Emmett McHenry, a former student of mine, is a technology graduate who just recently was granted a $4 million dollar contract with the U.S. government. Hal Singer, who was born on Latimer

Place in North Tulsa, has been a popular musician in Paris, France for forty years. There are so many people who have gone from Tulsa and who have done great things. The 'Tulsa experience' just seemed to bring out the best in all of us!

WILHELMINA GUESS HOWELL
b. April 25, 1907, McAlester, Oklahoma

When I was a little girl I used to visit my Dad's law office on Greenwood Avenue and also the office of my mother's brother, my favorite uncle, Dr. A.C. Jackson which was also located on Greenwood. My uncle was a very respected surgeon. In fact, my family has a document written by a doctor at the famous Mayo Clinic in Rochester, Minnesota in which my uncle was referred to as one of the finest surgeons in the nation. But all that medical stuff was unimportant to me. What was important to me was that this man was my favorite uncle and he had saved my life when I came down with a severe case of scarlet fever when I was eight years old. For a while my family feared I was going to die. But my uncle doctored me and I lived. From then on he was my hero! That is why I was just devastated when he was killed in the Tulsa Race Riot of 1921. The mindless acts of a bunch of thugs took him away from me and I will never forget that.

The fact that the riot which destroyed my father's office and which killed my uncle occurred in Tulsa seemed very ironic. My relatives had come to Oklahoma to get away from racism, violence, and death. In fact, my grandfather Guess just barely made it out of Tennessee alive. The night before he left Memphis, the mob came for him. But he had gotten word that the mob would be coming for him and he had fled to a neighbor's house where he was hidden until he could get safely out of Tennessee. If it had not been for those kind, courageous neighbors, the mob would have lynched nine black men that night, instead of eight, and I wouldn't be here today. We were always so proud of our ancestors. They had struggled so hard to take their families where they could be safe, get a good education, prosper, and serve the community. That is exactly what my Daddy did. He went off to Howard University in Washington, D.C. to become a lawyer. Then he returned to Tulsa to devote his life to helping his

Wilhelmina Guess Howell pointing to a picture of her uncle, Dr. A.C. Jackson, who was killed by mobsters in the 1921 Tulsa Race Riot.

people. When the riot burned down his office, he rebuilt and continued to practice law until his death in 1931. My Grandpa Guess was also proud of his other son, Dr. James Guess, who graduated from Meharry Medical College in Memphis, Tennessee and who practiced medicine in Okmulgee for over fifty years.

I never forgot my Daddy, my Uncle A.C., my Uncle James, and all my other Guess relatives on my father's side, and my maternal ancestors, the McMullens, who were equally strong, pioneer Oklahomans. I tried to uphold the family tradition of educational excellence and service to mankind. As an elementary teacher in Tulsa for forty years, I tried to give young black students a sense of pride in their ancestry and history. I tried to motivate them to develop their talents, to excel, and to contribute their talents and service to the community. Most of them did. I believe my grandfather would have been proud of me. I am sure glad that he got out of Tennessee that night before that mob got him!

EUNICE CLOMAN JACKSON
b. August 27, 1903, Lake Village, Arkansas

Racial discrimination affected black people from the cradle to the grave before the civil rights movement of the 1960s opened up accommodations to blacks. In the old days even in death black people had to take care of their own. White people wouldn't embalm black people in Oklahoma then. When a black person died, Mr. McBirney (a white funeral home owner in early Tulsa) and other white funeral home owners wouldn't pick up the body. If they went to a place and found out that the body was that of a black person, they would say 'What's the matter with Mr. Jackson? Call him!' They just wouldn't touch a black body.

Our first funeral home was located at 639 E. Marshall Place, just off of Greenwood, where the funeral home was downstairs and the living quarters upstairs. That building was burned down in the race riot of 1921. We relocated several times after that. Our last move was to our present location on 36th Street North.

That riot that destroyed our first funeral home and so much of North Tulsa was a terrible thing. When the riot began that evening we were sitting out in the yard and people were just running toward

Eunice Cloman Jackson, wife of funeral home owner Samuel Jackson, and race riot survivor.

us and hollering. Mama yelled, 'What's the matter? Where are you people going?' Somebody replied, 'There's a riot over on Brickyard Hill (Greenwood Avenue area). They're just shooting everybody they can!' More black people came running by. So we joined the running crowd — men, women, and children — all just running, running for our lives! We were stopped by the police at Pine and Greenwood, a place that was called 'The Section Line.' It was a big crowd of us black people by then. We were marched to the Convention Hall on Brady Street where we stayed all afternoon.

Later people who had a home were allowed to go home. We left although we didn't know if our house was standing or not. My mother had a bag with my brother's gun in it. On the way home a policeman stopped her and asked, 'What you got in the bag, Auntie?' All the black people were staring at the white policeman; they were just scared out of their wits. My mother slowly opened the bag. The policeman took the gun out and kept it. All he said was, 'You don't need this.' We went on our way and when we got to our house which was on the corner of Marshall and Elgin Streets, oh Lordy, it was still standing! We later found out how our house was saved. Every time a white mob would put a bucket (of burning debris) into our house, and go on to set a bucket in another house, some poor, white neighbors of ours would go in and take out the burning bucket. You hear a lot about the white mobs during the riot; you don't hear much about good, white Samaritans but they were there too. I will always be grateful to those white neighbors who saved our house during that riot. Most black people weren't as lucky as we were though. Most of their homes and businesses were just gutted, burned to the foundation!

After the riot, black people rebuilt. They just were not going to be kept down. They were determined not to give up. So they rebuilt Greenwood and it was just wonderful. It became known as The Black Wall Street of America. Of course it was a little on the wild side. Greenwood was always wild. When Mama used to bring us kids up to Tulsa before the riot we'd come by train. The conductor always announced the Greenwood stop (at the corner of Archer) with a little song:

> All out for Tush hog town,
> Greenwood Street, the battling
> ground!

There was a lot of fighting on Greenwood too. There was always some knifing or shooting down on Greenwood. But people also took great pride in the beautiful homes and businesses in the Greenwood area. That's why it is so sad to see what's left of Greenwood today. Urban Renewal and the highway just took away our Greenwood. First the riot took it away and we rebuilt. Now Urban Renewal and that highway (I-244) took it away and we haven't been able to build it back.

The funeral home business has changed too. For one thing black funeral homes have many more supplies than they had in the old days. In fact in the 1920s and early 1930s, the bodies of black people were embalmed right in their homes where they had died. The mortician would put the person on an ironing board or something flat like that and embalm the body right there. The deceased would then be placed in the coffin that the funeral director had brought and the families would then be ready to receive visitors. The selection of coffins has changed too. Then people bought simple sad-looking coffins. Now they want elaborate satin-lined, padded, elegant caskets. Behavior at funerals has changed also. In those days preachers preached long sad funerals and relatives would just cry, scream, jump and fall out during their grief. We would stand around with bottles of smelling salts, handkerchiefs, and fans. Funeral directors taught us how to catch the falling strickened people so they wouldn't hurt themselves or us. Some of the changes in the funeral business are good. In fact most of them are good. There are better and nicer supplies. Preachers don't preach funerals to make people fall out and have fits like they used to, and black people are no longer discriminated against from the cradle to the grave. That final trip — to the funeral home and the cemetery — is integrated now. And that's a good thing for the American democracy and for human beings no matter what their color!

REVEREND BILLY JARRETT
b. November 3, 1923, Tulsa, Oklahoma

Jarrett's Grocery Store was such a part of my life. It gave me my first knowledge of the work world. Our home was just four blocks from the store so all of us kids spent most of our time in the store. My first job, a janitorial job, kept me busy cleaning up, sweeping, and helping Daddy put groceries on the shelves. I was thrilled when I worked up to delivery boy. I got to deliver groceries by bicycle!

I learned a lot about people and about society in general in that store. I remember how people suffered during the depression years in the 1930s. There were even some break-ins where people broke into the store and stole food. But break-ins were different then. People just took food items or other merchandise that they could sell to get food for their families. Today there is a lot of mean-spirited, senseless vandalism. The thieves don't seem to be stealing out of necessity. They aren't starving to death like people were during the depression. They're not stealing out of hunger. Who knows why they steal now?

I learned my first lesson about credit when I was a boy clerking in that store. A lady and her son came in and selected a lot of merchandise. When I had finished bagging everything and had totaled her bill, the woman looked at me and said 'I don't have any money.' I didn't know what to do. So I asked her if she would wait while I went and got my father. She agreed. When my Dad came in, he said to her 'Things are rough now, but I think they will get better. Let's just keep looking up.' He never mentioned the money. When the woman and her son left the store, I said 'Daddy, I don't understand. What about the money? Why didn't you ask the woman about the money?' Daddy looked at me and said 'Son, when you are older, then you will understand.' Daddy was right. I do understand now.

Our store was a life-line to many people in the days when Tulsa was so segregated and black people had to look after themselves and after each other. When people didn't have money, my Daddy let them put their groceries 'on the ticket.' People were so honest then. They most always paid their bills. Sometimes they would be slow and could pay just a little at a time, but they kept plucking along

Rev. Billy Jarrett, former janitor and delivery boy for Jarrett's Grocery.

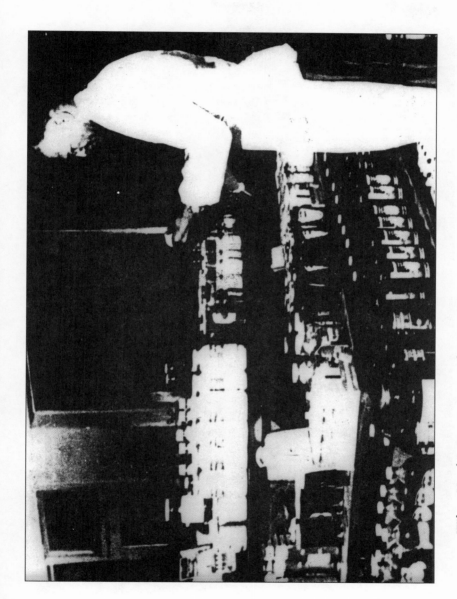

Wilson Hendrix Jarrett, owner of Jarrett's Grocery at 1122 North Greenwood Avenue.

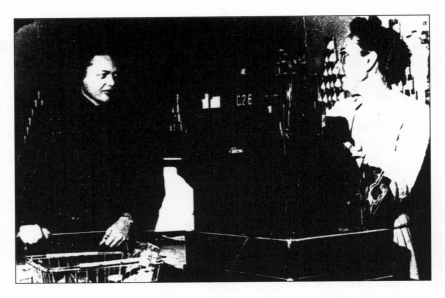

Jarrett's Grocery

Jo Pearl Jarrett waits on a customer in Jarrett's Grocery.

until they got their credit paid off. I long for the return of that kind of integrity. Some people think that integrity is a characteristic of only the rich and famous. That is not true. In that little store on Greenwood Avenue, we saw integrity in poor people. It might not have been easy, but these people were decent, honest, and hard-working despite their poverty.

HENRY JOHNSON
b. April 18, 1914, Taft, Oklahoma

I guess the turning point in my life was when I went away to Tuskegee, Alabama to attend college. Tuskegee Institute was such a fine institution. Founder Booker T. Washington's philosophy permeated every phase of life on that campus. There were superb faculty and staff there and the students were not only trained well in the classroom, they were exposed to hands-on learning experiences. Students in the trade fields made the brick that was used in campus building projects, electrical students did the wiring, agricultural students grew the crops, etc. No talent was wasted on that campus. But there was time also for the arts and for sports. I was on the football team in 1934. I was a good catcher and whenever a player threw the ball to me, it was a given that I was going to catch that ball! But I didn't like pain, so whenever I caught the ball, I stepped out of bounds because I just couldn't stand the idea of all those big guys tackling me. I was considered a small man on that Tuskegee football team. Coach Major was patient with me because I could sure handle that ball, but I quit the team. I just couldn't stand all that tackling.

My favorite person on the campus was Dr. George Washington Carver. He was one of my best friends. My roommate cut his (Dr. Carver's) hair for 25 cents a haircut. Dr. Carver had a very fine, high-pitched voice that caused a lot of young people to tease and mock him. But he was such a brilliant man; he was a master of language in addition to being a master scientist. His words were so powerful. And he knew more about science than any man I ever met. He could pick up a blade of grass and talk about it a half a day! He knew that much about the plant world. I sure did like Dr. Carver. I just enjoyed sitting down next to him on the campus and just talking. Sometimes guys would tease him about his voice or about his girlfriends (which I don't think he had any). A few times, I bruised my knuckles on some of them for teasing him.

Dr. Carver was a very private man. He lived in Rockefeller Hall on the Tuskegee campus and he didn't allow anyone in his room except one woman who cleaned it (and my roommate when he cut Dr. Carver's hair). But once there was a fire in his room and I was one of the persons who went into the room to help. That is the only time I ever saw that room.

George Washington Carver was a wonderful, unpretentious man. He put on no airs. Once when he came to give a science talk at Langston University, he sat on a bench a half a day just observing the comings and goings of students across the campus. Dressed casually and wearing an old floppy hat, he was unrecognizable. Students passed by never knowing that there sat one of the most eminent scientists in America!

Another thing about Dr. Carver, he never bore a grudge. Teasing or racist remarks never caused him to stir. He once told this story about the time he was on a train going to Fayetteville, Arkansas to give a speech at the University of Arkansas. Some white college boys on the train decided to have some fun with the casually dressed, old black man on the train. One of the boys said 'Hey, George get me a glass of water.' The old man got up and got the boy a glass of water. When the train stopped in Fayetteville all the university dignitaries were waiting for that old man — Dr. George Washington Carver! Can you imagine the horror those students must have felt when they found out that the 'Old George' who had brought the glass of water was their eminent, keynote speaker? Dr. Carver could have gotten those boys expelled from school if he had wanted to, but he never mentioned the incident to officials. That's the kind of man he was.

When Dr. Carver came to Tulsa to the dedication of George Washington Carver Junior High School in 1929, he was lovingly and exuberantly received by Tulsans. It was such an honor to have the most eminent scientist in America in our city. I am so grateful that I got my education at Tuskegee and that I got to meet such fine educators as Dr. George Washington Carver.

IMA WILSON JOHNSON
b. January 21, 1918, Rocky Mount, Texas

My experience as an art student at the University of Tulsa was one of the happiest experiences of my life. Actually, I graduated from Langston University in Oklahoma with a degree in music, but it was always art that I loved best. Ever since I can remember, I have always had a pencil, pen, or paint brush in my hand. I was always drawing.

In 1939, just after Henry and I got married, we were living in a little North Tulsa garage apartment. Our landlady, Effie Frazier, was the housekeeper of Dr. Adah Robinson who was the head of the University of Tulsa's art department at the time. Being around Dr. Robinson and the art students who were always around, Mrs. Frazier developed a liking for art. She noticed some of my drawings and liked them so much that she wanted to show them to Dr. Robinson. So I let her take them to her. That is how I first came into contact with Dr. Robinson. It was during the height of racial segregation in Oklahoma, so no matter how much Dr. Robinson liked my drawings, no matter how talented she thought I was, I couldn't have been a TU art student at that time. But Dr. Robinson and I just 'got around and got over' all that stuff. Every day Mrs. Frazier would take some of my work to show to Dr. Robinson who would critique the drawings (in a little blue notebook that I still have and treasure) and send the critiques back to the little garage apartment by Mrs. Frazier.

I learned so much from Dr. Robinson. She was a superb water colorist! I could already do pen and pencil drawings and oil paintings. I learned those things at Langston University, but I didn't know anything about water color art. Dr. Robinson said that an artist needed only three colors — red, blue, and yellow. She said that the white would come from the white of the paper. She taught me how to make a wash of colors, and how to do still life paintings. She was a master at that and I am so grateful for what she taught me.

Soon Dr. Robinson wanted to meet me. Effie Frazier had taken a still life drawing of some apples that I had done for Dr. Robinson to critique. She had written in the little blue book 'You draw apples better than my students; come and visit my art classes.' And so I did. I even modeled for the class (I was always fully clothed!).

Ima Wilson Johnson and Henry Johnson.

Later, when the University of Tulsa integrated in 1950, I enrolled and received a Master of Arts degree in art. It was a marvelous experience. I had excellent instructors such as Brad Place, Dwayne Hatchell, and Alexandre Hogue, the late artist noted for his superb western-themed art. I purchased one of Mr. Hogue's paintings, *Sage and Cedar*, number 38 out of 50. That painting has increased in value tremendously since I purchased it, and since Mr. Hogue's death in 1994, but I will never sell it. It is a link to my past that I will never sever. I loved being an art student on the TU campus in the 1950s, but long before that, I had been exposed to TU's superb art department thanks to that wonderful woman, Dr. Adah Robinson.

MAXINE JOHNSON
b. December 8, 1927, Tulsa, Oklahoma

When Freddie Rudisill suggested that I become active in the community so I could overcome my shyness, I took her advice. I got involved with the local NAACP because I liked what it did to try to secure rights for all citizens. In 1980 I decided to run for President of the local NAACP chapter. I wanted to serve a couple of terms and then step down. It was my firm belief that leaders served too long in their positions. I felt that they didn't give our younger people enough chances to train for leadership. The older leaders once in just stayed and stayed until they died off and the young never had a chance to train for leadership.

My philosophy as leader of the local NAACP was that we had to give people hope. We just couldn't sit back and wait for things to get better. We had to go out and make things get better. And if you encourage people and give them hope that they can help to make things better, they will work with you. Otherwise they'll just sit around and stew in their hopelessness and disillusionment; some might even react with rage and violence. Well we went to the people. We didn't wait for them to come to meetings. (Meetings are all right, but people are tired of meetings. They want action.) Everywhere that there were people we were there. We went to the people in supermarkets, beauty shops, barber shops, and similar places. We went to the people wherever they went in their normal daily routine. And they saw that we were doing something — registering people to

Maxine Johnson

vote, petitioning city hall, filing lawsuits. That's the answer — education plus action. That's what I do. I stay in the community. I'm always in the street, in people's houses, in stores. I'm always out and about trying to make Tulsa a better community. We were successful. Two of our biggest successes were the *NAACP v. The City of Tulsa* lawsuit that challenged unfair, at-large elections in the city, and *Greg Robinson v. The State of Oklahoma* which challenged at-large elections of judges.

When I had served two terms I kept my word. I stepped down as president of the local chapter of the NAACP so a young person could lead. That young man who replaced me, Joe Williams, is now a city councilor. Was it worth all the hard work? Did the city change? There was some change but the city still has a long way to go before all of its citizens enjoy equality and justice. But it is better. In the old days when black citizens would show up at city hall meetings with their long lists of grievances city officials were less than receptive. There was one official who openly dozed as black citizens poured forth their poignant stories of neglect! Can you believe that there would be a commissioner forever sleeping while people were pleading their hearts out about injustice in the city? Well, he did! He would often awaken with a start and pretend to know what was going on, but he didn't; he didn't know a thing about what was going on.

There have been some positive changes in the city of Tulsa like blacks being represented on the city council and Tulsa now having a black district judge. But there is still more rhetoric than reality in the city. Tulsa is still not an equal society for women and minorities. The 'Good Old Boy' system is still alive and well in Tulsa. It doesn't take a rocket scientist to see who is doing most of the building and contracting work in the city, or to see who holds the higher level management positions in society, and who holds the lower-rung, entry level positions. Still we must not give up. Keep educating, keep up action-oriented activities, and stay 'in the face' of people until they get the message. The message is that everyone in every city and state in the nation is entitled under the law to the same equality. I won't stop hitting the streets until that is a reality!

Waldo Jones, Sr.

WALDO JONES, SR.
b. February 16, 1909, Muskogee, Oklahoma

In the 1920s and 1930s, Tulsa was a very segregated place. 'Colored' (as we were referred to then) lawyers could not have their offices in the downtown area. They were allowed in the old courthouse, which was on 4th Street, when cases were being heard and they wanted to observe, but they were not allowed to use the rest room in the courthouse. But I remember that my father-in-law, B. C. Franklin, just ignored the segregation rules. He did use that white rest room! But I don't think any of the rest of us black lawyers were brave enough to defy Jim Crow laws then. There were lots of good, black lawyers in the area such as Amos T. Hall, H. A. Guess, Primus Wade, P. A. Chappelle, I. G. Spears, O. B. Graham and others. Most of us had our offices on Greenwood or somewhere in the Greenwood and Archer region. My office was on Greenwood directly across the street from Vernon AME Church. Amos T. Hall and Primus Wade were down the street from me.

There were some interesting cases then, high-dollar cases involving land claims, riots, murders and such. I remember that my father-in-law worked the Lee Corbin oil case for thirty years. He made $35 or $40 thousand dollars on that case. That was a lot of money then. B. C. gave each of his children (my wife Mozella was his daughter) some cash money and then he went on a trip to New York. His wife had passed away, so he went to New York alone.

After the Tulsa Race Riot of 1921, B. C. Franklin, I. G. Spears, and P. A. Chappelle made a name for themselves handling riot lawsuits in their little law 'office' which was a tent on Greenwood Avenue!

Case loads have sure changed. Then we had oil lease cases, land conflict suits, and the usual crimes of passion. Today there are more cases involving arson and drugs, hate crimes by Ku Klux Klan and Skinhead advocates and such, drive-by shootings, carjackings, and other youth-related crimes. We didn't have much youth crime in the old days. I believe that the root of all this drug and violence-oriented crime today is the breakdown of spiritual and family values. Until society restores moral and spiritual values, and provides economic stability to all segments of society — not just to the upper

Ed Lacy

and middle classes — these problems are going to continue. We especially have a problem with young black males. We must steer them away from negative behavior and activities that will lead them into the criminal justice system. They must be shown the dangers of ever getting involved with the criminal justice system. It is a deadend to nowhere. Once into that system, many of them forfeit their chances of healthy, happy, harmonious, productive lives in the future. This country needs to focus more on prevention of crime than on punishment after crimes have been committed. We must provide more positive opportunities for young people so they won't end up in the criminal justice system. It's cheaper, more humane, and more in line with the spiritual and democratic values of the counrty.

I am so proud to have been a part of Tulsa's legal profession. Tulsa is in good hands today. There are lots of good lawyers in the city. We have a fine crop of young, black lawyers who are carrying on the tradition begun long ago by lawyers like my father-in-law, B. C. Franklin, and the cadre of other lawyers who paved the way for them. Among them are Carlos Chappelle, Judith Colbert, Sandra Alexander, Walter Benjamin, Otis Williams, Jr., Steve Broussard, my own son Waldo Jones, Jr., and there are plenty of others. Yes, the city is in good hands with its fine lawyers today!

EDWARD J. LACY
(b. September 13, 1921, Dallas, Texas)

I have always loved two things in life — learning and sports. I always managed to do justice to both and to reap the benefits of both. I was too short and too small to play on college teams, but I have always been grateful for the lessons that I learned during intramural games in Tulsa public schools' athletic programs. In college I majored in physical education because of my love of sports and my entire professional career was in athletic education. I can't believe that I got paid for doing what I loved so much!

I am well aware of the controversy involving athletics and academics. Some people believe that athletic activities are emphasized too much and ought to be downsized or outright eliminated so students can concentrate on what they are in school for in the first place

— to learn. Other people feel just as strongly that athletics can often be the carrot-on-the stick to motivate students to stay in school and to do the very thing that they are there for — to learn. I can see validity in both views. I know that the primary focus of schools must be on academics, on the basics, on teaching the skills, knowledge, and behaviors that will help students survive in our highly competitive, technological world. On the other hand if students drop out of school, teachers won't be able to do that training. Athletic activity is a prime motivator of youth, especially young males who comprise the highest percentage of dropouts. If athletics lures them to school and keeps them there, then we'll stand a chance of educating them. Otherwise they are lost to the streets where their pathological behavior hurts them and the overall society. So we must walk a tightrope and carefully balance both. All the scientific studies that I have read seem to support this philosophy of balancing academics and athletics to ensure that students stay in school and learn the skills they need for success as adults. I always stressed academics first; but of course I loved athletics too. And the students could see that. As a result I was able to balance those two goals.

Another problem that we have in American society is that people tend to idolize athletes and entertainers too much. They either make them Gods and expect them to do no wrong, or they make them Gods and fall apart when the athletes and entertainers display normal, human characteristics and make mistakes. Here we need some balance too. Instead of unduly worshiping athletes and entertainers, students need to learn to recognize, appreciate, and pattern their behavior after real role models — their hard-working, loving parents, dedicated teachers, firemen, policemen, postmen, etc., the nuts-and-bolts, salt-of-the-earth type role models that made this country great! They need to learn to appreciate mathematicians, scientists, and inventors as much as they do athletes and entertainers. After all it was these creative people who gave us all the technological know-how and inventions that enrich our lives today. During Black History Month, teachers focus on the contributions of black mathematicians and scientists. We need to stress those contributions throughout the whole year.

Athletes need to remember that they do have a disproportionate amount of influence on young people. They really are role models to millions and millions of unseen, unknown children. That ought to make them think twice about what they do, knowing that they have all that influence on children. They should choose the good, positive behaviors that will guide children in the right direction. Before they do anything, they ought to ask themselves, "What if a child were watching me?" Then they ought to behave in an appropriate manner, for whether they want to be or not, they are role models to our youth. It is a sad thing to see anyone make a mistake, fall out of favor, or fail in society. It is especially tragic to people when that person is a popular athlete or entertainer. Just look at all the fuss over the O.J. Simpson trial. That is a classic example.

I have always tried to live my life where my actions would be a positive example for youth. I was deeply honored when the city of Tulsa renamed a park in North Tulsa for me. That was the nicest tribute the city — my friends of all races, creeds, colors, occupations — could have given me. I will always strive to deserve that honor.

CAESAR LATIMER
b. January 26, 1927, Tulsa, Oklahoma

Ever since I was a child I have been concerned about law, order, justice, and equality. When I was a student at Booker T. Washington High School in Tulsa, I played the part of a lawyer in a school play. I was hooked; I wanted to be a lawyer from then on. But it was really three things that compelled me to go into the legal profession:

1. My anger and frustration over racism — the racism that I had grown up with in Oklahoma and especially the racism that I observed in the U.S. military during World War II when I was a Marine in uniform risking my life for my country which afforded me only second class citizenship;
2. The death of my father (and the serious injury of my sister, Julia) in a freak automobile accident in Tulsa in 1951 in which the city of Tulsa was clearly negligent, but unapologetic, and in my opinion, grossly unfair and unjust;
3. The persistent, unending nagging of my mother, Maria Latimer (who died in 1985).

A look at the overall history of the U.S. military shows that racism has always permeated the institution, from stem to stern, as it did all other aspects of the American culture. It is obvious that

Caesar Latimer

military assignments, promotions, awards and honors, and everything else, were determined by race. As in the overall society blacks
received the worst assignments, the fewest awards and honors, and
were generally just given the 'leftovers' that nobody else wanted.
(Of course, there were some exceptions. A few blacks were promoted to high ranks and received awards such as Brigadier General
Roscoe Cartwright, the highest ranking black military person ever
to come from Tulsa, and Colonel Major Clark of Tulsa.) I just felt
that racism in the military was the most unfair of all racism. If we
were good enough to fight and die for our country (and many
blacks have done so from pre-Revolutionary days to the present),
then we were good enough to be treated like first class citizens!

My father's accident greatly influenced me into becoming a
lawyer. The accident happened at a traffic circle at Admiral and
Mingo in southeast Tulsa. There had been construction work in the
area to widen the circle and a big mound of dirt had been left in the
center of the road. There were no flashing lights, no warnings and
Dad just didn't see that mound. He ran right into it! He and my
sister, both seriously injured, were taken to the segregated hospital
in North Tulsa. Because their injuries were so serious, they were
then taken to St. John's Hospital, the white hospital at 21st and
Utica in South Tulsa. Dad was the more seriously injured, but he
insisted that the hospital staff treat Julia first. She was and then he
was treated. They were both treated in the hallway and were not
allowed to be admitted to rooms. Dad later died of a severely
crushed chest. Julia recovered, but had permanent facial scars. The
roof of her mouth had to be restructured (with plastic) and she
received not one penny for her injuries, and our family received not
one penny of compensation for Dad's fatal injuries. That made me
mad and I vowed to go to law school and work to prevent such
injustices in the future.

But I must say that of all the incentives for me to complete my
law school studies, none was more effective than my mother's nagging. The woman never let up! So I entered Indiana University's
School of Law because the University of Oklahoma wouldn't admit
me when I first wanted to enter after I got back from World War II.
But I dropped out after two years. My mother stayed on me for two
solid years. Every day for two years she nagged me to return to law
school. Thank God she did. I finished my law studies and returned

Josie Lewis

The moment that law is destroyed, liberty is lost; and men, left free to enter upon the domains of each other, destroy each other's rights, and invade the field of each other's liberty.—Timothy Titcomb.

IT MUST NOT BE AGAIN

SUCH a district as the old "Niggertown" must never be allowed in Tulsa again. It was a cesspool of iniquity and corruption. It was the cesspool which had been pointed out specifically to the Tulsa police and to Police Commissioner Adkison, and they could see nothing in it. Yet anybody could go down there and buy all the booze they wanted. Anybody could go into the most unspeakable dance halls and base joints of prostitution. All this had been called to the attention of our police department and all the police department could do under the Mayor of this city was to whitewash itself. The Mayor of Tulsa is a perfectly nice, honest man, we do not doubt, but he is guileless. He could have found out himself any time in one night what just one preacher found out.

In this old "Niggertown" were a lot of bad niggers and a bad nigger is about the lowest thing that walks on two feet. Give a bad nigger his booze and his dope and a gun and he thinks he can shoot up the world. And all these four things were to be found in "Niggertown"—booze, dope, bad niggers and guns.

The Tulsa Tribune makes no apology to the Police Commissioner or to the Mayor of this city for having plead with them to clean up the cesspools in this city.

Commissioner Adkison has said that he knew of the growing agitation down in "Niggertown" some time ago and that he and the Chief of Police went down and told the negroes that if anything started they would be responsible.

That is first class conversation but rather weak action.

Well, the bad niggers started it. The public would now like to know: why wasn't it prevented? Why were these niggers not made to feel the force of the law and made to respect the law? Why were not the violators of the law in "Niggertown" arrested? Why were they allowed to go on in many ways defying the law? Why? Mr. Adkison, why?

The columns of The Tribune are open to Mr. Adkison for any explanation he may wish to make.

These bad niggers must now be held, and, what is more, the dope selling and booze selling and gun collecting must STOP. The police commissioner, who has not the ability or the willingness to find what a preacher can find and who WON'T stop it when told of it, but merely whitewashes himself and talks of "knocking chairwarmers" had better be asked to resign by an outraged city.

FOR TULSA

Don't let your eye escape the coupon on the first page. Put your pencil to it. The honor of Tulsa is at stake. For the commercial stability of Tulsa stands in jeopardy. For reasons of justice, for simple, plain, good business reasons, Tulsa must do the right thing and do it NOW. Are you a Tulsan? Give. And give NOW.

children, one a baby a month old. Mrs. M. R. Travis of 1702 South Boulder, who is in charge of this case, is anxious to hear from anyone who knows of the whereabouts of Mrs. Love and the children. Her telephone number is Osage 2447.

JURY SUMMONS BEING ISSUED FOR RIOT QUIZ

BIDDISON ASKS THAT FREELING BE SENT HERE AT ONCE

OKLAHOMA CITY — Attorney General S. P. Freeling intends to go tomorrow to Tulsa where he will conduct an investigation into the race riot, as ordered yesterday by Governor Robertson, he said today. Evidence secured in the investigation will be presented to the grand jury, which meets June 8.

It was said at the governor's office today that an message had been received from Judge Biddison of Tulsa asking that the attorney general be in Tulsa Monday. Mr. Freeling had planned previously, however, to go tomorrow and to start work on the date asked by Judge Biddison.

Jury summons were being issued today for service on the grand jury for investigating and fixing the responsibility of the race riots in district court, while a call was under way to Governor Robertson from Judge W. Valjean Biddison asking that Attorney General Prince Freeling be sent here Monday to prepare his case for the quiz on Wednesday. Freeling has already been ordered here by the governor.

Judge Biddison said today that jury summons were already under way and that he was in active direction of the empaneling of a grand jury ordered by Governor Robertson. The date set for the first sessions of the jury is June 8. The investigation by the state authorities will be carried on separately from that ordered by the department of justice at Washington.

no more right to invade it than a professional burglar. If the search warrant is not available, then it is the duty of the police to exercise common sense in their selection of houses that might justify a search.

The suggestion of the Real Estate Exchange that the negro district be moved out farther, the present burned-over area to be given over to industry and switch tracks is a sensible one. If Tulsa business is to expand, the ground now in ashes is by all odds one of the most necessary to such expansion.

The honor of a large number of Tulsans is being put to the test by the gun store men. They want their property returned.

Sat. June 4, 1921 Tulsa Tribune

— photo courtesy of Robert Hower

Archer Street/Greenwood Avenue Corner Building, west side. KATY Railroad tracks. Photo courtesy of Jean Houston, widow of Merton Houston, photographer, channel 6, CBS, KOTV Television, Tulsa;
— photo identification by Robert Fairchild.

Greenwood Avenue looking north from Archer.
— Houston photo; Fairchild identification.

Corner of Brady Avenue, looking south to Greenwood.
— Houston photo; Fairchild identification.

West side of Greenwood Avenue.
— Houston photo; Fairchild identification.

Tulsa Race Riot of 1921 destruction.

— Houston photo.

Tulsa Race Riot of 1921 destruction.

— Houston photo.

East side of Greenwood Avenue where the Dreamland Theater was located.
— Houston photo; Fairchild identification.

Unidentified woman, Greenwood Avenue.
— Houston photo.

Charles Page, Wisconsin-born Sand Springs oil millionaire who was noted for befriending widows and orphans; During and after the Tulsa Race Riot of 1921, he befriended Tulsa black riot refugees.
— Sand Springs Leader

Tulsa Race Riot of 1921 destruction.
— photo courtesy of Sand Springs Leader newspaper,
Sand Springs, Oklahoma.

Tulsa Race Riot of 1921 destruction.

— Sand Springs Leader

Ashley Nicole President, 12, San Francisco, California Bay Area resident, in front of the Black Wall Street Memorial .

Greenwood Cultural Center, 322 North Greenwood Avenue, Tulsa, Okla.

Mabel B. Little Heritage House, 322 North Greenwood Avenue, Tulsa, Okla. Formerly the Mackey House. Includes furnishings, clothing, and memorabilia circa 1920s, 1930s.

Vernon A.M.E. Church, badly damaged during the riot. Located directly across the street from the Greenwood Cultural Center. Used for Summer Arts Youth activities sponsored by the Greenwood Cultural Center.

Sen. Maxine Horner, Democrat, Dist. 11, Tulsa, the Oklahoma Senate, Oklahoma City, Okla.

Rep. Don Ross

Dr. Lawrence A. Reed, long-time Tulsan (a native of Okmulgee), Director, Greenwood Cultural Center, Inc.

Mount Zion Baptist Church, June 1, 1996.

L to R. Eddie Faye Gates, the Rev. Benjamin Hooks, former director of the National NAACP, keynote speaker, 75th Anniversary Commemoration, The Tulsa Race Riot of 1921, held June 1, 1996, Tulsa, Okla.

— Photo by Davetta Petite Thibeaux, Oakland, CA

Greenwood Cultural Center Grounds. Across the fence is Rogers University (formerly The University Center at Tulsa, UCT). The university is on the site occupied by the old Booker T. Washington High School during the race riot. Adjacent to the North Campus extension is the site where the old Brickyard Hill (Acme Brick Company) area was during the riot. In the newly opened Conference Center at Rogers University is the B.S. Roberts Room which was named for Rev. B.S. Roberts who is featured in this book. The photographic/historical exhibit of Don Thompson and this author are on permanent display in the Roberts Room.

to Tulsa and took the Oklahoma Bar exam in 1955. I passed. I've never regretted my decision to become a lawyer. I have tried in my own small way to make America a more just and equal nation. Changes have been made, but we still have work to do before this is a color-blind society. I've lived in North Tulsa all of my life. I've lived at the same address for the past forty-three years and I have voted in every major election since then in this same district. And I have worked hard to make our judicial system work better for all citizens. We can't stop now. I know I can't ever stop. I can still hear the voice of my mother urging me to keep on working for justice and equality. I will never let her down!

JOSIE LEWIS
b. July 24, 1896, Swarn, Texas

I only finished the eighth grade so I didn't have the opportunity to get any higher education, but I never wanted for a job. And whatever job I had, I did to my highest ability. No employer was ever dissatisfied with my work. It was just the opposite. Everywhere I worked I was quickly promoted to higher, supervisory positions because my bosses said I had a sharp mind and learned things quickly, I was prompt and always on time, and I got along well with other workers. But I was so soft-hearted. I didn't want to hurt no one's feelings. Sometimes I didn't want to move up. The bosses had to sometimes drag me screaming, a hollering, and a kicking to those higher positions!

Once back in the 1920s, I substituted as a maid for a friend when she had her days off. Oh, that was a good maid's job. She took care of Mrs. Mayo's private quarters at the Mayo Hotel in downtown Tulsa. Well Honey, Mrs. Mayo got to like me and my work so much that she asked me to become her full-time maid. I was so disturbed I couldn't sleep that night. The next day I told Mrs. Mayo that I couldn't accept the job because I didn't want to undermine my friend. Mrs. Mayo said she was the one to decide who she wanted for a maid and she wanted me! So I became her permanent maid, but only after I got my friend's blessing.

It sure was interesting working for Mrs. Mayo. The Mayos suite was on the top floor and it was so beautiful — just full of the most elegant furniture, and Mrs. Mayo's closets were just stuffed full of beautiful clothes. Mr. Mayo had the reputation of being a stiff (a stern man) who didn't give tips. But he always tipped me. Every Monday morning, I'd hear his gruff voice calling 'Josie, Josie.' I would come and he would hand me a tip. I remember that Mrs. Mayo was a religious woman. She knew I was religious and she would ask me a lot of questions about the Bible. When she was sick, she would have me read aloud to her from the Bible. I sure enjoyed doing that. I also liked shopping for Mrs. Mayo. Because I was the Mayos' maid, I could go into stores that other colored people couldn't go into. Child, I went everywhere! When I would go into a store that didn't wait on colored people, I would pull out my pass that Mrs. Mayo had given me and I'd say loudly, 'Mrs. Mayo sent me.' And Honey, they would wait on me then. Yes Sirree, money sure does talk!

When I went to work at Douglas Aircraft, I started on the lowest rung of the ladder, but soon I was put in charge of five workers. One day I was called in by management. I got so scared. I said to myself 'Lord, what did I do wrong?' I hadn't done nothing wrong; the boss offered me a raise and a better position. But I didn't want to go. I didn't want to leave my four good lady friends that I was working with. I was crying because I didn't want to leave, my four friends were crying because they didn't want me to leave, so management just sent all five of us to the new position and I was made the leader! That's the way it always was everywhere I worked. I was always moved up to better positions, with better pay, and I was made the leader.

That's the advice I always give to young people today. No matter what you are called on to do, do your very best. Do such a good job that your bosses are always pleased with you. Then you will always be moved on up to bigger and better positions.

Yes, that really works. It didn't take no college education for me to learn that. I learned it right on all the jobs I had in my lifetime — jobs in Texas, Kansas, and Oklahoma. It's still true to this day.

CLARENCE LOVE
b. January 26, 1908, Muskogee, Oklahoma

My mother said that the train ride from Muskogee, Oklahoma to Kansas City in 1912 was one of the worst experiences in her life. My parents had decided to leave Muskogee, just like they had left other places before, because they had not found the Promised Land that they expected to find. They had searched so much for a better way of life. My mother came from South Carolina and my father from Mississippi. They first came by covered wagon to Ft. Smith, Arkansas. But they found too much segregation there, so they moved to Muskogee, but it wasn't much better. So the four of us — my parents, my two-year-old sister, and me — set out

Dapper young musician Clarence Love, 1940's, Kansas City, MO

on that train bound for Kansas City and a better way of life at last. Not only did we 'coloreds' have to sit in a segregated railroad car, but that segregated car was also the designated smoking area for the train. Mother was incensed because my little sister and I were literally choking due to the dense smoke coming from all the whites who came into the car for their nicotine breaks. Not only did they fill the car with smoke which burned our eyes and throats, but their language was very crude as well. My poor mother was besides herself, but what could she do? That was the law of the land. There was no other recourse for her. We just had to suffer. My mother never forgot that train ride and the indignity and injustice that we had to bear. But we sure did like Kansas City when we got there.

We just fell in love with the public school system in Kansas City. At Attucks Elementary School, I met the first of the many good music teachers in Kansas City and I learned to read music there. I learned the significance of being able to read music. Any musician who could read music was always welcome in my band! At

Clarence Love at his induction into the Oklahoma Jazz Hall of Fame, 1990

Heavyweight boxer Joe Louis and Clarence Love, circa 1940

Lincoln High School (LHS), I met the greatest high school music teacher that ever lived, William L. Dawson, who left LHS to become director of music at Tuskegee Institute in Alabama. When I was fourteen, I formed my first band in Kansas City. In addition to being the leader of that band, I played the violin, mellophone, trumpet, clarinet, and saxophone in the LHS band, and I was also in the LHS orchestra. I tell you, I was a very busy lad, music wise! Later I was in the school's Reserved Officer Training Corps and played in the school's army band.

Being involved in all that school music wasn't enough for me; I sneaked out at night and went to Kansas City night clubs and became acquainted with the city's leading jazz and blues musicians. Among those that I heard and loved were Benny Moton, George Lee, Jay McShann, and many, many others who came from all over the U.S. to play in Kansas City's popular jazz clubs. In those days all the black bands knew each other. We had to stay on the black side of town when we played gigs and everywhere we played we kept running into each other. So we had to know each other. I knew them; they knew me. We became very close. I remember I once ran into Jimmie Lunceford in Portland, Oregon. Later, I ran across Lionel Hampton who had two boys from Tulsa in his band. One of them played more sax than Charlie 'Yardbird' Parker! Both of those boys ought to be in the Oklahoma Jazz Hall of Fame.

One of my favorite gigs during those golden jazz years was the Grand Terrace Ballroom in Chicago. I played the same clubs as Count Basie, Duke Ellington, Billie Holiday, and other now-famous musicians. The last time the Grand Terrace was open, Billie Holiday was on the bill. She was a lovely girl with a beautiful, haunting voice. But she had some serious emotional and medical problems. Speaking of female musicians, I believe I was the only musician in the nation to have an all-girl band and an all-boy band at the same time. Those girls, *The Darlings of Rhythm*, were trouble. The girls just couldn't hold their liquor, and they were always bickering with one another. They were just not respectful to each other, although they were very polite and respectful towards me.

Oh, I had it all — all aspects of the music world — and I loved every minute of it!

DR. G. CALVIN McCUTCHEN
b. March 1, 1927, Rockfield, Kentucky

When I was growing up black and poor in Rockfield, Kentucky it was expected that the young black males would grow up to be farmers. But as a child I decided that I wanted to be a minister. But the ministry was not looked upon as a good occupation in our little community. Most of the black ministers in the area were untutored. But I couldn't help it, all I wanted to be was a minister. It was not my own doing. The Lord put me in the ministry. Even as a youngster, I had a real interest in spiritual things. So I stood firm in what I was going to be and there was one person who encouraged me, my elementary schoolteacher, Mrs. Ida Nell Finch. It was Mrs. Finch who taught me to have respect for my dreams and to reach for the higher things in life. She took me to larger towns so I could hear more skilled, tutored, and educated ministers. She told me 'Calvin, if the Lord has called you, you be proud of that and you stick with it. You stand by your convictions and you be the best minister that you can be!' I did just what Mrs. Finch told me to do and I have never regretted it. When Mrs. Finch came from Lexington, Kentucky to visit my wife and me in the 1970s, I was so proud to have that wonderful woman as my house guest. She has since passed on but I will never forget that marvelous woman.

Ministering is my life. I treasure the thirty-eight years that I have been pastor at Mt. Zion Baptist Church. The congregation has been just wonderful all those years and the church has such a rich and noble history. It literally came back from the ashes of defeat, the aftermath of the Tulsa Race Riot of 1921.

Although I am sorry for the grief that I caused my precious wife Adalene, I am proud of the role that I played in the civil rights movement in Tulsa in the 1960s. After working ten years at Moton Hospital as a registered nurse, my wife decided she wanted a career change; she wanted a less stressful job. So she decided to become Tulsa's second black policewoman. Mrs. Horne, a juvenile officer, was the first black policewoman. My wife worked twenty years for the Tulsa Police Department, fifteen years as a juvenile officer and five years handling sex offender cases.

My wife chose the wrong time for her career change. The 1960s in Tulsa were not stress-free years! They were the years when black protests brought down years of segregation in the city. The reason I

Rev. G. Calvin McCutchen, pastor, Mt. Zion Baptist Church, Tulsa

caused Adalene such grief was because I was in charge of some of the youth groups that she had to arrest. I joined Rev. B.S. Roberts' Christian Education protest movement when he asked me. He needed a younger man involved in the movement. We met weekly with the youth groups, training them for staging sit-ins to challenge segregation in public places. We'd go to a lot of places to test whether we would be served. We spent a lot of personal money because sometimes establishments would serve us and we had to pick up the tab for fifty or sixty students, but most of the time establishments wouldn't serve us. When we refused to leave there would be jailings.

Out of respect for my wife's position, and because we couldn't risk her losing her job because we needed her salary, I never allowed myself to be arrested. Rev. Roberts went to jail many times, but he knew my situation and encouraged me to always get up and leave when ordered to. My wife told me how it hurt her to have to book those black youth but she had to. It was her job. She told me that if I ever came down there to be booked, she just couldn't do it. She said she would just have to quit her job. So I never let myself be jailed.

Another tight spot that I got myself into was the time I chaperoned a youth dance for our young protestors at a Catholic church hall. Dances were our way of encouraging the children and of showing them our appreciation for what they were doing to make the city a better place. But I sure felt awkward. Here I was, a minister of the gospel, a Baptist minister, 'hosting' a dance! But I felt that it was a justifiable cause and from then on I chaperoned those youth dances.

The highlight of my civil rights experience was my participation in the civil rights march on Washington, D.C. August 28, 1963. I will never forget Martin Luther King, Jr.'s spell-binding 'I Have a Dream' speech. I almost didn't go on that trip. I had helped with all the fundraisers, I had helped the youth get ready for the trip, but I hadn't planned to go. Rev. Ben Hill said to me 'McCutchen, you're a fool! You've helped raise the funds, you've organized things for the youth, and you're not going? Go get your clothes and come with us.' And so I did. I am eternally grateful to Ben Hill for talking me into going on that historic trip. Knowing what I know now,

Augusta Mann

I wouldn't have missed it for the world. In fact I wouldn't change anything in my life. Every experience had its purpose and its reward. Well maybe there is just one thing I would change. I wish I could have spared my wife the grief that those youth bookings caused her. But there was just no other way. We had to show the community how unfair segregation and discrimination were and we had to do it in a visible way, in a way that our words and petitions had not been able to do. There was no way more visible than those jail cells full of our youthful black protestors. It was North Tulsa's finest hour!

AUGUSTA MANN
b. April 21, 1910, Coleman, Texas

The Mann brothers were all Tulsa businessmen and were active in the grocery business from 1919 through the 1970s. J.D. opened the first store in 1919 but it was destroyed just two years later in the awful Tulsa Race Riot. But he reopened just three weeks after the riot. My husband, M.M., and his brother, Obie, opened the second store in 1924. It was the largest grocery store in Tulsa — black or white — at the time. It had five butchers. I remember the names of two of them, Mr. Skinner and Mr. Malone. I can't remember the names of the other butchers but I do remember that one of them was peg-legged. Our store had the reputation of having the best meat in Tulsa and that included meat from the stores in South Tulsa! Both blacks and whites said that about our meat.

The grocery business was different in the old days. At that time people really cared about each other. There was especially a fondness for children in the community. It was like children belonged to the entire community, not just to their parents. Everyone looked after the children in the neighborhood. For instance my husband M. M. always gave water to the little children who played ball near the store whenever they asked for it. I remember that they would come into the store all hot and tired, and say 'Mr. Mann, we want some water!' No matter how busy he was, he would always stop whatever he was doing and give those children all the water they could drink, and anything else that they wanted. He would always say 'Y'all come on in here,' and then he would give them water, and some little treats. People just cared about each other then, and they especially cared about the children.

Of course the races hadn't learned to live together in peace

George Douglas Monroe, race riot survivor

then. Bad race relations led to that riot in 1921. The night that the riot broke out my husband and his brother were working in the store. When they heard about the riot, they quickly closed up and went home. Their mother begged them not to go back down on Greenwood. My husband listened to her but his brother did not. He joined some other angry young black men who armed themselves and went down to fight the white mobs. Because of that action my brother-in-law had to flee Tulsa when the riot was over. He was gone for three years and his family didn't know whether he was living or dead. My poor mother-in-law grieved so while he was gone. When he returned she and the entire family was just overjoyed! There were so many casualties from that riot, not only the dead and wounded, but all of the survivors suffered too. Our store was far enough from the riot that it wasn't damaged, but the brother who had his store on Greenwood was burned out. That's the way it was then. Some of the white mobs didn't know where the black living area ended and where the white living area began. So some black property survived because whites thought it was white property.

I've been very active in my church and I've served in community and state organizations to try to help make Oklahoma a better place. I hope that we learned some lessons from that riot and from the past history of strained race relations. I hope that Tulsans of all colors can live together in peace and harmony from now on.

GEORGE DOUGLAS MONROE
b. May 27, 1916, Tulsa, Oklahoma

One memory that I just can't forget is the night of the Tulsa Race Riot in 1921 when I was five years old. When white mobsters broke into our home which was next door to Mt. Zion Church, they went straight to the curtains and set them on fire. My mother, who had seen the mob coming, had hidden my two sisters, brother, and me under a bed. When the mob walked past the bed one of the men stepped on my finger. I was about to let out a scream, but my older sister Lottie put her hand over my mouth. Thank God she did. I shudder to think what that mob would have done to us if they had found us under that bed! That riot was so terrible — not only the loss of life, but of property that the Negroes had worked so hard to acquire. Our family business, a skating rink in the Greenwood area, was totally destroyed and never rebuilt. My dad Osborn Monroe was just devastated by this loss. Later on, the only job he could find was as a janitor in a white theater. That riot did so much damage to so many people. The beautiful Mt. Zion church, which had just been renovated and paid for, was burned down to its foundation. There had been false rumors that it was an arsenal for weapons and ammunition during the riot. That riot is something that I will never forget as long as I live!

When I was in high school I lived across the street from Booker T. Washington High School. My classmates used to tease me that I was so close to school that I could get up at 8:28 in the morning and get to school before the 8:30 bell! Dad then built us another house on a street that was called Exeter Street. What I remember most about that house is that there was a skating rink nearby on the corner of Elgin and Haskell Place. I sure did love Greenwood Avenue in those days. Of course living so close to Greenwood and absorbing all that wonderful music that floated from down there I couldn't help but develop a love of music. While I was still in high school in Tulsa I formed my own band. When I went away to Wiley College in Texas, I formed a band there called *The Rhythm Aces*. We played all over the Dallas area.

After college I had a lot of jobs. In 1934 I opened up a little place, *George's Sandwiches, Shoe Shine Parlor, and News Stand* at 1005 North Greenwood Avenue. I still have the menus and some publicity articles about that little place. In 1939 I made history by becoming the first black Coca Cola route salesman in Tulsa. The route was limited to Greenwood Avenue and other black areas but for that time in history it was considered an economic and social milestone, a breakthrough in race relations. It was such a successful route that a second black route salesman Greg Hawkins was hired. Black people were so proud to see us two black men in Coca Cola uniforms driving that Coca Cola truck. Somebody was always taking pictures of us. I still have some of those old photographs.

During World War II I served two years, as a Sergeant, in the U.S. Army in Europe. I was with the 3914th Quartermaster Gasoline Supply Company. It was our job to get gasoline to the troops all over Europe — England, France, Belgium, Luxembourg

— just everywhere in Europe where our boys were fighting. I remember those buzz bombs falling everywhere! That war was something else. I got all kinds of medals for service in the European theater. When the war was over I came back to Tulsa and here I am!

When I got back from the war, a soldier with medals, I was appointed a Tulsa County Deputy Sheriff under George Blaine. I guess Tulsa was trying to show that it appreciated the war service of all of its soldiers, black and white. I served as a deputy from 1945 to 1947 and then I began my 'real' life-time job as a sanitation inspector for the Tulsa County Health Department which I held until my retirement.

Oh yes, one other thing. From 1962-1982, I operated my own nightclub, *The Pink Lady*. I had my own band there and I played the drums in the band. I sure did enjoy that club and that music. Another hobby of mine is baseball. I was a big Tulsa Oilers fan. I've had my pictures taken with lots of baseball celebrities including Casey Stengel and Warren Spahn.

People who are trying to learn about the history of North Tulsa are always asking about Simon Berry. Yes I knew Simon Berry, but when I knew him I was just a boy and you know how young people are. They don't pay any attention to anything but themselves. I didn't pay any attention to Mr. Berry. To me he was just an older man who lived in my neighborhood and who had a garage on the corner of Hartford and Archer Streets. I remember that he was a tall, stately man and that he was well respected in the community, but that's about all I remember about the man.

Actually, I do know quite a bit about Simon Berry, Jr. In fact, we are related by marriage sort of. When I grew up and married Martha Simpson, we lived at 528 North Elgin Place and Simon Berry, Jr. was always coming 'round. Old man Berry was dead then. Well I knew Simon, Jr. because of his name, because I had known his father. I thought Simon was coming 'round because he liked my good company and conversation; but I found out that he was coming so he could see my wife's sister, Ella Pearl Simpson! So I had a little talk with Simon Berry, Jr. I said, 'Simon, now if you've got serious things in mind, that's all right. But I don't want no playin' 'round. I'm goin' to keep my eyes on you.' It was all right. Simon and Ella Pearl got married and have been married for more than forty years now. They live in Los Angeles and Simon, Jr. loves air-

Tennessee Washington Perryman accepting the coveted National Association of Community Health Centers' Public Award, Boston, 1979. She was selected from 600 delegates from 296 health centers.

planes just like his Daddy did. In fact, he wound up being a pilot for *The Flying Tigers* which flies out of L.A.

TENNESSEE PERRYMAN
b. April 21, 1907, Roff, Oklahoma

I have always loved people and wanted to help them. I thought there was no better way to help mankind than by being a nurse. So when I graduated from Booker T. Washington High School in Tulsa in 1927, I enrolled in the Hubbard Memorial Clinic in Tulsa, an affiliate of the Maurice Willows Hospital which was founded June 1, 1921, the second day of the infamous Tulsa Race Riot of 1921. Maurice Willows was a young white Red Cross worker who had been sent from St. Louis, Missouri to set up the first Red Cross Center in history to deal with a 'man-made disaster.' The Red Cross was used to dealing with floods, fires, earthquakes, etc. but it had never had to deal with a riot before! Mr. Willows was the perfect person to send — he was sensitive, caring, and efficient. The North Tulsa community just loved him. There are all kinds of documents that show this, like letters of appreciation sent to him after he helped Tulsa through the riot aftermath, letters from individuals, black and white, and from churches and other organizations. But the highest honor the community could give him was to name this hospital after him. I was so honored to be a student in a hospital affiliated with Mr. Willows.

I graduated from the Clinic as a licensed practical nurse. I just loved nursing. The doctors were all so very nice, so dedicated. I especially remember Dr. Charles Bate, Dr. E.E. Bowser and Dr. Warren Bowser. While we were in training the rules had been very strict. The curriculum was broad and varied and the student nurses studied very hard. We were very well disciplined. After graduation the rules were very strict also. Nurses could not wear any make up at all — no lipstick, not even powder on our faces. Our uniforms were white and blue with wide white bands on the apron. Cleanliness was stressed very much. We just had to be nice and clean for our patients. When we graduated we usually performed a broad spectrum of duties unlike the narrow specializations of today.

I did all kinds of nursing — obstetrics, general, surgical — and I was also the C.N. (Charge Nurse) when I first started nursing.

I went back to nursing school and did further study at Douglas Hospital in Kansas City, Kansas. I came back to Tulsa and for thirty-four years I worked at Moton Memorial Hospital in Tulsa trying to help my people. I tried to help alleviate their suffering, to make things better for them. I just love people. I was overwhelmed, though deeply honored, by the awards that people were always giving me. (Tributes from the Catholic Daughters of America; the League of Women Voters; the American Red Cross; the State Assembly of the Afro-American Community; Tulsa Action Agency; and the National Association of Community Health Centers' Public Award, Boston, Massachusetts 1979, in which she was selected from 600 delegates from 296 health centers in the U.S.). I know that people call me 'The Florence Nightingale' of North Tulsa. But I still say I did what I loved best. I was no hero. I just loved people and tried to help others.

I credit my mother with instilling the right kinds of values in me. She taught me to love others and to do good; she also taught me what happens when you do bad things. The worst whipping I ever got in my life, she gave me because I did something wrong. It happened like this. When I was a child growing up on a farm in Roff, Oklahoma, it was my job to bring in the eggs every day. One time Mama sent me to get the eggs from under an old hen that had made her nest under the house. That was the crankiest old hen! Well one day when I went under the house to get the eggs, that old hen 'whupped' me good. I was so mad. The next day when Mama went to the fields, I took a butcher knife and I went under the house, grabbed that old hen, held her feet together, and chopped her head right off! Oh, Lordy, did I ever get a 'whupping' over that. Oh yes Mama gave me the 'whupping' of my life. I learned never to react in anger like that again. I am glad that I chose the profession of nursing. It gave me the opportunity to show my love for people by helping them when they needed it most — when they were sick or dying. I think that it is the best profession in the world!

REVEREND ANDREW D. PHILLIPS
b. November 28, 1917, Morris County, Texas

I have always been very concerned about human and civil rights even before I knew exactly what they were. I knew that there was such a thing as fair play, kindness, goodness. Even during my teenage years, I worked for and insisted on those kinds of relationships in our East Texas community. When I became acquainted with Dr. Martin Luther King, Jr.'s philosophy, my efforts intensified. I longed to see him, to hear him. My life was changed as a result of hearing his message.

Martin Luther King, Jr. was a champion for poor people, the disenfranchised, the have-nots. He also had a message of sympathy for those who were well off in a material sense, but didn't know the real value of life such as recognizing their responsibility to the have-nots. He was just a wonderful man who preached true love and brotherhood. He didn't just stress black rights, he stressed human rights, rights for all people, rights for all races, all religions, all classes, all people!

In 1960 Dr. Martin Luther King, Jr. came to Tulsa to speak at Rev. T. Oscar Chappelle's Morning Star Baptist Church. How I wanted to hear the speech of that fiery young preacher-activist! But wouldn't you know it, I had an unbreakable speaking engagement myself that day. But before my appointment, I slipped into Morning Star church and caught a glimpse of the dynamic young man I had grown to admire so much. I listened to a few resonant phrases roll from the eloquent, southern tongue then I had to go on to my engagement. But just seeing Martin fortified and revitalized me. That's the kind of influence he had on people. He was indeed a vessel from God that brought out the best in mankind.

After Dr. King was assassinated, Tulsa city officials and Tulsa's black ministers got together and held an impromptu memorial, but I didn't think that was good enough. I felt that there should be an annual commemoration in Tulsa to recognize Dr. King's contributions to society, so I founded the Martin Luther King, Jr. Commemoration Society in Tulsa to provide an annual parade in honor of the great fallen leader. From a humble beginning in which just a handful of participants showed up at the first event, the celebration has become the largest parade in Oklahoma with hundreds

Rev. Andrew Phillips, pastor, Greater Mt. Rose Baptist Church, Tulsa

Rev. Andrew Phillips and his beloved round church on North Cincinnati in North Tulsa. NOTE: the high rise building in the background is the Pioneer Plaza Senior Citizens Complex which is located on the exact site of Standpipe Hill where white mobsters used a mounted machine gun to shoot fleeing black refugees during the Tulsa Race Riot of 1921.

of participants in the annual parade (floats, cars, bands, marchers, horse events, etc.) and with thousands of spectators lining the streets even in frigid weather.

The Martin Luther King, Jr. Parade is more than just fun, games, and revelry (though we have that, too); it says visually what we are unable to say verbally. It speaks in its own way of togetherness, unity, humanity, the oneness of us all. I sometimes wonder what Martin Luther King, Jr. would say about the Tulsa parade. I think that winning smile of his would crease his face. Then I believe he might say something like, 'This is what the Movement is all about!' I believe that he would be pleased. I think this parade atmosphere of brotherly love and unity is what he envisioned. There is more community bonding in this nation as a result of the King philosophy. We see it in our churches, in our schools, and in our cities.

Speaking of churches, Mt. Rose draws a lot of attention because of its unique shape (in addition to its healing ministry). I'd like to set the record straight about the church architecture. Since I have always marched to my own inner drum, some people say it's no surprise that my church should be different too. I don't know why I became fascinated with circular churches. I first saw one in Ft. Worth, Texas and then I saw another one in California. I just fell in love with those round churches and decided that I just had to have me a round church in Tulsa! But I got back to Tulsa, got busy, and forgot all about my round church. Then one day I was driving down North Peoria Avenue and the picture of a round church just popped into my head. I pulled my car off of Peoria and parked on Independence. I got a piece of paper out of my briefcase and hastily sketched out my future, round church. I took my rough drawings (very rough) to Tulsa architects Cecil Stanfield and William Elliot. I expected them to laugh me out of their office, but Mr. Stanfield looked up and said, 'When do you want to get started?' So that is how the little peach-colored, round church on North Cincinnati came about. It wasn't easy. We ran out of money and the half-finished church, and bundles of roofing materials, drew the attention of passers-by. Local churches, black and white, from all over Tulsa came to the rescue and the church was completed. We had a few problems though such as getting curtains to hang straight from curved walls, shaping carpet to fit a curved building, etc. But it was all worth it. We love our church. It is serving its spiritual purpose in the community, and it still draws the attention of motorists who are not used to seeing round churches. I don't know why I am so fascinated by round churches. I just know that I had to have me a round church in Tulsa. And God gave me one!

REVEREND BENJAMIN S. (B.S.) ROBERTS
b. January 6, 1916, Ft. Gaines, Georgia

People just don't realize the power that they hold over others, how an unkind word or act can cut one's heart right out! I had problems with what I saw as a youth in Georgia. There are hundreds and hundreds of examples of the racism that I saw, but some stand out more than others. For instance I remember that on icy cold days we black children had to walk miles to school as white children rode by in school buses and they would make faces at us and call us names. Even when I was young I knew that wasn't right, that it wasn't fair. I just resented that type of thing because I knew that I was a person. I saw all people as people, not as different races, but as people. But in the Deep South, black people were treated as if they were still slaves. That built something up in me and I vowed that when I grew up, if I ever had a chance I would do something about what had happened and was still happening to black people, people who had been humiliated and some even killed without reason.

When I moved to Tulsa in 1949, I thought that I had left racism behind me but I found out that was not so. I found that racism was just as bad or worse in Tulsa than it was in Georgia, but there was one difference. The police department here did not abuse black people. The department was more cultured than the system from which I had come. Discrimination in Tulsa was more subtle, more psychological, not like the open, blunt prejudice and discrimination I had seen in Georgia.

Of all the experiences that I have had, one that I am most pleased with is my involvement in the civil rights movement in Tulsa. I found that there was a need for the black Tulsa community to address its needs, especially the needs of its children. So some of us Tulsa ministers — Rev. Ben Hill, Rev. Calvin McCutchen, Rev. T. Oscar Chappelle and others — began an active civil rights move-

Rev. B.S. Roberts, retired pastor, St. John A.M.E. Church, Tulsa.

Rev. B.S. Roberts, city council office, The City of Tulsa. Roberts was elected Tulsa's first black councilor in 1990.

ment in Tulsa in the 1950s. Rev. Carl Theely, pastor of Prince of Peace Lutheran Church, worked diligently with us, as well as Father O'Neill, a priest of a Catholic Church. Fifty to sixty white students from the University of Tulsa joined our efforts. One of them was Rodger Randle who later became a Peace Corps worker, the mayor of the city of Tulsa, and a state senator. He is now the president of the University Center of Tulsa. We used Dr. Martin Luther King, Jr.'s plan as our guideline. I knew Martin personally. I first met him in Atlanta in 1944.

In our Christian education programs for youth, we let the children choose the focus of the movement. Oh those young people were wonderful. Some of them are outstanding citizens in the community today. There were Don Ross, Ray Freeman, Billy Rountree, brothers Melvin and Bertrain Bailey (both now Tulsa ministers), Hubert Bryant, Shirley Scoggins, Mae Katharine Jarrett Copeland, Wanda Jacobs, Opa Chaney, and many, many others. They just wanted to tackle everything! They wanted to be able to go to Mohawk Park, to swim in Tulsa's public pools, to try on clothes in stores before they bought them, to eat in public places. So we had sit-ins, wade-ins, voter registration — just everything!

We rented a little building on Pine and Madison streets where we could train the youth in the techniques of non-violent protest. We taught them how to picket without breaking the law and how to protect their bodies if they ever met force. National leaders like A. Phillip Randolph of the NAACP, Dick Gregory, and even Martin Luther King, Jr. himself came to Tulsa to help us with our movement! It's interesting how we got Dick Gregory to come. I had been calling and calling him, but he didn't return my calls. But when he read about Martin Luther King, Jr.'s visit to Tulsa in 1960, he called me. He said, 'Y'all are really doing things in Tulsa. I'll be there Saturday.' We were all so excited. We worked all day Friday and stayed up all night Friday getting things ready. We rented the Brady Theater and it was filled to capacity that Saturday night. It was a wonderful program. Dick Gregory used his comedian skills to spread civil rights activism and he captivated the crowd, both blacks and whites. He opened a lot of eyes that night.

Oklahoma City had a civil rights movement similar to the Tulsa movement which was led by the indomitable Clara Luper. In fact

Clara and her movement was more advanced than our movement. Clara used to come to Tulsa to give us a 'civil rights transfusion.'

When we first started to march we managed to stay out of jail. But when we speeded up our protest the jailings began to occur. I remember that one day we had 600 arrested, a record for Tulsa! A lawyer from the University of Tulsa came down to assist us. Mayor Garrett told me he was going to arrest every protestor. I told him, 'That's your job, you do what you have to do. But making America a just and equal society is my job, and I'm going to keep on doing it!' And I did, and so did all those wonderful youth, and all the other people who joined us. It worked, too. The walls of segregation began to break down. Some restaurants just quietly started to serve us. Mrs. Fannie Hill and the 'youth brigade' that she took to Mohawk Park every week like clockwork just wore down the park officials. They just gave up and opened the park to blacks. One thing I found out was how powerful the media is. The written word can sure bring about change. You see those who are in power have a deep desire to be seen in 'a good light.' They don't want their dirt to be uncovered and revealed to the world. Rev. Ben Hill was a trained journalist and worked at *The Oklahoma Eagle* newspaper. His uncovering of Tulsa's 'dirty deeds' and the publishing of them, or sometimes just the threat to publish them, brought about much needed change. I am so proud of what we did in the 1950s and 1960s. In a peaceful manner we showed the city the kinds of injustices that existed in Tulsa at the time and we helped to show them how to rise above that condition and to make Tulsa a better place. But we can't rest on our laurels. We must be ever vigilant to recognize injustice, point it out, and do something about correcting it. That's what I vowed to do when I was just a boy in Georgia. I have been doing just that ever since!

ROSA DAVIS SKINNER
b. November 6, 1898, Bonham, Texas

The evening before the Tulsa Race Riot of 1921 began May 31 1921, my husband Thomas and I went to a BTU meeting at Paradise Baptist Church just off Greenwood Avenue. The churches used to hold BTU meetings regularly, but they done quit holdin' them now.

Rosa Davis Skinner

Thomas got up and told the congregation about a vision he had. He said, 'I don't know what it's going to be, but it's going to be some kind of destruction.' Several of the church people questioned him about whether the message had really come from God, or from Thomas. My husband kept explainin' his vision and most of the people believed him. Some of them though made light of him. He just said to them, 'We'll see.'

When we got out of BTU that night we went on home to our little house at 519 West Latimer Street. Thomas didn't say no more about his vision. I went to bed but he was still up. A little after midnight he woke me up and said, 'Wife it's time for us to go!' I said, 'Go where?' He said, 'I told you something was goin' to happen; well it's happenin' now. A man just run by the house and he said 'Brothers, get your guns, get your guns, a riot has broke out.'

We found out that an old man who pushed a vegetable cart along Greenwood was one of the first blacks to be shot. Some eye-witnesses said that white people put a machine gun on the Hill (Brickyard Hill) and they shot through the middle of that little pushcart and the bullet killed that old man. That really did hurt the black people and scared 'em too. That's why we were all runnin'. We were just runnin' trying to get away from the guns and bullets. We heard that the Home Guards were doing a lot of damage too, just like the white mobs.

When we got to Greenwood, we met up with a lot more black people who were running trying to find a safe place. We ran into a couple — the man was one of Thomas' best friends. The wife had just had a baby that had died at birth. She had put it in a shoe box and was waiting until morning to bury it when the riot broke out. Well durin' all that runnin', and pushin', and shovin' when black people were trying to get safely away from the riot, that po' little baby got lost! Everybody was just runnin' and bumpin' into each other. They never did find that child!

That riot was a terrible thing. There was so much death and destruction. So much disorder. The National Guard was called to keep the peace. The women in my group had been taken to the fairgrounds and were raising a lot of sand — we were all hungry, thirsty, and just plain scared to death. A milk truck and a bread truck came and brought us some food. We were each given a bottle of sweet milk and some slices of bread. I never did like sweet milk. In fact I never did drink it. But this day I was so tired, scared, and thirsty that I drank that bottle of sweet milk right up!

The men had been taken to different places, some to churches and some to the Convention Center. The next day our husbands were brought to the fairgrounds and we were reunited. We sure were glad to see each other. If any white employer called for his black worker, the worker and his family would be allowed to go home. That's how we got to go home. We heard Thomas' boss calling, 'T.R. Davis, T.R. Davis, come on out.' Thomas answered and we got to leave. When we got to our house, thank God it was still standing, but it was such a mess! The door was standing wide open and when we went in we saw that the house had been ransacked. I was sure upset especially about the laundry. You see, Thomas worked in a sporting house, that's what they called them in those days, and there were two ladies who worked there that paid me to do their laundry. They didn't wear nothin' but the finest, expensive silk things. I had washed those silk things so nicely and hung them on hangers so neatly. Well those mobsters had thrown all those pretty silk things in a pile on the floor. I was so mad. 'Course, I picked up all those pretty things, put them back on hangers and took them to those ladies and asked for my money. The riot wasn't no fault of mine, was it? I'd done my job washin' those things, so I felt I deserved my pay.

Oh, that riot was a terrible thing. One of Thomas' best friends got killed and poor Thomas felt that it was his fault. It was two days after the riot before Thomas told me about Willie Lockard. He said, 'Rosa, when the guards rounded us men up over in Mohawk Park, I told Willie to get down off his horse and make himself seen or he was goin' to get shot. Well he didn't listen to me and they got him. The horse, with blood on his nose, run home. One of Willie's brothers jumped on the horse and the horse led him to Willie's body, which was straight down the road from Mohawk Park.' Thomas just repeating over and over, 'It's my fault. I should have made Willie listen to me.' But it wasn't Thomas' fault that Willie Lockard was hardheaded. I just couldn't make Thomas understand that. He sure did grieve over Willie. I did too. I sure did hate to hear how he was killed. Oh, I wish I could forget that terrible riot. I often think to myself, 'I wonder what happened to that po' little baby!'

JOSEPH WILLARD VANN, SR.
b. September 28, 1903, Lenepah, Cherokee Nation,
Indian Territory - Oklahoma

I get my stubborness and my persistence from my Dad. When my Dad made up his mind to do something, he did it. Dad already had a career as a schoolteacher, but he decided he wanted to be a lawyer so he went to school and became a lawyer. His specialty was putting people on Indian tribal rolls. He made many, many trips to Washington, D.C. to get Indians on those rolls. My mother helped him, too. She became a notary public and when she went to church, she would take the Indian roll sheets with her. If a person had three witnesses testifying to a person's Indian blood, Mother would put that person's name on the roll. When she got the list completed, she would mail it to my Dad in Washington. That was the way black people with bona fide ties to Indian tribes were put on the rolls. As a result of the Dawes Act, enrollers were given land allotments — usually eighty acres, but if the land was split in pieces, a person could get from ninety to 115 acres.

Those rolls could sure cause a whole lot of conflict though. In fact one conflict led to my Dad getting shot! There were two brothers and one had an Indian wife. My Dad got that wife duly registered on the tribal roll. Well the other brother came in and wanted his wife put on the roll too. Dad said he couldn't do that because this second brother's wife wasn't Indian. The man kept insisting that the Dad put his wife on the roll and Dad kept insisting that he couldn't because the wife wasn't Indian. Suddenly, the man just pulled out a gun a shot my Dad. Funny thing though the bullet didn't go into his skull; it just went under the skin and then traveled all along the side of his head. I saw it all. I ran home, got a gun and came running back. My Dad stopped me. He said, 'Son, don't do it. Put that gun up! If you had had that gun on you right here when the man first fired the shot, and if you had fired at him, that would be all right; that would be self-defense. But to go home, get a gun, and return and shoot someone, that is pre-meditated murder.' I did just like my Dad told me to do. I took the gun home. Do you know that years later a similar thing happened to me? The motive was dif-

J. Willard Vann, Sr.

ferent but the results were the same. I wasn't seriously hurt either. I just had a superficial gunshot wound, just like my daddy had the time he got shot.

I learned a lot of lessons from my parents, especially from my Dad. I try to help other people just like he did years ago. I like working with youth. They need people to show them how to live and learn and act so they can have peaceful lives. Yes there is so much that we need to do today to help people especially our youth. I always remember my Dad and how he worked all of his life to help people especially Indians who had been given a bad deal in this country and who were so needful then. That's why I am so concerned with today's youth and I do anything that I can that might help these young people to 'do the right thing.'

THELMA WHITLOW
b. September 2, 1908, Bremond, Texas

When Katie Duckery, Mabel Little, Opal Dargan, some other Tulsa oldtimers, and I got disturbed about Urban Renewal and highway construction tearing down the significant buildings from our past on Greenwood Avenue, we decided to do something about it. Don Ross, who was then a journalist and public relations consultant, did a study of the situation and made some recommendations. Then us 'little old ladies' hit the streets and we never stopped until we had $100,000 in donations to begin our memorial to the Tulsa pioneers. We wanted some monument on Greenwood that recognized what the black settlers had accomplished in the face of tremendous odds and had passed on to us. They gave Greenwood (and the entire black community) its spirit, its dream, a dream that we continue to carry on until this day. We formed the North Tulsa Heritage Foundation then and the organization is still working to preserve the Greenwood area.

We wheedled donations out of everybody. We begged and borrowed at every North Tulsa door. We just wouldn't take 'No' for an answer! We just told the North Tulsa story and it touched the hearts of the people. They saw that it just wasn't right that we as a people should lose all that our ancestors and leaders had struggled so hard to build. We just couldn't let our culture die. And we didn't! Thanks to all those Tulsans who shared our dream, we soon raised that

Thelma Whitlow giving the keynote address at a United Nations Association of Eastern Oklahoma Human Rights program, December 12, 1989.

$100,000. People responded more generously than we expected, especially the women. It was hard work but it wasn't really work. It was a labor of love. Later when Don Ross became a state representative, and when Maxine Horner became our district's state senator, they were extremely helpful and successful in getting generous funding for our North Tulsa projects from the local and state governments.

Of course begging, borrowing, and wheedling were not new to me. I'd always been doing that especially for the girls in the North Tulsa community. For twenty-five years I worked with girls who are now grown women, to help them see a better way of life. Now they in turn work with girl groups in Tulsa. When I first began working with the girls, we had girls come to us from all over the city. We had camp, ballet, art, and anything else I could beg, borrow, or get free that would enrich the lives of those girls. People would see me coming and run the other way because they knew I was going to be asking a favor. But most people did respond. Once I talked a nurse into working for us free. She was just fixing to go off on a vacation. I talked her into postponing her trip so she could work with those girls. I told her, 'These girls need you. We can't have this event we have planned and have worked so hard on. Can't you give two weeks to these girls?' She did too! It was that kind of love, dedication, and service in Tulsa that I shall always remember.

I didn't just minister to the needs of girls either; I helped the boys too. Once when my husband Whit was teaching and coaching the boys' basketball team at Carver Junior High School, the boys decided that they wanted their names and numbers put on their basketball sweatshirts. They didn't have enough money to purchase professionally-lettered and numbered uniforms, so the young coach's wife — me — took it upon herself to sew the numbers and letters on the sweatshirts. You can ask some members of that long-ago team, like Julius Pegues who is now an engineer in Tulsa and a business contractor-developer who is carrying on the tradition of his Latimer ancestors, and they will tell you that those were the crookediest numbers and letters that you could ever see! But that's the way it was then. We did whatever had to be done to help our children and to help our community.

While we never expected, or wanted, public recognition for what we did, Whit and I were always getting some kind of award from the Tulsa community, black and white. We also received state and national awards which deeply humbled us. It was good to have our efforts appreciated, but just accomplishing what we did for the boys and girls of Tulsa, and to help the North Tulsa community was reward enough. I was especially proud of one breakthrough that I made however. I was the first female to be appointed as a board member of the Tulsa Housing Authority. Whit and I were able to break down a lot of barriers for which I am grateful.

I will never forget the days of Greenwood's glory and the legacy that the black settlers of North Tulsa left for us. I am proud to have had a part in the preservation of this legacy through the North Tulsa Heritage Foundation. Black Tulsans are so proud of the Greenwood Cultural Center. It is the focal point of the black community. The Chappelle Goodwin Gallery and the Mabel Little Heritage House on Greenwood are the focal point of the North Tulsa community. Key community events such as civic and social meetings, honors awards and banquets, school tours, weddings, etc. are held there. The third phase of construction, a $2.5 million dollar expansion of the Greenwood Cultural Center, is underway and is expected to be completed by the fall of 1995. It will include a large auditorium, a museum area, and other rooms where the memorabilia of our past may be stored and where the events of our future can be held. I am so proud to have been a part of this memorial to the black pioneers of Tulsa.

I don't 'hit the streets' anymore on fundraising efforts. I still attend North Tulsa Heritage Foundation meetings and a few other meetings besides my church work at Wesley AME Church. But mostly I stay at home and paint. And I love it when my son Clay (Henry Clay Whitlow, III a Denver lawyer) and his family come to visit. I can't believe that Kirsten, Abby, and Joy are now all grown up. It seems like yesterday that they were little girls spending the summers with me. Now they are college graduates! Abby just graduated from Smith College. When I look at them I am so proud of them. I am also proud of all those boys and girls that Whit and I were able to help in the early days in Tulsa. They were lovingly disciplined and taught by dedicated teachers and given a good basic education under not-so-ideal situations (segregated schools, inadequate supplies, etc.). They were exposed to whatever cultural, enriching experiences we could find for them in Tulsa and they did what students are supposed to do. They followed directions and they learned. Today they are successful, mostly professional men and women carrying on the Tulsa tradition. Yes, I am so proud of them!

WESLEY YOUNG
b. September 2, 1917, Beggs, Oklahoma

When I was twelve years old, my cousin Raynes Belton put me on an old ropin' horse named Levi, gave me a rope, and turned me loose to practice ropin' goats and I been ropin' ever since! When I caught my first goat I was hooked. It was such a thrill. I knew that I wanted to do this all of my life.

My mother supported me but my Daddy sure didn't. He never did like my ropin'. He said 'A horse ain't for 'rodeo playin' round with. A horse is for plowin'!' He didn't want me to have no rope, no horse, no bridle, no saddle! He just wanted me to plow. I sure wish that he had liked ropin' and could have supported me. I know I could have been really good. I could have been another Will Rogers. I just wish my Daddy could have been proud of my ropin'.

When Mama died in 1929, I became serious about my ropin'. Oh, those were some good old days for cowboyin'! Us black cowboys stuck together like glue. There was Emory Metcalfe, Homer Silas, Jim Shoulders, Jess Goodspeed, and some others. All of the Metcalfe family was into rodeoin'. Emory's boys, Emory, Jr., Benny, and Clyde performed just like their daddy. But Benny got killed in a car wreck and Emory, Jr. got shot to death by his woman; she just shot him in the head during an argument! Clyde Metcalfe is still rodeoin' and makin' movies and television shows out in Hollywood and in Tucson, Arizona. He was in that movie, *The Young Guns*, which starred Emilio Estevez and Keefer Sutherland. Two Tulsa cowboys were also in that film, thirty-nine year old twins Donald and Ronald Stephens who are also Tulsa firemen. Metcalfe and them Stephens twins were also in the television series, *The Desperados*. Metcalfe was a stand-in for one of the leads, Billy Dee Williams, and the Stephens twins played Buffalo soldiers. That's the way it is today. In addition to rodeoin', cowboys also make films and movies, and some of them write articles and books about rodeoin', like Donald Stephens does. But in the old days, we just rodeoed.

It was rough for black cowboys in those days. There was so

Wesley Young, wily old cowboy! 1995

Wesley Young holding "Oklahoma's Oldest Cowboy" Trophy, 1994

much prejudice and discrimination; blacks didn't get a fair chance. We weren't allowed to participate in the main events. They let us pass the hats to collect the money or they let us perform in the unimportant opening 'acts.' And when we began to break through and perform in the bigger events, there was resistance from some of the white cowboys and from the paying spectators. We were called racial names by some white people in the audience. You know the big 'N' word! That is why some of the black cowboys just stopped trying to break into white rodeoin' and formed their own all-black rodeos, like the LeBlancs in Okmulgee. Rodeoin' was real popular with black folks. In the '40s and '50s, I opened up my farm here in Boynton to accommodate Tulsa rodeo fans. So many Tulsans came to my weekend rodeos, you could hardly walk out here!

It's true that there was a lot of racism then and that some white folks mistreated us black cowboys, but there were some good white folks too, and I have some pleasant memories from them rodeoin' days. For instance there was Red Holmes who sold cars and trucks in Henryetta, Oklahoma. Henryetta was an-all white town that was noted for its prejudice towards blacks. In fact it had a 'Sundown' law which meant that blacks could not be in the town after sun down. Well, I broke that law all the time. I was always in that town talking to the cowboys who lived there. I didn't have no better sense than to be in that town any time of day or night. One time someone jokingly said I was gonna get in trouble in Henryetta some night. But Old Red spoke up. He said, 'Wes, if anybody messes with you, you just get to a telephone and call me. I'll have them rascals put away for good if, they bother you!' Old Red was a good friend. He sure did like me. Course he sure caused me a lot of friction with Little Mama, (wife Valdonia). You see, it was Red that got me on the rodeo circuit which took me away from my wife and three children so much of the time.

Red got me on the rodeo circuit this way. One day we was just sittin' 'round talkin' about rodeoin' and Red said to me, 'Wes, why don't you rodeo for me?' I said, 'Man I can't rodeo for you. I got a wife and three kids, and we're all on starvation.' He said, 'You don't have to stay on starvation no more.' He kept pesterin' me to go on the rodeo circuit under his sponsorship. He said I was good at calf ropin' and that I could make some big money. He said I could get started in Fort Worth, Texas right away. I said, 'Man, I ain't got no car, no truck for rodeoin.'All I got is that old beat-up second-hand truck settin' over yonder.' Red said to me, 'See those cars and trucks over there. I got acres of them. Go pick you one and don't worry 'bout payin' for it.' So that's how I got the truck and trailer to carry my ropin' horse in. That's how I got into the rodeo circuit.

I went home and talked it over with Little Mama. She wasn't too happy about me goin' on the rodeo circuit, but she tolerated it if I wasn't gone too long and if I came home when I said I was comin'. Once she chewed me out good because instead of comin' home like I had promised, I went and hooked up with another rodeo. When I got home, she chewed me out good! She said, 'Now you looka here. You're gone all the time away from me and these children. I'll tell you one thing, I'm not gonna put up with it. When you say you're gonna be back a certain time, I want you back then, or on the road comin' back. I don't want you meetin' someone by the side of the road and loadin' your horse onto somebody's trailer and goin' off somewhere else!' She was right. Course even after her ultimatum I just couldn't resist loadin' up my horse and hookin' up with some other rodeo sometimes when I should have been goin' home. I still got into hot water with Little Mama sometimes.

Things have changed in rodeoin'. Cowboys were more flexible then. We competed in many events; today, everything is so special-ized. Performers compete in just one field. Then we did everything! Cowboys are faster today due to faster horses, better ropes, and better-fed, healthier cowboys. Records are being broken everyday. In the old days ropin' a calf in sixteen or seventeen seconds was considered great; today it had better be done in seven to nine sec-onds. The first time a cowboy tied a calf up in twelve seconds, it was like a man going to the moon! Yeah, things sure have changed. But I liked it best in the old days. I sure do miss them days, and I miss all of my all cowboy friends and Old Red. I even miss the little spats with Little Mama over my rodeoin.' She was a good woman, a good wife and mother. And the children turned out just fine. Sometimes I get out my rope and practice just like I did when I was twelve years old and Cousin Raynes turned me out to rope them goats. I still get a thrill ever time I rope a calf. Rodeoin' is just in my blood. I'll be a ropin' 'til I die. There's just one thing I regret. I sure wish that Papa had liked my ropin.' I wish he could have supported me.

SIMON BERRY

Simon Berry

5

The Promised Land At Last

Memorials

SIMON BERRY
"The Father of Tulsa Transportation"

Simon Berry, a black North Tulsa businessman and pioneer aviator, did not sit around waiting for the attitudes of whites to change or for racial segregation to end, so he could be successful. He didn't accept the lie that he couldn't be a part of "The American Dream" because his skin color was black. He reached out and grabbed with gusto the golden fleece of opportunity wherever he saw it; and if the golden fleece was slow in presenting itself, he sheared his own sheep and wove his own opportunity.

The colorful, flamboyant Berry first arrived in Tulsa in 1915 where he began driving a cab. Later he established Berry's Jitney Bus Line, charging customers five cents a ride. That bus line became the first black-owned transportation system in the southwest. Before long Berry made a deal with the City of Tulsa in which the city bought out Berry's line and incorporated it into the city's expanded bus routes which provided bus transportation to North Tulsa. Simon Berry, always a shrewd businessman and smooth-talker, knew that he had a good product and that the city wanted it. He used this leverage to apply pressure on the city to "do better by blacks." Before he sold his transportation line, he insisted that the city hire black bus drivers for the northern routes, a practice unheard of in southern and border states during this rigid period of racial segregation. The city obliged. That lesson of economic leverage to bring about needed economic and social change bears repeating. Simon Berry proved that one "can fight city hall" and win! To this day Simon Berry is affectionately remembered in Tulsa as "the father of Tulsa transportation."

Berry's other distinction was that he was one of Oklahoma's first black aviators and that he owned his own airplane. He and his partner, James Lee (J.L.) Northington, a leading black Tulsa building contractor, were the only two licensed black pilots in Oklahoma at that time. It was even worse for black females who dared to dream of becoming pilots. Oklahoma's Bessie Coleman had to go to Paris, France to receive her pilot training and license. She was killed in a barnstorming accident in 1926. She is revered by all who remember her or by those who have read about her heroic efforts to become a pilot. A street in her adopted hometown of Chicago is named for her and a U.S. postage stamp now bears her image!

Simon Berry and Northington operated an airline charter service in Tulsa during the mid-1920s which was utilized by white businessmen and others for weekend flights. Julian Northington, son of J.L. Northington, said, "Flying was more a passion than a business for my Dad and Mr. Berry. They just loved flying!"

Simon Berry was indeed a colorful character and a shrewd businessman who knew when and how to take risks and how to use his property as economic leverage; he was also a passionate man who loved adventure. He successfully combined both! His son, Simon Berry, Jr., of Los Angeles, California, carries on the tradition of his famous father. He too is a pilot and flies for the *Flying Tigers*.

(Information gathered from interviews with Alice Andrews, Ernestine Gibbs, Juanita Lewis Hopkins, Eunice Jackson, George Monroe, and Verna Taliaferro, 1994. See the following interviews with J.L. Northington's two sons for more information on the colorful Berry and Northington.)

James Lee Northington, Sr., business and aviation partner of Simon Berry, Sr.

From Wilber Lee Northington June 21, 1996:

I believe that my Dad James Lee Northington was the first black person in the United States to get an aviation license. I am presently working to document that. I know that my family has a photograph dated 1925 of my Dad flying after he had gotten his license. Dad just lived and breathed flying, but neither my brother Julian or I had any aviation desires. Of course we admired our Dad and he would often take us up in his plane. The planes that my Dad and Mr. Berry flew were bi-planes, open cockpit, two-cockpit planes. Dad was always taking somebody up for a ride — my mother, grandmother, other relatives, friends and acquaintances. Mrs. Jeanne Goodwin says that many Tulsa residents would go out to Berry Park Sundays after church and go up for a ride in Dad's plane. My mother did not share my Dad's enthusiasm for airplanes. She went up once or twice with Dad but she never really cared for flying. Dad got his pilot's training at Northwestern University but he didn't buy his plane until he moved to Tulsa in 1924 or 1925. My father is pictured in the souvenir booklet of the National Negro Business League which held a meeting in Tulsa August 20, 1925 just four years after the race riot had devastated Greenwood. That bears witness to the resilience and persistence of black Tulsans then, doesn't it?

Now that I am older I am often asked about my impressions of Simon Berry. When I knew Simon Berry I was just a child. You know how children are. I didn't pay any attention to Mr. Berry. I knew he was a nice man, well-respected in the community, and that he was my Daddy's business and aviation partner. But that's it. Speaking of my childhood, we had a nice house at 547 North Detroit Avenue. Some of the neighbors that I remember were Mrs. Cynthia Petit Bankhead who lived at 401 North Detroit and Dr. Bryant and his family who lived on a corner lot which was part on Detroit and part on Haskell Street. Yes those were some good old days, the days when black businesses were booming in Tulsa. My Dad was part owner with Dr. Dickey of a drug store located at Greenwood and Archer. Later he purchased an interest in the newspaper that later became the Goodwin family's "Oklahoma Eagle." Dad was also a major stockholder in the first black bank in Tulsa which failed during the depression. Dad died in 1954. He was well respected by the Tulsa community.

When I got grown I never forgot about Tulsa and my growing up years there. But I was never interested in business and aviation like my Daddy was. I became a music and band teacher. I taught in Okmulgee and Beggs, Oklahoma. Later I moved to Dallas where I worked until I retired. Now I have moved back to Tulsa.

From Julian Northington, June 21, 1996:

My Dad, James Lee Northington, was a shrewd businessman, an entrepreneur in the finest tradition, and a well-known Tulsa contractor. And he sure expected his sons to be workers! We worked right along besides him on those building jobs. Some of the Tulsa buildings that my father constructed, or worked on, were the Big Ten Ballroom, First Baptist Church of North Tulsa, the Mason Building on Apache Street, Jarrett's Grocery Store and Hotel, and many, many residential building projects.

My brother Wilber Lee has told you about Dad and his flying, so I will tell you about a tragedy that affected our family. In 1939 the oldest son in the James Lee Northington family, my brother Cornell Mayo, was killed in a car wreck. Six young black seniors from Booker T. Washington High School in Tulsa had attended a Hi-Y Conference at Langston University.

On their return home the driver of the car swerved on a hill, lost control of the car, and hit a tree. Five of the six boys, including my brother Cornell Mayo, were killed. The following Friday or Saturday the funeral for the five boys was held at the Convention Center in Tulsa. No church could hold all the mourners. Even the Convention Center was filled to capacity with several thousand people standing outside.

From Harriett Cotharn,
Retired Chicago Public Schools teacher:

I've always had a sense of being incomplete. I have no history of family beyond my parents, siblings (three sisters and three brothers — all of whom are deceased except one sister and one brother, Artie Elizabeth Cotharn Ownes of University City, MO and Garfield H. Cotharn of Chicago, IL) and my father's nephew Mr. Simon E. Berry, Jr.

My parents, Robert Provine Cotharn and Lula Whitehill Cotharn, related little amusing stories of local color about their childhood without revealing a continuity of family and community or neighborhood.

During my childhood, 'Children were seen and not heard.' Translated to its full meaning, grownups in my generation limited their conversations with children to the issuance of orders concerning behavior, chores, etc.

Perhaps they didn't discuss family members because slavery had succeeded so well in the dissolution of the family, or they didn't know the whereabouts of many relatives or neighbors who therefore are forever lost to posterity.

Oft times if relatives were mentioned, it was in a conversation of whispered tones among adults always about brutal tales of slavery and the aftermath. I learned early in East St. Louis, Illinois the names of family and neighbors were those of slave masters or acquired names used to erase past slavery ties which could still be disastrous although long after the Emancipation Proclamation.

So it was in such an atmosphere with a sense of wonder, pride, admiration, albeit extreme apprehension and fear, I met my uncle Mr. Simon E. Berry Sr. sometimes in the 1930s. All these emotions were accompanied by a joyous feeling of happiness which made me feel I would simply 'bust open.'

Mr. Berry Sr. was wearing a finely checkered suit (which gave an overall illusion of being gray) with a perfectly clean white starched shirt and tie. His shoes were polished to a high shine. He was so clean; his finger nails were completely void of dirt or grime.

He arrived in a big shiny automobile. Years later as a freshman at Fisk University, I learned a term which explained perfectly how I would have (if I'd had the words) described him at the time. I was amazed, enthralled!!! He appeared larger than life and when he emerged from that car, truly he was a *deus ex machina.*

He gave my father a hundred dollar bill while standing on our front lawn. This exchange was seen by most of the neighbors who had gathered to see up close the big shiny automobile and the man so impeccably dressed.

I asked my father later how Uncle Simon got a job to make that much money. My father said he was a 'self-made man.' I knew then my destiny. I would be (whatever that was) a "self-made woman."

Although I didn't attain the financial and social status of Uncle Simon, I did learn that a successful 'self-made man' must of necessity possess 'mother wit' — common sense-basic intelligence.

Mother wit and/or common sense is what Miz Lucy imparted to Mrs. Eddie Faye Gates (author of **Miz Lucy's Cookies,** Tulsa, Oklahoma: Coman & Associates, 1996) and other children in their Preston, Oklahoma, childhood neighborhood. It is the type of community involvement embodied in the phrase 'it takes an entire village to teach a child.' Alas our children are giving birth to children and because of their immaturity are unable to pass on the mother wit of a Miz Lucy or Miz Lillian.

As a retired counselor/teacher of the Chicago Public Schools, as a parent of two beautiful daughters — Sabryna-Joi and Kymberli-Joi King, the answer to rcapturing our wayward young people is to 'teach', 'indoctrinate', 'imbue' them with 'mother wit' — common sense.

'Common sense ain't common' was a poster on my office wall and in a wall in our home library (I wish I knew the author of that most profound statement.)

I wrote a proposal in a 1972 **COPE** (Counseling Opportunities for Personal Evaluation). It is a program designed for discussion of common sense solutions to problems for our children of all ages and our child-parents. The proactive goal is to address our youngsters' concerns before they become <u>violent members</u> of our society or <u>victims</u> of our violent society.

I have digressed — It's because Uncle Simon, given all the obstacles with which he was confronted, succeeded nevertheless because of his extreme wit and intelligence. It gives reason to pause, applaud his accomplishments and underscore what ingredients produced such a productive person.

A week doesn't pass when I don't mourn his untimely death. It was whispered that his body was found, without a mark, next to his car in the southern state to which he'd gone to visit other relatives. I feel a sense of frustration and anger because I don't know the manner in which he died. It is a loss of historical facts to all citizens that the Simon E. Berry Park in Tulsa, Oklahoma, no longer bears his name as a celebration of his unique life.

Miz Lucy and Miz Lillian in Eddie Faye Gates' *Miz Lucy's Cookies* and Uncle Simon were each 'a village it takes to teach a child.' Eddie Faye Gates continues today in that vein as an active participant in education and civic activities.

And so even at my age in quest for continuing knowledge, if a genie would appear and grant me three wishes; I would unhesitatingly ask for:

1. a few minutes of dialogue with Simon E. Berry Sr.
2. a few minutes of dialogue with Simon E. Berry Sr.
3. a few minutes of dialogue with Simon E. Berry Sr

T. OSCAR CHAPPELLE
b. October 15, 1915, Sapulpa, Oklahoma; d. April 28, 1990

"A Man for all Seasons"

Dr. T. Oscar Chappelle was a revered Tulsa leader, dedicated servant of God since childhood, an education advocate, business entrepreneur, and a clown. A clown? Yes that is what his beloved spouse of forty-four years, Elizabeth Cooley Chappelle, says.

She has more to say about that wonderful man, the beloved T. Oscar Chappelle, minister of Morning Star Baptist Church on East Pine Street, not far from Greenwood.

From Elizabeth Chappelle, widow of Rev. T. Oscar Chappelle, September 29, 1994:

Many people think that Thomas was always serious, but he wasn't. He had a great sense of humor; he was a real comedian, a real clown! He was always just bubbling over with good humor. He was quite mischievous. I can still hear him coming through the front door and that big voice of his booming out, 'Cooley, where are you?' Cooley is my maiden name and that is what Thomas always called me. I always called him 'Thomas,' though everybody else called him T. Oscar which is what he asked them to do.

The fact that I referred to my late husband's humor in no way takes away from the wonderful things he did and his many accomplishments. He was held in high esteem by the Tulsa community and received numerous awards for his efforts. He was modest about receiv-

Elizabeth and Rev. T. Oscar Chappelle

ing such accolades and tributes, but he richly deserved them all for there was never a more dedicated servant of God or community leader than my Thomas. He probably got his sense of community commitment from his father, P.A. Chappelle, an attorney who had a law office on Greenwood Avenue until it was destroyed in the Tulsa Race Riot of 1921. It was P.A. Chappelle, I.H. Spears, and B.C. Franklin who set up a 'law office' in a tent after the riot. Those three dedicated lawyers handled $4 million worth of riot claims against the City of Tulsa and won a landmark case against the city which had passed a post-riot ordinance which would have confiscated riot victims' property without proper compensation. North Tulsans sure were grateful to those lawyers. It was a shame what the city tried to do to those riot victims. Without those lawyers justice would not have come to Tulsa.

Thomas did so many good things for the Tulsa community, especially for North Tulsa, and for his church family such as developing a one and a half million dollar credit union at Morning Star Baptist Church and a funeral home policy for Tulsans. One of the things he was most proud of was his efforts on behalf of civil rights. It was Thomas who invited Dr. Martin Luther King, Jr. to come to Tulsa to speak in 1960. Oh what an exciting day that was! Morning Star Baptist Church was filled to capacity the day that Martin spoke.

After the speech, and dinner at our home, my husband, other Tulsa ministers, civil rights protesters, and Martin travelled the Turner Turnpike to Oklahoma City to rally in front of the State Capitol. They had a highway patrol escort all the way. That visit to Tulsa by Dr. Martin Luther King, Jr. was a landmark in Tulsa's civil rights history.

From Opa Chaney, Martin Luther King, Jr. Parade,
Tulsa, January 16, 1995:

I shall never forget the day that Martin Luther King, Jr. came to Tulsa to speak in 1960. I was sixteen years old and so excited that I could hardly contain myself that day at Morning Star Baptist Church. I was part of the 'student brigade' in the Tulsa civil rights movement and we were just overcome by Dr. King's powerful speech. That man could make an ant want to get up and march for freedom! After his speech I got him to autograph my program. I still have that program to this day.

OPAL LONG DARGAN
b. September 21, 1916, Beggs, Oklahoma; d. March 11, 1994

"Risk-taker and Dream-Maker"

If there is a special place in heaven for people who took great risks, sometimes life-and-death risks, to help their fellow man, Opal Dargan is there. These risk-takers, those already there, and those still living but whose names are on a reservation list, are special people. They include "Righteous Gentiles" (people who saved Jews and other groups of people destined for gas chambers during World War II) such as Raoul Wallenberg, a Swedish ambassador who gave thousands of Jews "authentic" passports that allowed them to get out of the clutches of the Nazis in occupied Europe and escape the Holocaust; Swiss Red Cross nurse Elsbeth Kasser whose efforts at the Gurs, France concentration camp saved the lives of many Jews, especially teenagers, and earned her the nickname of "The Angel of Gurs;" Corrie Ten Boom who hid Jews behind the clocks in her father's Amsterdam clock shop; The Warsaw, Poland Catholic woman who gave a seventeen-year-old Jewish girl, Feiga, the birth certificate of her daughter who died at age three and who would have been the same age as the Jewish Feiga. That birth certificate became a "life certificate" for Feiga who, but for that birth certificate, would have surely perished at Treblinka concentration camp like the rest of her family did. Then there was Opal Dargan.

Opal Dargan didn't fight Nazis, but all of her adult life she fought the formidable enemies of ignorance, intolerance, injustice, poverty and racism, and she figuratively and literally saved the lives of many Tulsa children. And like people in World War II, she witnessed a cruel example of "man's inhumanity to man." She was an eyewitness to the Tulsa Race Riot of 1921. She never forgot the lessons that she learned growing up black in Tulsa, or the lessons from that riot either. When she grew up she became a schoolteacher who devoted her life to teaching, loving, and enriching the lives of young people. For her efforts she received numerous tributes from her beloved North Tulsa, as well as honors from the city, state, and nation. She wrote articles, gave interviews, appeared on radio and television, and gave guided tours at the Greenwood Cultural Center to visitors from all over the nation and foreign countries. The audi-

L to R: Eddie Faye Gates, Opal Dargan, and Norma Leshie discuss the Summer Arts Youth Program held at the Greenwood Cultural Center each year. June 1993.

torium of the new 2.5 million dollar extension to the Greenwood Cultural Center is named for Mrs. Dargan and contains a stunning, life-size color portrait of her. Her prevailing message to all of her audiences from elementary school classroom to visitors from state and national capitals was the same — learn to love each other, trust each other, respect each other, and live together in peace and harmony. Here are some excerpts from one of her guided tours at the Greenwood Cultural Center.

From an Opal Dargan guided tour,
Greenwood Cultural Center, October, 1993:

That riot was a terrible thing and I have never forgotten it; the memory of it is engraved in my thoughts as if it happened yesterday! I was home from school May 31, 1921 because I had the measles. The first day we tried to ride out the riot, but that second day, June 1, 1921, things got so bad that it became obvious that the black people could no longer remain in their homes and businesses on Greenwood Avenue or in the Greenwood area. There was burning and looting everywhere. Most of the men had been taken to the old Convention Center on Brady or to the Fairgrounds. Others were dead and in temporary morgues while some bodies had been unceremoniously dumped into the Arkansas River. Some of the women were taken that first day too, and were housed in schools and churches. Others like my mother had remained in their homes hoping that things would 'soon blow over.'

When the women saw that they were not going to be able to stay in the area, they reluctantly took their children and headed for safer ground. I remember that we all walked paralleled to the Frisco Railroad tracks heading south and east. What a sight we were — black mothers with babies in arms, and children of all ages by their sides, all of them walking down dusty paths trying to get to safety. We did make it to safety thank God. We reached a lovely three-story house in which a white doctor and his family lived. I will never forget that doctor as long as I live. He made the whole bottom floor of his house into a shelter for us tired, hungry, scared, dispossessed and homeless riot refugees. I will never forget the kindness of that man and his family. Other whites like him did the same thing. Rich oil men on Brady, and other streets, opened their oil mansions to helpless, homeless blacks. These oil men started out hiding just their maids and menservants; then those blacks kept bringing in other relatives and some non-relatives to those 'safety zones.' Soon, those oil men had virtual refugee camps in operation. We were sure grateful for those safe havens. We must never lump and label groups of people. We must learn to look at people as individuals. During the race riot of 1921 we saw some of the most despicable behavior imaginable which was committed by white mobsters; but we also saw some touching and tender behavior by some whites.

When the riot was over we went home, or to what was left of our homes. Most of Greenwood was destroyed — 35 blocks in all. Nothing remained but looted, burned, and desecrated buildings and a few buildings that managed somehow to escape destruction. It seemed so strange. Right next to a totally devastated building would sometimes stand a building that was untouched! When we got to our house, my mother was overjoyed, for our house was still standing. It had been looted however and the drapes, lamps, and my mother's 'pretty things' — vases, jewelry, hats, etc., taken. But the house had not burned and when we went into my parents' bedroom, we found out why. The white mob had tried to burn down the house. In the middle of the bed was a pile of burned papers and debris. But the fire had gone out because Mother had a feather mattress on the bed. The feather parts burned but the stem parts did not; they just melted together in a big blob. Oh it was a mess but that mess saved our house. Thank God for that feather mattress! We were happy about the house, but we were still sad because we didn't know whether my dad was dead or alive. Thank God, he was alive and he returned to us when the riot was over and order was restored. People were able to rebuild and restore their lives to order, but that terrible riot left marks on our minds that will never be erased.

From Theodore Dargan, widower of Opal Long Dargan, September 29, 1994:

Opal loved the North Tulsa community, did many wonderful things on its behalf, and was notably rewarded for her efforts but she belonged to us first! We were married fifty-seven years and we had a wonderful son and daughter. When Opal and I decided to do something we would discuss it, set our goals, and then do it. Then if we decided to do another project, we would do the same thing — discuss it, set goals, and do it. We were always a team. She gave her best in everything that she did, and she expected the best in others. She always said to our children, and to the thousands of children that she taught at

Johnson Elementary School, 'If you are going to be a ditchdigger, then be the best ditchdigger in the world!' She was proud of our son, Adrian Dargan, who graduated from Oklahoma State University and became a forester out west, and our daughter, Dr. Oleta Dargan Harris, who also attended OSU for a while but transferred to Rocky Mountain College in Denver where she got her degree. Later she got her doctorate and today she is a college professor.

The Tulsa community loved Opal nearly as much as we did. She was always receiving some kind of award. I asked her what she was going to do with all her awards, honors, and memorabilia. She said she wanted me to give it all to the Greenwood Cultural Center, and to include a typewriter that had belonged to her father and a 1917 sewing machine that had belonged to my family. So that's what I'm going to do with her things. One of the last things she said to me was, 'Don't let the Greenwood Cultural Center get a little old dinky piano out of that Helmerich donation ($50,000). Make sure they get a grand piano for the North Tulsa children!' She was adamant about that and I'm going to see that her wish is honored. Opal served on the Tulsa Park and Recreation Board with Walter Helmerich III. She was just crazy about Walt, his wife Peggy Helmerich, and their five wonderful boys. Walt Helmerich has donated $10,000 for the creation of a statue of Opal to be unveiled at the Greenwood Cultural Center. I know that she would be so grateful to Walt for that.

A. D. DAVIS
b. May 4, 1866, Denison, Texas; d. 1955

"One of Tulsa's First Black Policemen"

Tulsa's first black policemen in the 1920s and 1930s received their appointments at the whims of white politicians, served at the whims of white politicians and businessmen, and it is a tribute to their character and tenacity that they usually served long and well. They were a colorful lot — A. D. Davis, C. L. Alexander, Sr., and the other "foot patrol" black policemen, and the few members of the elite *Motorcycle Cops* brigade.

One of the most flamboyant of the *Motorcycle* cops was Herbert "Roughhouse" McGill who was famous for being able to give a ticket to a cornered motorist without ever getting off his

Early black Tulsa policemen.

— Photo courtesy of Leon Davis

motorcycle. He accomplished this mean feat by pulling his motorcycle up beside the unfortunate vehicle, putting his foot on the car's running board, and writing the ticket while he sat astride his gleaming motorcycle! Another interesting black policeman from this era was John Smitherman who had the dubious distinction of having an ear partially cut off during the infamous Tulsa Race Riot of 1921. McGill had a son who was called "Roughhouse Two." He died a couple of years ago.

But this vignette is about A.D. Davis who was one of the oldest pioneers featured in this work. No one living today knows more about the man than his son, Leon Davis, who is a budding author. His soon to be published book, *Corn Whiskey, Gambling, Choc Beer, Crack Cocaine in Black Wall Street, 1836-1994: A True Story*, promises to be an eye-opener! Davis says his book will add more information about the wonderful legacy of Greenwood, North Tulsans, and black Oklahomans, including mixed black and Indian settlers. But it will have a different slant from most other chronicles about North Tulsa settlers; there will be more of a focus on the "underground and illegal elements" in the city at that time. Davis promises to hold nothing back!

From Leon Davis, son of
A.D. Davis, Tulsa, September 29, 1994:

In my research I have found that there was a lot of discrimination in the Tulsa police force in the 1920s and 1930s. The black policemen were given their jobs as political plums for services they had rendered to white politicians. That was the case of all black policemen then. There was no such thing as a merit system. There was a lot of friction and bickering. White policemen wanted black policemen investigated because they said the blacks were too lenient on their own race, especially toward bootleggers who whites said were allowed to cook their liquor in 'Choc houses' all over North Tulsa! Black policemen wanted white policemen investigated because they felt there was a double standard (just as there is today) which resulted in harsher treatment of blacks for the same infractions that were overlooked when committed by whites.

I always heard my Dad talk about those days when he was one of Tulsa's first black policemen. Dad was one of the 'foot patrol' policemen. He knew and admired Roughhouse McGill who was one of the 'elite' Motorcycle squad cops. That Motorcycle squad was started by the police department so policemen could run down bootleggers who were driving cars. The foot patrol couldn't outrun them on foot, so the Motorcycle Cops were entrusted with the duty of tracking down those lawbreakers. Back then the Strip — Greenwood — where the black policemen patrolled was only about a mile. Now what we call the Strip covers about seven miles.

My father was well respected as a policeman on the Strip, and he was also respected as a businessman. He had come to Oklahoma from Mississippi in search of the Promised Land. When he was sixty-nine years old he married my mother and started a new family (four sons including me, the youngest). He didn't find Tulsa to be a Promised Land, race-wise, but he did prosper financially. He started by buying up real estate property in North Tulsa. We lived in the main house at 520 North Elgin Street and Dad rented the other houses. He also had the largest shoe shine stand in Tulsa at Fourth and Main in downtown Tulsa where the shoes of Tulsa's elite white citizens were shined! When he died, when I was ten years old, my father left his family well provided for. We lived in the original family home until Urban Renewal took it over in 1975, and there was even enough money left by my Dad to send all four of us children to college. I think my Dad would be proud of us if he could see us today. The oldest, A.D. Davis, Jr. is a retired full bird colonel in the U.S. Air Force, M.B. is employed at American Airlines, Ernest D. is a teacher, and I am a free-lance writer and businessman.

My mother, Bertha Townsend Davis, was an interesting person too. She just died recently at the age of 87. She was the daughter of Tama Franklin (who was kin to B.C. Franklin and Dr. John Hope Franklin), a black Creek Freedman who gave the land for the first school for blacks in Haskell, Oklahoma. She also had 160 acres of land that overflowed with oil. Some kind of way she and her heirs were beaten out of their oil rights. I am active in Black Creek Freedmen's meetings which are being held in Tulsa. Scott McIntosh is the chief of our organization and I am the chief spokesman for the group. We hope to reclaim our lands and our oil rights which were taken away from us by greedy whites.

My brothers and I treasure the mementoes we have of our Dad's days on Greenwood. One brother got Dad's service revolver which in those days was a 44. Another got Dad's field Winchester rifle, and all

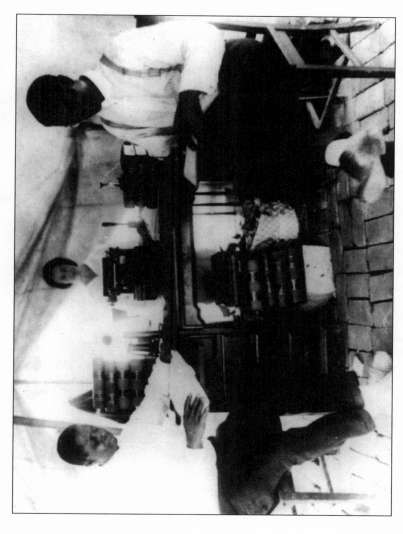

Far Right: B.C. Franklin in his tent "law office" on Greenwood Avenue after the Tulsa Race Riot of 1921.

of the 32nd degree Mason materials went to a third brother, and I got the family photographs including a long, long picture that shows all of Tulsa's black policemen who served at the same time as my Dad. I think Tulsa can be proud of the record those policemen left. Though their jobs were political plums for past services rendered to white politicians, they took their positions seriously and most of them served with great courage, dignity, discipline, love, respect and loyalty in the North Tulsa community, the only part of the city where they were allowed to patrol.

BUCK COLBERT (B.C.) FRANKLIN

"The Father of Tulsa Attorneys"

From a telephone interview with Dr. John Hope Franklin, son of B.C. Franklin, Durham, North Carolina, April 4, 1995:

Buck Colbert Franklin in life was always known as B.C. and as a tenacious fighter for the legal rights of black Tulsans. In death he is still remembered as B.C. and as the phenomenal fighter who "fought city hall" (and state and national courts, as well) to ensure that black victims of the Tulsa Race Riot of 1921 were properly compensated for their losses. Helping to keep his name and accomplishments alive in Tulsa is B.C. Franklin Park in the Springdale Area of North Tulsa, near the intersection of Pine and Lewis Street, just a couple of miles from the upper end of Greenwood Avenue where so much Tulsa history was made.

EDWIN LAWRENCE (E.L.) GOODWIN, SR.
b. December 6, 1902, Water Valley, Mississippi;
d. September 12, 1978

"Rebel with a Cause"

If E.L. Goodwin could see all of us peering at his photograph, reading about him in print, or viewing clips of him on film or videotape, he would no doubt be a bit perplexed; he might even characteristically say a few "choice" words if he thought our tribute to him was too flowery or "out of hand." But this is more than a tribute to a noble man (and E.L. Goodwin was that!). E.L. Goodwin's

Atty. Edwin L. Goodwin, Publisher, the Oklahoma Eagle newspaper, Tulsa, Oklahoma.

life is a "how-to" lesson to the Tulsa community, a lesson about holding onto and perpetuating one's dream, about strong family values, about standing up to and even conquering adversity. That is what Mr. Goodwin did all of his life. Strong-willed E.L. Goodwin even had the last word in death. He had told his family how his funeral should be. He said, 'I don't want some preacher who never knew me standing over me telling lies about me.' He said that since his son Robert did know him and since Robert was an ordained minister, he should say a few truthful words about him at his funeral. That is exactly what Robert Goodwin did.

I hope that this tribute would have met Mr. Goodwin's approval, and since Ed Goodwin always liked to "cut to the chase," only two short examples of his legacy to the North Tulsa community will be cited here — his newspaper, *The Oklahoma Eagle* and his law profession. The newspaper was purchased by Mr. Goodwin in 1936 because he was piqued because the *Tulsa Tribune* had once again written an article that was negative toward blacks which was typical of most of the white press at that time. An angered E. L. Goodwin said, 'I'll just have to print my own (expletive deleted) newspaper!' And so he did. The *Eagle* has forever since remained the main media focal point of the black community in Tulsa. It is the one source that the community can depend upon for accurate, consistent, balanced and positive reporting on political, economic, and social events relating to blacks in the city, state, and nation. It has never missed a deadline in fifty-eight years despite catastrophes such as fire and tornadoes.

Mr. Goodwin's law profession grew out of his frustration with prejudice, discrimination, and racism that had plagued his family in the deep South and in Oklahoma. In Mississippi his father, James H. Goodwin, had been so conditioned by the persistent racism there that he once tipped his hat to a white-faced cow! Mr. Goodwin thought the fleeting glimpse of white that he encountered on a Mississippi road was a white man and Southern custom required that he, a black man, step off to the side, bow, and tip his hat. So that is how a white-faced cow got tipped in Mississippi one long-ago night! But centuries of ingrained racism, injustice, and inequality could not restrain Goodwin's free spirit; instead unfairness and injustice made him more principled and more determined than ever to stand up and fight against those conditions that black people faced routinely, and persistently every day of their lives. Simply unwilling, and unable, to tolerate any more the legal inertia and apathy in Oklahoma regarding racial issues he enrolled in the University of Tulsa law school when he was fifty-eight years old in order to learn how to better focus his assault on racism. He kept up that battle against racism until his death.

From Jeanne Goodwin, widow of E.L. Goodwin, Tulsa, May 6, 1994:
My father-in-law, James H. Goodwin (who was always called Papa by his children and grandchildren) was a fine, strong-willed, hard-working, family man and he passed those traits on to his children. He was also always interested in community affairs. He and my mother-in-law were always playing host to dignitaries who came to Tulsa in the pre-open accommodation days. They had as their house guests such notable black Americans as Mary McLeod Bethune, George Washington Carver, Marian Anderson, Teddy Horne, husband of Lena Horne, Dinah Washington, Yolanda DuBois, daughter of black author W.E.B. DuBois, and noted Chicago scientist Percy Julian. There was a large lake behind their house and the ducks that were always paddling there were quite a hit with their famous visitors. And of course there was always some jazz band staying there and practicing at all hours. My husband carried on that tradition of 'open house' for visitors to Tulsa. We had some very interesting house guests. Once Dinah Washington, the famous blues singer, was our guest. My husband was taking a nap when he awoke with a start. He said, 'What is all that noise?' It was Dinah Washington and her band who had gone down to the lake to rehearse and they were loud! I went down and told them to lower the decibel because my husband was trying to take a nap. They did. Dinah was a delight and loved staying with us. It was refreshing for her to get away from all the clamor of big city life. She loved to ride horses when she came to Tulsa. I still have this picture of Dinah and E.L. riding a horse.

From James O. Goodwin, Attorney, and Publisher of **The Oklahoma Eagle** *newspaper, Tulsa, Oklahoma, December 9, 1994:*
The "Oklahoma Eagle" newspaper really began in 1918 and was then known as "The Tulsa Star." My father purchased the paper in 1936 and renamed it "The Oklahoma Eagle." Dad had great respect for the press. He knew as the grandson of a slave that there was a legacy of prohibiting communication between black people. During slavery

and even after its abolition there was suppression of freedom of the press and all other freedoms for black people in the U.S. But the written word is powerful and it could not be suppressed. "The Freedom Journal," published by Frederick Douglass in 1826 was the first recorded black newspaper in the country. Black newspapers continue to flourish to this day.

Our general circulation is small, but the significance of "The Oklahoma Eagle" can not be measured in just numbers. We provide a voice — actually many voices — for the North Tulsa community. We fulfill a need that the larger, metropolitan newspaper can not or will not meet. We are a community within a community acting as a vanguard for maintaining and keeping alive the Bill of Rights because our target audience is an example of the underdog, the victim whose cause cries out for attention. It is ironic that the large, metropolitan papers shun these issues. Being 'the only act in town,' they tend to write about the status quo, not about dissent. They do not champion the cause of people who cry out for justice. Our newspaper fills that void in Tulsa. Plus people just like to read about themselves — about births, graduations, marriages, deaths, what's happening in the religious community, and other significant social and economic events in their culture! The fact that our paper stresses religion so much speaks of the character of the black community, notwithstanding the serious problems such as illegitimacy, drug addiction, and violence that plague society in general, and the North Tulsa community specifically.

Dad's philosophy was that the service that our paper provided to the community outweighed any economic benefits to be derived from it. He said he never expected to make a fortune from the paper. I do understand my father's philosophy, but run correctly, a black newspaper can be run 'in the black.' (No pun intended.)

We are proud to be carrying on "The Oklahoma Eagle" tradition of our father. Goodwin children always played an active role in the newspaper, starting with proofing and publishing duties at the tender ages of nine, ten, and eleven years. Dad's philosophy of meeting the needs of an underserved and neglected population in the city is still benefitting and blessing the North Tulsa community. We've been around a long time and we intend to be around for a long time to come!

AMOS T. HALL
b. October 2, 1896, Bastrop, Louisiana;
d. November 12, 1971, Tulsa, Oklahoma

"On the Judicial Battlefield for Civil Rights"

Amos T. Hall is renowned as one of Tulsa's most distinguished and revered citizens who led the civil rights challenges (with the help of national legal representatives from the NAACP) that brought down segregation in higher education in Oklahoma. But long before those legal challenges in the late 1940s and early 1950s, Amos T. Hall was a warrior for God on behalf of the religious community, a champion of Masonic brethren and their families, an advocate for education, a protector of youth (via YMCA programs, scholarships, etc.) and above all else a loving and devoted family man whose extended family was as close as a walk from his Greenwood law office where he often went for lunch to satisfy his enormous "sweet tooth," or as far away as Detroit, Michigan where two of his sisters Bertha Simms and Callie Fulp lived.

Hall was a member of First Baptist Church of North Tulsa for many years where he served as a member of the Board of Trustees. He was an activist on behalf of the Tulsa community, especially North Tulsa, and spearheaded a capital fund drive to build the Carver Youth Center. For this service to the community he was named an "Outstanding Citizen of Tulsa" by the Tulsa Chamber of Commerce, one of only two blacks to receive that award at that time.

The law career of Amos T. Hall began in the 1920s. A member of the Tulsa Bar Association and the Oklahoma Bar Association, Hall soon gained a reputation as one of Oklahoma's finest trial and criminal lawyers. In the 1940s and 1950s, he gained fame as Oklahoma's most famous civil rights lawyer. With Thurgood Marshall from the National Legal Defense Fund of the NAACP, he successfully challenged Oklahoma's separate-and-unequal higher education institutions, handling such cases as the watershed Ada Lois Sipuel case vs. the University of Oklahoma. In 1969 he was appointed Special Judge of the District Court of Tulsa County where he served through 1970. In 1970 he was elected associate district judge of Tulsa County and served in that capacity until his death. He was the first black to be elected a judge in Oklahoma.

Amos T. Hall's services as a Mason were phenomenal. He was

L to R: Edward Williams, Thurgood Marshall, Judge Amos T. Hall, 1946.

Family of Judge Amos T. Hall. Seated: Jean Williams McGill, niece of Hall, her mother, Lucille Hall Williams, sister of Hall. Standing: Hall's nieces Dorothy L. Gordon, Edith G. Johnson and Carolyn Williams Tolliver.

a member of the Coal Creek Lodge Number 88, Free and Accepted Masons, Jurisdiction of Oklahoma. In addition he was Grand Master, Masons of the State of Oklahoma, 1941-1971. He was instrumental in establishing Masonic lodges in Alaska, Germany, and Korea.

The death of Amos T. Hall, under mysterious circumstances in 1971, left the North Tulsa community in shock. Tulsans of all races, creeds, and colors, from all geographic regions of the city turned out for his funeral. His beloved First Baptist Church in North Tulsa couldn't accommodate such a crowd, so Rev. Warren G. Hultgren, pastor of First Baptist Church in downtown Tulsa, volunteered his church. Dignitaries from local, state, and national government attended — Thurgood Marshall and Wiley A. Branton from Washington, D.C., Governor David Hall, State Rep. Archibald Hill and State Senator E. Melvin Porter of Oklahoma, Mayor Robert LaFortune of the city of Tulsa, Brigadier General Roscoe C. Cartwright, a North Tulsa native, from the Pentagon in Washington, D.C., Dr. Oral Roberts of Tulsa, plus many, many judges, attorneys, businessmen, members of his XI Omega Chapter of Omega Psi Phi Fraternity, Tulsa YMCA officials, and "the general public" that loved him too. Masons came from all over the world including George Swansdon, secretary, The Prince Hall Lodge of Masons, Bamberg, Germany.

From Jean Williams McGill, niece of
Amos T. Hall, Tulsa, Oklahoma, March 21, 1995:
Of all the people who visited my childhood home at 535 E. Oklahoma Street in North Tulsa, my favorite visitor was my mother's brother, Amos T. Hall whom everyone in the family called 'Son.' I always called him 'Uncle Son' except when as an adult I worked as secretary to Mr. Eugene Harris, administrator at Moton Hospital. When my uncle first came into Mr. Harris' office, I said 'When you are here, you are 'Mr. Hall.' And that's the way it was! We never knew when Uncle Son was coming. The phone would just ring and he'd say to my mother, Lucille Hall Williams, 'What you got up there? Put on the coffee. I'm on my way.' Most of the time he just walked from his office on Greenwood. His first office was at 107½ North Greenwood. Then he moved to a larger office at 121 North Greenwood which was located between Williams Drug Store on the

south and *"The Oklahoma Eagle"* newspaper on the north. Other times, he'd just show up, step in the house, and ask, 'What you got sweet?' The man just loved sweets! One time he drove his car from his office and left it in front of our house with the keys in it. When he had his fill of my mother's cakes and pies, he went on back to his office by foot. When he got there he called my mother and said he couldn't find his car, and asked her was he driving when he came to lunch. She said 'Yes Son, you were driving and you left your keys in the car again didn't you?' He had done just that and some boys had stolen the car. The police found the teenagers driving down North Peoria! We all had a good laugh about that, but my mother scolded Uncle Son for being so careless again with his keys.

Uncle Son was a very religious man and attended First Baptist Church near Greenwood and Pine. My family lived near Paradise Baptist Church and we went there just like most of our near neighbors who were also in walking distance of Paradise, like our neighbors McKinley and Margaret Anderson Petit who lived at 1173 North Frankfort.

My uncle was such a good man and was so loved and respected by the community. It just about killed us when he was found dead in his car. I was the one who had reported him missing and I was the one who went to identify his body in his car at 43rd Street North and Garrison Avenue where he had been found. He had failed to return to court in downtown Tulsa after he went home to lunch. The court house people called me and I verified that he had eaten lunch and said he was going by his Greenwood office to pick up a file, and that he would then go on back to the courthouse. We knew he would never miss court like that, so I reported him missing at 3:00 P.M. When the police found the body later that evening, I went out to the death site. But when I got there some policemen didn't want to let me through. But I was just charging them, and just trying to 'bust through.' The policeman in charge of the scene came and said, 'Let her through. She's the family member here to make the identification.' And I saw right away that it was Uncle Son. The police let me enter the car after I promised I wouldn't touch anything. My uncle was sitting upright, but kind of slumped over to the right. His hat had fallen off and was kind of crushed by his right knee. The first thing that I noticed was that he wasn't wearing his glasses. I said, 'Where are his glasses?' We looked up and his glasses were on the sun visor above his head. Someone had to have removed those glasses. Uncle Son never took off his glasses until he was going to bed. There were many mysterious things about his death — why he was in that area, why his face was bruised, why his glasses had been removed, etc. Aunt Ella, his widow, signed the papers acknowledging the cause of death as a massive heart attack, but we family members never believed it. To this day we believe that his death was foul play. He had inherited some of Judge Robert Nelson's cases (Judge Nelson was killed in a car bombing in Tulsa), so maybe there was some connection between Uncle Son's death and Judge Nelson's.

Interview with Carolyn Williams Tolliver, niece
of Amos T. Hall, Tulsa, Oklahoma, March 21, 1995:
My sister Jean Williams McGill is the talker in the family, and she is a doer too. I don't talk much. I'm the quiet one, but I am a doer also. I'm the one in the family that collects and takes care of all the photographs, like this one of my Uncle Son (Judge Amos T. Hall) who is shown here with Thurgood Marshall who later became a U.S. Supreme Court judge, and my father's youngest brother, Edward M. Williams, who was Worshipful Master of the Coal Creek Lodge Number 88 of the Masons when Thurgood Marshall became a member. I also take care of the antiques and collectibles that once belonged to Hall and Williams relatives. My sister Jean and I have inherited some wonderful pieces like this eterge and this circular cabinet that belonged to our great grandmother (Judge Amos T. Hall's mother) and all these china and pressed glass pieces.

I talked to an expert on antiques and he said don't dust them too often. He said many people make the mistake of dusting too much, often every day. He said it was best to just let them be for six months or so, then give the china and glassware a good sudsy washing, and polish the wood pieces good. Then leave everything alone for a while. Don't be rubbing everything everyday, spreading dirt and dust and damaging things. That suits me just fine! That's what I do. And I don't feel guilty about doing it. When it gets to where I can write my name on things, I give everything a good cleaning like that antique dealer said. Then I let it alone for a long time. Yes Ma'am, that's what I do. That suits me just fine!

Interview with Clarence Love,
Tulsa, Oklahoma, March 17, 1995:

Amos T. Hall was one of the greatest Masons that ever lived! He was directly responsible for me becoming a Mason in Tulsa. When I joined, I was the youngest Mason in the city. The Masonic order was very significant for black people. It was a brotherhood thing. You took the oath, you lived by the oath. It allowed us to help each other. We helped the entire community — all ages, groups, all people. Of course I mean black people. For in those days, the Masonic lodges were segregated. Black lodges were called 'Clandestine lodges.' There was a special bond between Masonic brothers. We were never to divulge our secrets. Most of the workers on trains were Masons. Any Mason could give the sign and stop a train! I still have my fez and my leather apron from long ago. They don't wear leather aprons any more but we did then.

REVEREND BENJAMIN HARRISON HILL
b. November 1, 1903, Sidney, Nova Scotia, Canada;
d. September 17, 1971

"Religious and Secular Leader Extraordinaire"

Like a tricycle-riding acrobat juggling four balls in the air, Rev. Benjamin H. Hill successfully balanced the religious, personal, community, and state components in his life.

Rev. Hill, an African Methodist Episcopal minister and later bishop, spent a lifetime ministering to church congregations all over the U.S., the last years at Vernon AME Church on famed Greenwood Avenue in North Tulsa. His secular work took him into the newsroom of *The Oklahoma Eagle* newspaper and to the impressive, marbled, but domeless state capitol building in Oklahoma City where he served as the second black legislator in the history of the state. Always vigilant in protecting the rights of the oppressed in this world, either with the pen or with laws, or preparing them for a harmonious sojourn in the future world, his influence was greatly felt, and is still being felt in both religious and secular realms in the city of Tulsa, in the state, and the nation.

Born in Canada and reared in Pueblo, Colorado, Ben Hill found it hard to adjust to the prejudice, discrimination, and racism

Rev. Benjamin Harrison Hill, pastor, Vernon A.M.E. Church on North Greenwood Avenue and Oklahoma's second black state legislator.

that he found in Georgia and Oklahoma. Perhaps that is why he became so active in civic organizations — Hutcherson YMCA, Urban League, NAACP, in fraternal organizations such as the Masons, where he was a 32nd degree Mason, and the Alpha Phi Alpha Fraternity.

His church mission was similar to his secular mission and had its roots in founder Richard Allen's philosophy, "God our Father, Christ our Redeemer, Man our Brother." Rev. Benjamin Harrison Hill was committed to right conduct, high motives, and Christian service. When he came to Vernon AME Church in November of 1949, he was following a noble heritage of dedicated black ministers of God, beginning with Richard Allen who reacted to being literally pulled from his knees during worship at a white church in Philadelphia by founding his own church in protest. Oklahoma has a rich religious history. Gospel pioneers trudged many a weary mile, forded rivers, faced dangers from the elements, animals, and feuding mankind to spread the "Good News" of the gospel in the days before statehood. From humble dwelling places, such as the one-room house at 549 North Detroit Avenue where Vernon's first church service was held, the church has expanded and progressed. It has overcome "Acts of God" and "Acts of Man," and is today a strong beacon light in the North Tulsa community.

Interview with Fannie Ezelle Hill, widow
of Rev. Benjamin H. Hill, November 9, 1994:

When my husband was in the state legislature, he introduced a number of bills into the House of Representatives including one that divided school districts into zones from which school board members would be elected. That made it possible for blacks to elect someone to represent them and their issues. Also he was responsible for introducing the amendment to the Oklahoma Constitution to allow eighteen-year-olds to vote. He helped to organize the "Black Elected Officials" organization in 1970 whose goals were to improve the welfare and to satisfy the needs of blacks in Oklahoma, to serve as an inspiration to young blacks of Oklahoma, to show that Oklahoma does afford them a future with equality..." That was his way; he was always looking for ways to improve the conditions of mankind, and to promote brotherhood and self-government.

I guess that of all the civic things that he did in his life, his coordination of the Tulsa participation in the 1963 Martin Luther King, Jr. Civil Rights March on Washington, D.C. stands out most in my mind.

With all of his religious and secular activities, my husband never neglected his personal life. His family (my son and I, plus all the extended family that I took in) always came first. When he traveled so much when he was bishop, he most always brought a doll back to me for my collection. He knew of my special love for cuddly baby dolls and I have cabinets full of them now. They are beautiful tokens of his love for me. He was just a wonderful man, a true servant of God, and a revered and respected community leader. But most important of all he was my husband!

THE LATIMER BROTHERS
(WILLIAM SHAKESPEARE, JAYPHEE CLINTON, MAJOR SYLVESTER, ELIHU, AND FRED)

"Barbecue and Buildings: The Latimer Legacy"

In researching the history of North Tulsa — its homes, churches, schools, stores, and other buildings — one family name turns up frequently, that of LATIMER! It seems that two of the brothers, William Shakespeare and Jayphee Clinton (J.C.) were well-trained at Tuskegee Institute in the building/contracting business. In the heads-hands-and-heart philosophy and tradition of Tuskegee founder, Booker T. Washington, they knew the business literally and figuratively from the ground up. Strapping young college students learned agriculture by tending the poultry, sheep and cattle that ended up on the dining table in Tompkins Hall; mechanical industries students learned building and electrical wiring by making the bricks themselves from red Alabama clay, and building magnificent buildings which are still standing today; electrical students did all the wiring. The Latimer brothers used those "Tuskegee skills" to build much of the housing for blacks in North Tulsa before the riot, and just as much housing after the riot so decimated the Greenwood area. With the Latimer family's religious values, and strong work ethic, reinforced by the "Tuskegee tradition," the Latimer brothers were groomed for success.

The parents of the famous Tulsa Latimers, James Harold and Julia Latimer, had come from the deep South in search of a better way of life, James coming from South Carolina and Julia from Florida. Today, Latimer relatives love talking about the people who inspired them to success, their role models — teachers, community

The Latimer Family L to R: Jaypbee C., Elibu, Fred, William Shakespeare, and Major. Standing Women (next to seated men).

leaders, etc., but especially those famous Latimer relatives. In addition to the five brothers there were five sisters, equally strong and determined — Alice, Ella, Maggie, and twins Patella and Thella.

Julius Pegues, son of Patella Latimer Pegues and Allan Pegues, becomes so animated when he talks — about his parents, his famous "building uncles," and all the other wonderful role models including teachers at Dunbar Elementary School, Carver Junior High School, and Booker T. Washington High School, and other community leaders who helped to mold him into the success that he is today — that he can't sit down! His eyes twinkle, the large hands make circles in the air as he illustrates a point, and he frequently walks out of the range of the interviewer. It may be difficult to keep up with the physical body of Julius Pegues as he talks about Tulsa's history and the marvelous legacy that our black pioneers left for us, but his message is loud, clear, tangible, and in focus, and as valuable and necessary today, if not more so, than it was all those years ago.

Interview with Caesar Latimer, Attorney, Tulsa, September 26, 1994:

My uncles, William Shakespeare and J.C. Latimer, were the famous 'building brothers' in Tulsa. They built lots of Tulsa homes before the 1921 Race Riot and they had an especially heavy building schedule after the race riot. They rebuilt churches, homes, businesses, and recreation facilities. My Dad, Major Sylvester Latimer, was the one that invented the famous Latimer barbecue sauce. He kept the ingredients secret and didn't write them down, but all of us, his four children, knew the recipe by heart. How could we not know it? From childhood all of us had to help cook that sauce! We grew up in the barbecue business. We were always in and out of that barbecue place, Latimer's on Pine and Greenwood. We helped to prepare and to serve the food there. There are three of us survivors of Major S. Latimer and we still know that recipe by heart. It feels good to see Dad's sauce on the shelves of major supermarkets today.

The Latimer name came in handy during the 1921 race riot. My Uncle J.C. was interred in one of the detention camps during the riot. It was customary if a black worked for a white man, that officials would release the black man to his white employer. A lot of blacks who were interred during the riot were released that way after things calmed down and control was restored in the city. J.C. explained to the white officials that he was a self-employed building contractor, that he was his own boss. The officials believed him and he was released on his own recognizance.

Interview with Julius Pegues, engineer, American Airlines, Building Contractor, Sunset Plaza Apartment Complex, North Tulsa, Consultant, Oklahoma City Building Complex, September 30, 1994:

I was always in awe of my famous Latimer uncles, William Shakespeare and J.C. When I was twelve years old, I hung around them trying to learn everything I could from them about the building trades. Well, you know what? They were patient with that inexperienced twelve-year-old and they began to teach me. In fact my cousin J.C., Jr. and I were groomed from that point on to become successful builders! We had so much guidance in those days — guidance from parents, extended family, teachers, ministers, and others who believed in the collective approach to childrearing. We desperately need to get back to that philosophy if we are to save our youth today.

Everybody can be a mentor; you do not necessarily need a formal education. My Dad, Allen Pegues, had only an 8th grade education, but he was a self-trained man. He was the best auto mechanic and the best electrician that I have ever seen. His real occupation was as a winch builder for the Tulsa Winch Company at First and Admiral, a job he held for thirty-five years. But he mentored and taught young boys how to repair autos, how to do electrical wiring, and other mechanical-type things.

The Latimer women were great role models, too. My mother's twin, Thella, had a B.S. degree from Tuskegee Institute and went on to earn a Master's degree from Hampton Institute in Virginia in the 1940s. She was one of the first black women in Tulsa to earn a Master's degree. Other Latimer women became famous musicians, one having trained at the famous Julliard School of Music.

In addition to family mentors, I had wonderful mentors in school, Mrs. Jobie Holderness at Dunbar Elementary, and for junior high and senior high schools, there were Jesse Greadington, Clyde Cole, George Homer, Fred Parker, Mr. Riley, Mr. McGill, Mr. Hughes, and the best principal that ever lived, Mr. Henry Clay Whitlow, Jr.

Oh how our mentors encouraged us then. I remember that when I was in a wood shop class, Mr. Homer oversaw a project that I did. I won a city-wide competition with that project. Mr. Homer was prouder than I was! Do you know how good that made me feel? We had really active Boy Scouts troops then. And North Tulsa leaders such as Dr. Lloyd H. Williams and Attorney Amos T. Hall were active in YMCA programs that molded and mentored young males. Those wonderful role models were there for me, from my earliest age, guiding and encouraging me. Because of the men and women of character that I had around me, I am what I am today!

When I built the Sunset Plaza apartment complex just off North Cincinnati, I could see whole blocks of Latimer-built houses in the area. Those Latimer buildings have always been my inspiration. From the back of the complex, I could see the three houses that my uncles built for the E.L. Goodwin, Sr. family. From Easton back to Fairview Streets, from Elgin to Detroit, I could see Latimer-built houses. We have to teach our youth today of their rich heritage, and we have to be there for them as mentors and role models, just like the wonderful ones that I had in my youth.

JAMES NAILS, SR.
"Tulsa Entrepreneur: Businesses, Parks, Dance Halls and Transportation in Early Tulsa"

In life James Nails, Sr. was an up-by-your-own-bootstraps black business entrepreneur who used to repair 50-75 pairs of shoes a day in his combination shoe shop/record store in the Archer/Greenwood area of North Tulsa in the late 1920s and early 1930s. In death he is an enigmatic figure in North Tulsa history. Most Tulsans recognize him as the astute businessman that he was. But other Tulsans feel that he was cheated of the recognition that was due him for his real estate, transportation, and parks connections which they feel was given, unconditionally, to Simon Berry. In fact his daughter, the late Dr. Cecelia Nails Palmer, the first black professor at the University of Tulsa, did extensive research on Tulsa history and was preparing to write a book when she died. Her brother Claxton Nails has inherited all of her research and plans to write a book utiliz-

News clipping photograph of James Nails, Ft. Custer Military Facility, Michigan, 1944. Mr. Nails is shown performing his specialty — repairing shoes.

ing his sister's materials. He says that evidence that has been uncovered will vindicate his father's place in Tulsa history.

Interview with Claxton Nails, son of
James Nails, Sr., Tulsa, September 23, 1994:

In the early 1920s my father and his brother Henry Nails owned the Lincoln Park area in North Tulsa (now Lacy Park). They later sold the land to Simon Berry. Dad owned a record shop and 12 shoe shine shops in the Greenwood area. I heard my Dad talk about those days. He said his parents had come to Oklahoma from Honey Grove, Texas and first settled in McAlester. They had moved to Tulsa by the time of the Tulsa Race Riot of 1921. He said that there was such chaos on the first day of the riot — people were just running everywhere. He said that the majority of blacks where his family lived and worked escaped to Golden Gate Park in the present Mohawk Park region of Tulsa. Many didn't make it to safety though. My father said that over 300 people were killed and that the bodies of riot victims were hastily carried away from the riot scene and buried. He said most of them were buried in the cemetery at 11th Street and Peoria Avenue.

I have this yellowed 1944 news clipping (I wish that the name and location of the paper had been included). This article describes my Dad's duties as a civilian employee of the Quartermaster repair depot at Ft. Custer. It describes how he repaired shoes for WACS, officers, and filled prescription orders for the Orthopedic Clinic of the Station hospital. My father was quoted as follows:

> 'I started to repair shoes back in 1917 when I graduated from Prairie View Normal and Industrial College in Texas and I have been at it ever since. When this war is over, I intend to return to Tulsa, Oklahoma to shoe repair work there, but as long as Uncle Sam needs me here, I'll stay but I do miss my family and the Southern climate. I have enjoyed my shoe repair work here however. The largest shoe that I have repaired here was a size 16 and the smallest, a size 3.
>
> In the old days on Greenwood Avenue in Tulsa, I would sometimes repair 50-75 pairs of shoes myself in a day, but now that I do this prescription work, I average about a hundred pairs a week. Before this Ft. Custer job, I worked in Kansas City, Topeka, and Chicago for awhile. In Chicago I took a civil service exam and passed. Then I was assigned to Ft. Custer in October of 1941.'

My father and my uncle Henry Nails are both deceased now. Their only surviving sibling is a sister, Allie Mae Walker, who lives in

Claxton Nails, son of James Nails.

The late Dr. Cecelia Nails Palmer, the first black professor at the University of Tulsa.

Mary Elizabeth Jones Parrish, author, The Event of The Tulsa Disaster, 1921 *(only eyewitness account of the Tulsa Race Riot written by a professional journalist).*

Kansas City, Missouri. I do intend to complete the work that my sister started. She left so much material, so many resources about Tulsa history. It must be told. Her home is a tribute to Tulsa's art history. Every room has a beautiful mural by Tulsa's outstanding artist Felix Cole who has gone on to achieve national fame as an artist. I must not let all of my sister's research, work, and love of history be in vain. It will be completed someday!

MARY ELIZABETH JONES PARRISH
Author of *The Event of the Disaster,*
The Race Riot of 1921

Mary Elizabeth Jones Parrish, a black woman, wrote the only eyewitness account of the Tulsa Race Riot of 1921 by a professional writer. The significance of her book is acknowledged, not only by the black community, but by leading American historians such as Scott Ellsworth, whose *Death in The Promised Land* is considered the definitive account of the Tulsa race riot.

It is not known exactly how many copies of the Parrish book were published; it is believed that about two dozen were printed and paid for by a white donor. Only a few copies are known to exist today. Mrs. Parrish left her book (and copyright) to a brother and sister-in-law, both of whom have passed on. The copyright has now expired and the book is in Public Domain according to the national copyright office in Washington, D.C. A few copies of the book remain in the hands of Tulsans including Clarence Love, a nephew by marriage, a few Tulsa pioneers, and a few researchers. Mr. Love tells the following story about Mrs. Parrish:

Interview with Clarence Love,
Tulsa, Oklahoma, March 17, 1995:
When I was a young boy living in Kansas City, Missouri, Aunt Sweet came to visit my family. To the rest of the world she was known as the writer Mary Elizabeth Jones Parrish, but to my sister Etta (Etta Aretha Love Green who died in 1948) and me, she was always, 'Aunt Sweet.' She was not our blood aunt, but you know black folks. They claim kinship right down to the last drop of blood, or even when there

Professor Henry Clay Whitlow, Jr.

is no drop of blood! Anyway Aunt Sweet's brother Harrison Jones, was married to my mother's sister Daisy Smith Jones. So that was the 'family connection.' Aunt Sweet and her husband had one child, a girl named Florence Mary who married a Bruner that lived in Tulsa but his folks were originally from Okmulgee. There are still a lot of Bruners in Okmulgee. My sister and I used to play with Florence who died years ago. That is how my mother Mattie Smith Love came to inherit the Parrish belongings including the book, 'The Event of The Tulsa Disaster.' When I moved home to look after my mother in 1946, I didn't realize the significance of that book. It was autographed 'To my sister Mattie Smith Love from Daisy Smith Jones.' I didn't know until much later how important that book is because it is the only eyewitness account of the Tulsa Race Riot of 1921 written by a professional writer.

HENRY CLAY WHITLOW
b. January 22, 1909; d. April 15, 1994

"Master Teacher Before the Word was Coined"

Henry Clay Whitlow, Jr. was an outstanding Tulsa principal (George Washington Carver Junior High School and Booker T. Washington High School) and a well-known and loved community leader. His unrelenting, visionary focus on educational excellence, his fairness, and his loyalty endeared him to faculty and students alike. He was always "willing to go to bat" for his teachers and students. In 1955 when black teachers began to lose their jobs after the *Brown v. Board of Education* Supreme Court decision in 1954 had abolished racially-segregated schools, he as chairman of the Oklahoma Association of Negro Teachers' Integration Committee, Tulsa Attorney Amos T. Hall, and the National Defense Fund of the NAACP "went to bat" to stem the tide of black teacher dismissals.

But it was Henry C. Whitlow Jr.'s influence on youth, especially young black males many of them trouble-bound, that made him a legend in the Tulsa community. He is credited with literally saving a number of black youth from the McAlester Penitentiary in Oklahoma or from an early grave! One of those youth was Don Ross.

Interview with Rep. Don Ross, Democrat, Oklahoma House of Representatives, District 73, Tulsa, October 12, 1994:

For some reason Mr. Henry C. Whitlow, Jr. always took an interest in me when I was a student at Booker T. Washington High School. I never knew why. I wasn't appreciative; in fact I just wanted him to leave me alone so I could do what I wanted to do in high school — socialize with the students, visit with the kind and dedicated teachers, and even read a book every now and then.

I wasn't a bad kid. I was just unmotivated. Well that's not true. I was motivated but not in the way Mr. Whitlow and my mama wanted me to be. I wanted to be a pool shark and I always cut my sixth hour shop class (Motor Mechanics in 10th grade, which I flunked; Wood Shop in 11th grade, which I flunked; and Tailoring which I was flunking during my senior year) so I could go to the Big Ten Pool Hall and work on the skills that would earn me big money hustling pool. But Mr. Whitlow had other plans for me. I wasn't worried that I might not graduate with my classmates because I wouldn't have a passing grade in a mandatory class. I just shrugged my shoulders and told Mr. Whitlow, 'I ain't got nothing else to do, I'll just come back next year.' But he wasn't buying that! He cornered Ben McKinney, the tailoring instructor, and told him to get me out of there (BTW High School) whatever it took! It took Ben McKinney's getting Bettie Downing to type my study book and Yvonne Hopson Hatcher making a pair of pants for my project, but I graduated with my class in May 1959! Mr. Whitlow still wouldn't leave me alone though. He, Wyonia Bailey, and Dr. Nancy Feldman, who was teaching at the University of Tulsa at the time, tricked me into college. They told me I had won a scholarship to study at TU. I really thought I had won something and I wanted to take advantage of what I had won. Years later I found out that those dear people had paid for me to take those hours. That is how I became a perpetual student. That study at TU ushered me into a new era — a lifelong process of learning. It was thirty years before I got a B.S. degree and thirty-five years before I got a Master's degree. It all started because of Henry C. Whitlow, Jr.!

But as grateful as I am for the help Mr. Whitlow gave me education-wise, I am even more grateful for another Whitlow intervention in my life — the time he saved me from a felony conviction. It happened this way. During the 1960s civil rights movement, there were lots of sit-ins to test whether blacks would be served in public accommodations. One day Billy Rountree, a classmate and previous partner in truancy and I decided to test Bob's Cafe at Third and Detroit in downtown Tulsa. If refused service we would file a civil rights complaint before the Community Relations Commission (CRC) of Tulsa (whose chairman was Henry C. Whitlow, Jr.). Wouldn't you know it. When we got there, Bob's Cafe was locked tight, but Billy and I decided that had Bob actually been there he would not have served us anyway. So we filed our complaint.

Mr. Whitlow knew that Billy and I were lying because the very time we said that we had been denied service at Bob's, Bob was appearing before Mr. Whitlow and the CRC to answer a legitimate complaint about refusing service to a black! Billy confessed and put all the blame for the Bob incident on me. I never wavered from my story of the event although Mr. Whitlow tried to enlighten me about the seriousness of a felony conviction. Mr. Whitlow and CRC Director Lois Gatchell discarded the complaint. I never admitted a thing. If I had received a felony I could never have served in the state legislature. I owe so much to Henry C. Whitlow, Jr. The man never left me alone. To his dying day he never stopped being concerned about my well-being. I loved the man and would have done anything for him. When I was grown up he asked only two things of me — (1) that I would never disappoint his wife, Thelma, and (2) that I would never lie. I have kept half of my promises to that great man!

Interview with Thelma Whitlow, widow of Henry Clay Whitlow, Jr., September 6, 1994:

Whit dearly loved this community especially the children, and especially the young black males who seemed to need him so. Whatever it took to make the ball roll, whatever it took to make education work, he did. I took my cue from him and worked with him. Our volunteer work took a lot of time but it was worth it. We were awarded together The Tulsa Hall of Fame Award in 1990. This was one of the rewards he treasured most. It was a wonderful tribute. Another award that Whit treasured was The Silver Beaver Award from the Boy Scouts. He was the first black person to receive that award. He was always so proud of that award and kept it hanging in a conspicuous place in the den as long as he lived.

DR. LLOYD HUME WILLIAMS, SR.
b. April 8, 1906, Coweta, Oklahoma; d. May 30, 1961

"A Drug Store that was a Social Center"

The Williams Drug Store at 119 North Greenwood was not the largest nor the oldest of black businesses in North Tulsa, but it was and still is one of the most enduring. I have found conflicting information in my research regarding exactly who was the first black businessman in Tulsa. Some sources say that it was Mr. Wesley Williams who came to Tulsa from Mississippi. He was an engine mechanic who was hired by some white Tulsans to power the downtown Tulsa ice cream factory. He became a prosperous entrepreneur and was the first black Tulsan to own an automobile. Other sources point to O. W. Gurley's little grocery store on the corner of Greenwood and Archer, in 1905, as the first black business in Tulsa. Despite not being the oldest, or the biggest, the Williams Drug Store was one of the most popular entities in North Tulsa for many reasons:

> **Location:** It was on Deep Greenwood (unlike other drug stores that were toward the upper end of Greenwood — nearer Pine Street) and was right in the "heart" of Greenwood activity;
> **Timeliness:** It thrived during an era where there were few "socializing" facilities for teenagers;
> **Diversity:** It offered something for all age groups, a little bit of everything for everybody — sodas and socialization place for teens; wide variety of beauty products for the courting and the young-marrieds; medicine on credit for the elderly!

Dr. L. H. Williams and his schoolteacher wife, Ethel Mildred Peeviehouse Williams, had interests that went beyond their merchant interests. Mrs. Williams' Dunbar Elementary School connections were legendary. Many of the courting teens sipping sodas in Williams Drug Store once sat at desks in her classroom where she was a popular teacher. Dr. Williams' interest in youth extended outside the drug store, also. He was an active member of the Hutcherson YMCA. Both Lloyd and Mildred Williams were civic and community leaders and received numerous tributes and honors

Dr. Lloyd Hume Williams, owner, Williams Drug Store on Greenwood Avenue.

from the Tulsa community for their outstanding, long-term efforts on behalf of the community. Dr. Williams' philanthropy and community service was cut short by his untimely death at age fifty-three of a heart attack.

Dr. Lloyd Hume Williams, Jr. carries on his father's tradition. His Greenwood Pharmacy on North Greenwood Avenue has its roots in his Dad's old drugstore (which had its roots in the A.L. Ferguson Drug Store, which Dr. Williams, Sr. purchased in 1940 after he had worked there for ten years). Gone is the soda fountain with its stools occupied by giggling, conversing couples. But the oldtimers still can get their medicine on credit there! Below are some comments by Dr. Lloyd H. Williams, Jr.

Interview with Dr. Lloyd Hume Williams, Jr.,
Tulsa, Oklahoma, November 3, 1994:

The Williams Drug Store today is located at 105 North Greenwood Avenue, a few doors south of where the original Williams Drug Store (formerly A.C. Ferguson Drug Store) was located at 119 North Greenwood, between "The Oklahoma Eagle" office and Amos T. Hall's law office.

Greenwood Avenue was the focal point of the North Tulsa community then. All the business needs of the community could be met there, as well as the social and recreational needs. These old photographs on the walls of the drug store today tell the story of the Greenwood of the past. Here you see St. Monica's band marching down Greenwood in 1940. Other photographs show the bustling activity in the drug store especially on Sundays the busiest days of all! All generations of North Tulsans converged on the drug store on Sundays after church. They came from Mt. Zion, Vernon AME, Morning Star, Paradise Baptist, and other churches in the area. The soda fountain was the meeting place for teenagers who would be sitting at the counter sipping sodas and courting, women would be replenishing their beauty supplies, and old people would be getting medicines for their ailments. And everybody would be talking and visiting with each other. Oh it was a lively, hectic, wonderful sight to see!

The store had one of the largest selections of beauty products in the city — powders and perfume, lipstick and lotions, and all kinds of hair products for both men and women, and all kinds of tobacco products mainly for the men. It was a full line drug store and could supply

Lloyd Hume Williams, Jr., graduate, Booker T. Washington High School, Tulsa, 1951.

any medical need for any patron. And of course as I said before it certainly satisfied the socializing need.

Williams Drug Store was a multi-purpose institution. My Dad was very proud of the store and its role in the North Tulsa community, (and so was my mother). I strive to keep the tradition alive and to continue to meet the needs of the North Tulsa community just as my father did in the old Greenwood days.

Interview with Robert Fairchild,
Tulsa, Oklahoma, November 8, 1994:

In the old days in the days when Greenwood excelled, we genuinely cared about each other and about the community. We encouraged each other and helped to lift each other up. When one of our classmates from Booker T. Washington High School went off to college, he or she came back and encouraged others to follow. That's what Lloyd Hume Williams, Sr. did. When he went to the University of Nebraska, he came back to Tulsa and told such stories about the great opportunities there that he encouraged others to enroll there. That was the beginning of the Tulsa/University Nebraska connection.

And when we got our education in those days, we didn't hoard our good fortune; we came back to the community and gave back to those who had nurtured us. Dr. Williams did that when he got his degree. He returned and worked ten years for the A.L. Ferguson Drug Store where he had worked summers when he was a college student. Then he bought the drugstore, himself, and devoted the rest of his life to giving back to the community.

Don Ross was one of the youth who enjoyed patronizing the Williams Drug Store on Greenwood Avenue (interviewed October 12, 1994):

Dr. Lloyd Hume Williams, Sr. was a man who was very dedicated to the North Tulsa community. His drug store on Deep Greenwood was a landmark. It was a popular meeting place for all generations in the North Tulsa community. It was especially popular with young people with my peer group. It was the main socializing area in Tulsa for teenagers. In addition to his drug store and its role in promoting wholesome socialization among teens, Dr. Williams was also very active in YMCA work. He was one of the charter members of the Hutcherson YMCA and he worked all of his life with youth groups. The role of Y's in those days was even more significant than it is today, for there were very few other options for black youth then. Segregation laws excluded them from access to public accommodations in the city — parks, pools, larger theaters, etc. were off limit to them. So that is why I have such a warm spot in my heart for Dr. Lloyd H. Williams, Sr. He gave us teens somewhere to go and something worthwhile to do. Because of him, a lot of us stayed out of trouble and became the successful men and women that we are today.

MAURICE WILLOWS
b. April 16, 1876, Clinton, Canada; d. January, 1953, Santa Monica Veterans Hospital, California

"An Honorary Black Tulsan"

Access to the Maurice Willows papers and memorabilia proved invaluable to me as I was doing research for this book. Others who have researched the Tulsa Race Riot of 1921 have interviewed eyewitnesses, have used the inflammatory *Tulsa Tribune* articles and editorials in their research, and have drawn the conclusion that those racist writings did contribute to (if not precipitate) the riot. But no researcher before has had full access to the Willows materials (both public and private records and journals).

In all my studies of history, in all my historical research, I have never seen a more meticulous, carefully detailed account of an event than Maurice Willows' account of the Tulsa riot. He documents everything — right down to the last sack of flour, bucket of nails, bolt of cloth, jug of kerosene, and last bottle of medicine that was used to help restore order to riot-torn Tulsa!

His materials corroborate the findings of others regarding media stereotypes and the incitement of the Tulsa riot, the ineptitude of city officials, and the deep and perverse racism that permeated every layer of Tulsa's society at the time.

From analyzing Mr. Willows' writings, from observing what others, black and white, said about him, it is obvious that Maurice Willows was a good, decent, loyal, honest, and loving family man and humanitarian. Like all good people he was blessed just as much as the people that he befriended. He reaped numerous rewards for

Maurice Willows, sent from St. Louis, MO to minister to Tulsa race riot refugees, June-December, 1921

his goodness — health, peace, harmony, love, and respect from peers and from family, and a long life.

Interview with Robert N. Hower, former KTUL,
Channel 8 Television Anchor, grandson of
Maurice Willows, September 20, 1994:

From all that I have heard and learned about my grandfather Maurice Willows I have determined that he was a fine, honorable, and compassionate man. He was born in the United States but raised in Canada. As an adult his whole life was dedicated to public service to helping his fellow man. One of his first acts of humanitarianism was to volunteer to serve in the Spanish-American war in the place of a buddy who was about to be married. Noting that he was about the same size as the buddy he said to him, 'Why don't I go in your place?' And so he did! Of course like it usually happens, that act of kindness blessed not only the young bridegroom to be, but my grandfather as well. It gave him the veteran benefits that allowed him to live his final days in the Veterans Hospital in Santa Monica, California. You never know when an act of kindness will turn into a blessing for yourself. My grandfather always seemed to be thinking about the welfare of others. He started some of the first boys clubs in America, like the one he founded in Birmingham, Alabama where he met my grandmother. He came to Tulsa on a humanitarian mission — as director of Red Cross operations to help the riot-torn community in 1921. He stayed six months and before he left, he wrote two versions of what he observed:

> (1) The official Red Cross report contained the accounts of actual expenditures by the Red Cross, and by other organizations to alleviate the suffering of riot victims;
>
> (2) His personal memoir to the family was more explicit, more personal, and he gave his candid views on what he believed to be the causes of the riot, the cause for such destruction and violence, and what he thought the city needed to do if its people were to live together in peace and harmony in the future.

My grandfather was convinced that the riot was a conspiracy spawned by greedy and corrupt businessmen, railroad officials, real estate dealers, inept politicians, the Ku Klux Klan which had infiltrated even the local and state government in Oklahoma, and an inflammatory press, especially "The Tulsa Tribune."

When Grandfather Willows died, his collection of Tulsa Race

Robert N. Hower, former anchor, Channel 8 ABC television station KTUL, and grandson of Maurice Willows.

Riot of 1921 memorabilia was given to his daughter, Maurine Willows Hower, my mother. I wanted to use the materials then but my mother asked me not to. She said, 'Let's not kindle old flames.' She felt that it would open up old wounds. But just before she died she gave me permission to use the materials. What spurred me to use the collection was the Rodney King beating incident in Los Angeles in 1992. After the riot occurred there, I kept hearing that the L.A. riot was the worst riot in history. I said, 'No that's not true. The Tulsa Riot was worse! The Tulsa riot caused over 300 deaths and destroyed 35 city blocks. It obliterated the North Tulsa community.' So I felt the time had come to use the Maurice Willows materials to set the record straight regarding the Tulsa Race Riot of 1921. I was just looking for the right source to trust this material to. I am glad that Mrs. Eddie Faye Gates is writing a book about Black Tulsa's history. I feel that if we are to learn the lessons of history, we have to know history. That is why I wanted this Willows material made public. I know that my grandfather would be pleased with Mrs. Gates' book. He felt great compassion and love for the North Tulsa community and they returned that love. In his collection are numerous letters and tributes from blacks who were grateful for his concern and care after that awful riot. He treasured those outpourings of love. That makes me feel good. I have always felt close to the black community. My popular television show, "Waiting Child," which tried to find parents to adopt children, featured mostly black children. I grew up in North Tulsa — on North Elwood and Denver Avenues. So my roots are in North Tulsa. I hope that this collection of my grandfather's will help, in some way, to ensure that the people of Tulsa learn to live together in peace and harmony from now on. I know that would please that wonderful, loving, humanitarian Maurice Willows who just happened to be my grandfather!

ELLIS WALKER (E.W.) WOODS
b. June 22, 1885, Louisville, Mississippi; d. November 29, 1948

"The Best Principal that ever Lived:
Or the Quintessential North Tulsan"

The epithet on Ellis Walker Woods' gravestone ought to read, "The Greatest Principal Who Ever Lived," for those are the words most often uttered by North Tulsans in describing the beloved principal of Booker T. Washington High School (who, for a short time, previously, was principal of Dunbar Elementary School) in Tulsa.

He is considered the "Quintessential Tulsan" by most Tulsans, black and white. Those who were not yet born when he died feel the influence of his education philosophy which has come to epitomize North Tulsa's focus on educational excellence. His sole surviving child, Homer Dexter Woods, describes his famous father.

Excerpts from an article written by Homer Dexter Woods, Ogden, Utah, the second of four sons born to Ellis Walker Woods and his second wife, Anna. (The other sons, Ellis Walker Woods, Jr., Isaac Rider Woods, and Clyde Andrew Woods, are all deceased):

My father Ellis Walker Woods was born June 22, 1885 in Louisville, Mississippi on what was once plantation acreage in the red clay hills of eastern Mississippi. Penniless and weary from trying to coax a living from worn-out, unproductive soil, he longed for 'book learning' so he could escape the vicious cycle of poverty and exploitation that was the lot of most Southern blacks at that time. Hearing about a school for 'coloreds' in Holly Springs, Mississippi (Rust College), he set out by foot for this institution where he worked his way through both the secondary and collegiate levels there. Later he would recall that Rust experience as one of the greatest joys of his life — working and receiving an annual gift of one dollar from his mother. That was all that my loving grandmother could scrape together, but each Christmas that my Dad was in college, she sent him a dollar 'to enjoy the Christmas season.'

Upon graduation Dad set out with his college diploma to find his fame and fortune, but found the pickings meager. It was while job hunting in Memphis, Tennessee that his eyes came to rest on a flyer proclaiming an urgent need for 'colored' teachers in a place called Oklahoma, a strange land 500 miles to the west. Dad was not to be stopped by the minor nuisance of having no money for transportation to Oklahoma; he did what he always had done — he started with what he had and worked his way up to better things. All he had was his two feet for walking and that is what he did. He started walking towards Oklahoma! Crossing the Mississippi River bridge, he went on to Arkansas where he split rails, picked cotton, and did other jobs until he had enough money to get to Oklahoma.

His first dwelling in Oklahoma was a barn loft which a generous Sapulpa farmer allowed him to use. He considered that loft an

Professor Ellis Walker Woods, Principal, Booker T. Washington High School, Tulsa

improvement over his Arkansas dwellings — which had been the hard ground of Arkansas! The stay in Arkansas was brief for he got the call to come across the Arkansas River and start a new high school for 'colored' students in Tulsa. The school prospered, Dad became a legend during his thirty-five-year career there as principal, and his influence is still felt in Tulsa until this day.

My father was so respected for his intellect, integrity, and good common sense that it was an unwritten but standard practice, for all leaders in Oklahoma, black and white, from the Governor down to local authorities, to consult him on any matter dealing with the race issue or with North Tulsa in general.

When Dad died in 1948 at the age of sixty-three, there was no black church or facility in North Tulsa large enough to hold all the people who wanted to come and pay their respects to him. So his funeral was held in the Convention Center in downtown Tulsa. Elizabeth Stubler, a "Tulsa Daily World" reporter, wrote of his funeral:

> Hundreds of friends of E.W. Woods — from the littlest Negro children to big businessmen from the south side — gathered at Convention hall today to say goodbye to the Negro school principal, who died Monday.
>
> It was a quiet ceremony, punctuated by low murmurs of 'Hear, hear,' as speakers recalled the accomplishments of the educator. Women wearing white dresses and gloves were at the entrances of the hall and passed out programs. An organ, piano, and three singing groups provided music, the choir of Vernon AME church where Principal Woods was a member, The Booker T. Washington High School chorus, singing 'The Lord is My Shepherd,' and Alpha Phi Alpha club members who gathered around the casket to sing the organization's song.
>
> The scriptural selection was read by Rev. C.L. Netherland, Baptist minister, and the obituary and eulogy were delivered by J.T.A. West, a teacher, and Rev. L.C. Browning, pastor of Vernon AME Church.
>
> After a solo, 'His Eye Is on the Sparrow,' by teacher T.T. Moore, and the recessional, ushers lined the exit with sheaves of flowers and the group went to Crown Hill cemetery for final rites.

Pallbearers included John I. Claybon, W.D. Combs, Ben McKinney, U.S. Mitchell, A.L. Thompson, and H.C. Whitlow.

Interview with Inez Black, niece of Ellis Walker Woods, Tulsa, October 27, 1994:

My uncle E.W. Woods was a very dignified man who expected everyone else to be just as dignified. But I remember Saturday morning breakfasts in the Woods home that were anything but dignified! My cousins, Ellis Walker, Jr., Isaac, Clyde, Homer Dexter, and I would be frying bacon and eggs and just making a glorious mess of the kitchen, all the while laughing, talking, and joking — just being mischievous. My uncle would come and look in the door at us and just shake his head and leave. He just couldn't take our undignified kitchen behavior. But when we had dinner in the Woods home, that was a different matter. We would all mind our P's and Q's then! We held our knives and forks so-so, and talked about 'right' things, not silly things like we did at those breakfasts. That's just the way it was. That's what he demanded of us. And we did what was expected.

Uncle Ellis wasn't just watchful of his kids or me but of all children. At Booker T. Washington High School I was a student monitor. At lunch time students who were returning to school from lunch would stand in the school yard and socialize (including me). I was aware that Principal Woods (that's what I called him when I was at school) was watching me from the window in his office. He wasn't just watching me; he deeply cared for all the students and he never ceased to monitor and direct us. He was always concerned about our welfare and wanted the best for us. He was a great influence on my life. It was he who encouraged me to go to college, and he helped me to get my first teaching job in Haskell.

Even those who never met him have felt the influence of E. W. Woods in their lives:

Interview with Rep. Don Ross, Tulsa, October 12, 1994:

I never met Ellis Walker Woods, but like many who were not born when he was Tulsa's quintessential leader, I have benefitted from the wisdom of that fine man. I think it was E.W. Woods' influence that caused Henry Clay Whitlow, Jr. to become such a great educator and motivator of youth. And it was through Mr. Whitlow that I got exposed to the Woods philosophy of education. Perhaps Mr. Whitlow was passing on Professor Woods' tradition of working with youth and that motivation, direction, and guidance was passed on to me and to my generation. So, indirectly, I too am a product of Professor E.W. Woods!

6

Reflections of White Pioneers
Friends or Foes of Black Tulsans?

JOHN BULLOCK
Tulsa, Oklahoma, Age 88

I was a thirteen-year-old delivery boy for the popular Kansas City (K.C.) Market grocery store located between First and Second Streets in Tulsa when the race riot broke out in 1921. My daddy was a cripple and drove his Model T Ford all over Tulsa delivering groceries which I unloaded. Among the best customers of the K.C. Market were the restaurants in the Greenwood area. I was such a popular delivery boy in the colored community then. Some customers would tell the K.C. Market managers, "Send John or don't come!" One of my favorite deliveries was to Mrs. Jackson on the corner of Greenwood and Archer. She baked the best sweet potato pies in Tulsa!

On May 31, 1921, the evening the Tulsa Race Riot of 1921 began, my Daddy and I were over by the Brady Theater. We soon witnessed something that I will never forget as long as I live — the total destruction of a community, the colored community of Tulsa. That night and the next day, I saw things that no human eye should have ever had to see. There was smoke everywhere, and flames, and heat. Oh, the heat! Everything between Archer and Pine Streets was burned to the ground, and also the area from Peoria back to

243

Detroit Avenue. And there were lots of deaths too. I saw bodies stacked up like cord wood on the north side of the Brady theater. Just stacked up like so much cord wood! It was a crying shame. There was a much higher death rate of blacks than the newspapers let on. I know because I saw so many of the dead colored folks with my own eyes. That riot had been brewing for a long time. There was so much hatred in Tulsa at that time. I once saw a Ku Klux Klan cross burning myself before the riot. It was in my neighborhood on the south side of Old Rose Hill Church on Richmond Avenue near the present Rose Hill Cemetery near Admiral Boulevard and Yale Avenue. My neighbors didn't like it that the Klan was burning a cross in our neighborhood, so twelve community men armed with shotguns surrounded the Klan and told them to move on. They didn't argue a bit. They moved on! But of course, that didn't stop the overall race hatred in Tulsa. Hateful people were just waiting for an excuse. It doesn't take long for things to get out of hand when there's an excuse for violence. That's what that elevator incident provided. It just gave the mobsters an excuse to do what they wanted to do all along. Oh, that riot was a tragic thing.

— **Interview with John Bullock, age 88, December 8, 1995**

MAXINE CARNAHAN
Tulsa, Oklahoma, Age 86

I was eleven years old when the race riot broke out in 1921. I awoke to the sound of gunshots but I thought they were firecrackers. My Dad told us that a riot was on and he took all of us family members downstairs. Noon the next day, June 1, 1921, Daddy took us down to "colored town" and I was shocked by what I saw. Everything was burned to the ground and there was rubble, heat, smoke, and white ashes everywhere! People were milling around and talking about the riot. Someone said that the bodies of some of the colored dead had been dumped into the Arkansas River.

My parents, William and Pearl Strong, were not used to all the race hatred that existed in Tulsa at that time. They had come as newly weds to Pawnee, Oklahoma in 1907. Dad had been born and raised on an Indiana farm and Mama on an Iowa farm. They moved to Tulsa and rented a house at Ninth and Elwood Streets. In 1911 they built a house. They had three children, another girl and a boy both of whom are now dead. My dad and mother both died at age 80. Their property was sold to the city of Tulsa and is now the site of two luxury apartments. Today it seems like a dream, what I saw after the race riot of 1921. But it was no dream. I'll never forget the sight of that burned rubble, that smoke, the heat, and the white, hot ashes that was all that was left of the colored community in Tulsa after that awful riot.

— **Interview with Maxine Carnahan,
age 86, January 8, 1996**

VIOLA CLOWES
Tulsa, Oklahoma, Age 81

My parents John and Ida Allen came to Tulsa the spring of 1921 when I was six years old. We were staying temporarily in a hotel in West Tulsa when the riot broke out the night of May 31, 1921. My Daddy was out driving and househunting the second and worst day of the riot. The police commandeered his pickup truck and forced him to pick up and dispose of the bodies of dead colored people. He didn't want to do it, but he had no choice. He was appalled by what he saw. It bothered him so that he just shut out of his mind what he saw that awful day; he was real tight-lipped about it. He just wanted to forget it! I'll never forget that riot either. I remember that we children were kept cooped up in that hotel room the entire time of the riot. The manager wouldn't let us go outside. That was such an awful feeling for a child — to be kept cooped up inside with all the noise and fervor of a riot going on outside! And we were so worried about our Dad. We didn't know if he was all right or not. He was alright, physically, but the sight of those stacked up colored bodies and him having to load them in his truck and dispose of them under police orders, affected his mental condition the rest of his life. My memory is still good and I remember those two days of the riot like they were yesterday. I am just always writing things down. I am glad that I have kept a written record of the things that happened in my childhood.

— **Interview with Viola Clowes, age 81, January, 1996**

MRS. CLARA D. FORREST
Tulsa, Oklahoma, Age 84

I have lived in Tulsa since 1918. I was a secretary at Sinclair Oil Company. My father, D.A. Mullens, was an insurance agent and an active Mason. Our family (Dad, my mother, Neva, and us kids) lived in a little three-room house at 121½ East Haskell Street behind a little widow woman. I still remember that little widow woman well. On Armistice Day, November 11th, when the whistles blew, that little widow took a granite dishpan and nearly beat it to death with a wooden spoon!

The Tulsa Race Riot of 1921 was a terrible thing. And I think it was so unnecessary. That elevator incident was just an excuse for the mobsters to begin that riot. I truly believe that the young colored man (Dick Rowland) accidentally bumped into that elevator operator (Sarah Page). I rode that very elevator and got off on the fourth floor of the Drexel Building many times myself. No operator could ever get that elevator level. It would shake and jerk and would never stop level! I am sure that is what happened that day in May of 1921. I heard that when the elevator didn't stop level, the young fellow bumped into the elevator operator, his right hand touching her left shoulder as he stumbled.

Anyway because of that incident a riot was on. It was just terrible. I remember seeing militia everywhere. Our house was right on the property line. Dad had a little fox terrier that used to bark at everyone passing by, but that little dog never barked a single time at the government troops passing by. We knew two blacks, Dollie and Olive Robinson. Olive worked for my parents and Dollie worked for the Josh Cosdens. (Cosden was a famous Tulsa oil millionaire.) On the day of the riot, Dollie and Olive hitched up their mules and were fleeing to Sapulpa when they were picked up by the militia. The militia carried many of the blacks to McNulty Park on 11th and Elgin Streets. In 1923 I went to see Babe Ruth play baseball at that park. Babe didn't do a thing that day but hit foul balls, bless his heart!

Yes I still remember that riot vividly. I might have one foot in the grave and the other on a banana peel, but my mind is still good and I don't show my age. That riot was a terrible thing. It is a blot on Tulsa's history. I am so sorry it happened. It caused so much suffering for so many people.

— Interview with Mrs. Clara D. Forrest, age 84, January, 1996

ROBERT CLARK FRAYSER
Vinita, Oklahoma, Age 85

I was born in 1911 in Vinita, Oklahoma. In 1921 my family had a black maid named Mattie who lived in a little house right behind our house. We just adored Mattie. During the Tulsa Race Riot of 1921, when the colored people were desperately trying to find safety, many of them came to Vinita. Most of them were on foot and had no actual destination. They just wanted to get out of Tulsa where their neighborhood was on fire. But some had specific destinations and were trying to get to friends or relatives, or to former hometowns. Many blacks were walking to Vinita which was about a one and a half hour drive from Tulsa down the old Route 66 highway. It is not known how long it took the colored people to walk from Tulsa to Vinita but many of them did it! These wandering people were just walking — past Chelsea and right into Vinita. They had sacks on their backs and babes in their arms, and little children holding onto their hands. Some of them showed up in our back yard and Mattie, always known as a great organizer, took over. She had some of the refugees cut wood for fire, and others draw water from our well, and others setting up makeshift shelter for the homeless people. She put some of the women to work cooking for the crowd, or just doing whatever needed to be done. I was always glad that we helped those poor refugees who had lost everything they owned in that riot.

— Interview with Robert Clark Frayser,
Age 85, January, 1996

H. A. JOHNSON
Skiatook, Oklahoma, Age 90

I was fifteen years old when the Tulsa Race Riot of 1921 broke out. I lived on Pine Street and I saw much of the mob activity that day. Another boy and I just stood around all day, June 1, 1921, and watched. I have never seen such a thing in my life! I actually saw some of the shootings. And I saw the smoke, flames, and ashes of a destroyed neighborhood (35 blocks between Archer and Pine Streets). And I saw bodies lying in the streets, stacked up beside buildings, and piled upon flat bed trucks. Oh yes, it was such a terrible sight!

— Interview with H.A. Johnson, age 90, January, 1996

Hazel Leigh Whitney Parcel

RUSSELL KING
Tulsa, Oklahoma, Age 97

My parents came to Tulsa, Indian Territory, in a covered wagon from Terre Haute, Indiana in 1899. I was born on the way. During the Tulsa Race Riot of 1921, my brother and I operated a butcher shop in Sand Springs, Oklahoma (west of Tulsa). On the day after the riot I drove a Creek Indian lady's (a customer) Chandler automobile all over "colored town" (Greenwood/Pine area of North Tulsa) to see the ruins which were still smoldering. I will never forget the awful things I saw that day — oh the terrible ruins, and the smell of burning flesh. I can shut my eyes and still smell that flesh!
— **Interview with Russell King, age 97, January, 1996**

HAZEL LEIGH WHITNEY PARCEL
Wichita, Kansas, 83

I was born in Tulsa in 1912. I attended Lincoln Elementary School, Horace Mann Junior High School, and Central High School in Tulsa. I haven't lived in Tulsa since 1932, but I still consider it my "home town."

My grandfather J. W. Whitney was Commissioner of City Streets of Tulsa during the Tulsa Race Riot of 1921. He worked with the mayor, a Mr. Evans, and with other City of Tulsa officials. I was living with my grandparents just east of Peoria Avenue and South 13th Street and was a ten-year-old fifth grader at Lincoln Elementary at the time of the riot. My grandfather had several Model T. Ford one-seater automobiles and he was gone somewhere about the city streets on projects most of the time. My grandmother, Etta M. Whitney, lived in Tulsa from 1905 until 1934 and considered herself quite a "poet" and wrote some poems about Tulsa. The day that the riot started was just like any other quiet and peaceful day in my life. But how that riot changed things in Tulsa!

As a ten-year-old child, the events of those days were fixed in my mind. I remember hearing spasmodic gunfire and I remember that some of my friends were unable to come to school because they would have had to pass through danger zones. There was tension and considerable unrest the entire summer. The National Guard was called in and some of the troops patroled the city for at least three months.

The day that the riot started when I got home from school, I was astonished to find a whole family of black people on our porch. They were shelling peas. I suppose they were helping my grandmother and in return would get part of the peas for their supper. Up until that day I had had no contact whatsoever with black people. You must realize that I had been living in the Southern tradition. Blacks had their own schools, their own part of town, rode in the back of the street cars, etc. I don't say it was right. I just accepted it as it was. My grandfather owned several farms in northeast Oklahoma and hired black sharecroppers to do the farm work. For some reason, those black sharcroppers were in Tulsa the day the riot broke out. My grandfather got them out of danger and sheltered them until they could be safely settled elsewhere. We had a small house, but a big double garage. Those black refugees lived in our garage until the riot dangers were over.

That August, after the race riot of May 31-June 2, 1921, we wanted to take a trip to Colorado. I remember that we had to obtain permission from the National Guard to leave the city. These are some of my memories about the 1921 race riot in Tulsa. It started over a minor incident and should have stopped there. May there not be more trouble of that sort.

Interview with Hazel Leigh Whitney Parcel,
August, 1996

EVELYN PARKER
Tulsa, Oklahoma, Age 85

I was nine years old when the Tulsa Race Riot of 1921 occurred. I have written down my recollections of the riot. My parents, Ralph and Etta Middleton, owned a plumbing business at that time. During the riot, we lived in the 500 block of West Cameron Street. On the day the riot started, my Daddy didn't know that the riot was on. He was down to the Courthouse which was located at Sixth and Boulder in downtown Tulsa. As he was coming down the marble steps, which were about twelve inches or so wide, bullets whizzed by on each side of his ears. He instinctly dropped down and rolled down the rest of the steps. He had his car keys in his hand and he lost those keys. On the west corner of Sixth and Boulder was an old arcade and two large, two-story houses that had lilac bushes in front. When Dad rolled down those marble steps, he crawled to one of the lilac bushes to hide, but there were two colored men already hiding there, so Dad crawled on to one of the houses and crawled under it. There were lots of women and children hiding under there. They stayed there until after sundown and until it was quiet. When they were sure that the mobsters were gone, they crept out. Dad went back to the marble steps and there were his car keys right where he had dropped them! He drove home where Mother and I were anxiously waiting for him. He made us pull down the window shades and told us to keep the doors locked and to keep quiet. Then he left to find out what was going on.

The next day my Dad returned and we found out how terrible the riot had been. A colored man named Dan worked for Dad and we all just loved Dan. We were so worried about him. Dad took us in his car to look for Dan. We went to the Fairgrounds, near Admiral and Lewis, to the northeast section where the colored people were being held, but we couldn't find Dan. I remember seeing two big water trucks outside the gates. And I remember looking at all the colored people just milling around, aimlessly, behind the gates. I later learned that colored people had been picked up everywhere as they were fleeing the riot and were brought to the Fairgrounds, to the Brady Street area, and to other areas. But nowhere could we find Dan! I was just heartsick. About two weeks later, Dan walked in at our house and we were all just elated. My spirits just lifted when I saw Dan. He worked for many years after that for my father.

— **Interview with Evelyn Parker,
age 85, January, 1996**

Herbert Johnson, Supervisor, Denver Blvd. Fire Station, during Tulsa Race Riot of 1921. Was an admitted Ku Klux Klan member.

TONY PRINGER
Langley, Oklahoma, grandson of Herbert and Marie Eunice (Molly) Johnson. Herbert was a Tulsa firefighter and a Ku Klux Klan member during the Tulsa Race Riot of 1921; Molly was a soft-hearted, broom-toting housewife.

My grandparents, Herbert and Molly Johnson, lived near Sequoyah School in the 1,000 block of North Boston Avenue. Grandpa was a firefighter at the Denver Avenue station and he was a member of the Ku Klux Klan. It was just a common thing, a common practice, for white men in business and in government in Oklahoma during the early 1900s to belong to the Klan. It was more like a social organization, but then it could turn mean and violent if the occasion arose. Well the occasion arose with the race riot of 1921. My grandpa told me that on the day of the riot, a group of blacks (called "coloreds" at that time) were trapped in the train station by an angry white mob which included him and his friends. It is ironic that while Grandpa and his Klan friends were out terrorizing "coloreds," Grandma Molly was befriending "coloreds." (One of Grandpa's Klan friends was not too bright. When the group was just leaving to start their mob activities, this fellow accidentally shot himself in the foot. So while the rest of the mob went on jubilantly with their terrorizing, this fellow hobbled home on his wounded foot!).

It is understandable that my grandparents had different values and were on different sides during the race riot. My grandfather was from a region of the country that had racial views similar to Tulsa, and as I mentioned before the Ku Klux Klan mentality was "normal" for Oklahoma at that time. Grandma Molly on the other hand was a more refined lady. She was not from this part of the country. She was from Ohio. Grandpa was not so refined; he was originally from West Virginia. He was part Indian and part Italian, so with all that mixture in him, he shouldn't have been prejudiced. But he was. So while Grandpa was rounding up "coloreds" with malicious intent, Grandma Molly was using their house as a haven for fleeing "colored" women and children. Grandma Molly had known and befriended many of these women before the riot. You see, Boston Avenue where she and Grandpa lived was not far from the elegant Brady Heights and Osage Hills region of Tulsa where many of the

Molly Johnson, wife of Herbert. A feisty, broom-wielding Ohio-born, "genteel" woman who hid black servants in her basement while her Klansman husband hunted down black refugees.

oil millionaires lived. Their maids and other servants would often walk right past my grandparents' home on their way to their homes after work in the mansions. Grandma was a friendly woman and she would chat with these servants and would sometimes give them cool lemonade. My brother remembers that during the riot, when the militia was marching those black women down the streets and shooting at their heels, Grandma recognized one of the women, and she took her broomstick and marched right up to that line of militia and broke right through and pulled that woman out of the ranks of besieged black women. The militia men didn't do anything to Grandma Molly either. That grateful woman became one of the group of black women hiding in the Johnson house basement! Before Grandpa went to work for the fire department he and Grandma ran a little grocery store on Haskell Street near the Denver Avenue area. Well the riot destroyed the homes of the black people in the "colored area" and my kindhearted grandmother did what she had to do; she provided them with shelter. She hid eight women in her basement, and she carried food to them down there. Once while Grandma Molly was in the kitchen baking a cake for her "colored house guests," Grandpa Herbert came home to refresh himself. So while he was in the bedroom doing that, Grandma finished her cake and took it down to the women. Grandpa couldn't figure out why there was the smell of cake in the house but no cake to be found! When things cooled down a bit Grandma led the women to their neighborhoods. At first she was afraid that she being the only white woman with a group of "colored" women, might get shot in "colored town." But she felt that she had to go with the women to assure their safety. And so she did.

Years later, my grandparents laughed about their different roles during the riot. Grandma Molly was always a strong, determined woman. She did what she felt was right. She always felt that the blacks weren't treated right in Oklahoma. So she just ignored custom and treated all the blacks who crossed her path with dignity and respect. Grandpa Herbert on the other hand was prejudiced and went right along with the Klan mentality. He drank a lot too, at that time. But later in life he changed his attitude and regretted his past actions with the Klan. He died in 1962 and Grandma Molly died in 1967.

— **Interview with Tony Pringer, of Langley, Oklahoma, June 21, 1996**

Tulsan Philip Rhees, 1996

PHILIP RHEES
Tulsa, Oklahoma, Age 83

I was born in Delaware, Oklahoma on June 8, 1913. My parents, Herbert and Katheryn Ann Bloom Rhees, came from Pennsylvania via Ohio and Indiana. They settled in Morris, Oklahoma (home of Anita Faye Hill, the University of Oklahoma law professor who testified at the confirmation hearings of U.S. Supreme Court Justice Clarence Thomas). I was eight years old when the Tulsa Race Riot of 1921 happened. My dad, a general superintendent for Prairie Oil and Gas Company, my mother, and the five of us kids, lived at 720 South Elgin Street near downtown Tulsa. I was a happy child and enjoyed life in Tulsa. I didn't understand what race prejudice was. I was just a happy, carefree child.

My first contact with black people was with Cora whom Dad had hired to help Mother with us kids. I remember how sweet and kind Cora was. I remember her rocking me in a chair and singing to me. She was well loved by our family; in fact she was just one of the family! After the riot we hid Cora for about a week. Later, I heard people talking about the riot. They were upset about the rumor that that boy (Dick Rowland) had tried to rape the elevator operator of the Drexel Building. The people said that rape rumor was just an excuse for mobsters to go on a rampage against "colored" people.

Early that Tuesday night, May 31, 1921, before the race riot started, Tulsa's Central High School held a Junior/Senior Pow Wow like it did every year when school was out. My older brother and sister had gone to the Pow Wow which was held at the park in Sand Springs. When the Pow Wow was over they came home. We sat up and talked a while and then we went to bed. The riot happened but I slept right through it that first night.

The next morning I heard of some of the things that had happened through the night. One thing was that Mother had fallen out of bed during the night and broke her toe. When I looked out of the window that June morning, I saw some of the aftermath of the first night of the riot. It was just awful. Our house on Elgin Street was less than a block away from the Midland Valley Railroad (on the Muskogee route) and I saw hundreds of blacks fleeing Tulsa. They were all trying to get on the trains leaving for Muskogee. But the

8-year-old Philip Rhees who was so distraught at the sight of militia men marching black refugees near his Elgin Street home that he hid under his porch, poked his B-B gun through the lattice and shot the marching guards in their backs!

militia met the blacks at the Midland Valley Depot and took them off the trains (for their own safety, so they said). They were cordoned off and were just milling around until trucks could come and take them to the "holding places" — the Fairgrounds, the Convention Center, McNulty Park, Booker T. Washington High School, and other places. All denominations of churches made sanctuaries for the fleeing blacks so they would have a place to eat, sleep, and be secure. Many decent whites took blacks into their homes and hid them like my family did.

When the militia brought the blacks down Elgin Street to the old McNulty Park they came right past our house. Elgin was such a lovely street — pretty little, well-cared for houses, trees, bushes, flowers, etc. But this day, Elgin Street was being used to herd black people! I was only eight years old, but I felt so sad for the black people. I thought the militia was doing them wrong, herding them down the street away from their homes. So I hid under our front porch which had lattice work around it, about 30-50 feet of lattice work. I stuck my little B-B gun through the lattice holes and popped those militia troops as they went by! They didn't know what was popping them in their backs as they marched by. They'd get hit and they'd stop and look around and see nothing. Then they'd move on. I'd poke that gun through the lattice work and pop another guard! I thought they were just a bunch of "bad guys."

It was a shame what the white mobsters did during the riot. There was just an attitude at that time that any time was "open season" on black people. I remember that I got a haircut at my neighborhood barber shop the day that there was still some riot activity going on. One barber told the barber who was cutting my hair to "Hurry up and finish cutting that kid's hair so we can get our guns and go down to Midland Valley and shoot some niggers." I don't know whether they went and shot any black people or not, but I do know that that barber cutting my hair hurried up. He just botched up my hair! Whether they shot any blacks I don't know. I do know that they left the shop early with that intent.

There was just an attitude that black people didn't count for much. One of my own little playmates had that attitude. I'll tell you her name and show you her picture but keep it confidential. I don't want to hurt her family. Well she was about twelve years old during the race riot and her father was secretary of the local Ku Klux Klan.

The Klan used to march in downtown Tulsa right down Sixth and Main. The city would order all cars off Main Street at 6:00 P.M. and the Klan would march. My father would take us children to watch. Dad was not sympathetic to the Klan — people like us would just go and watch. It was like people watching the evening news today. We just went because it was something to do; it was sort of like entertainment. I remember standing and watching the Klan march. I would be holding my father's hand. Dad would recognize many of the sheeted Klansmen. Even the little children had sheets on and marched. Dad would say, "That's old so-and-so." We'd ask Dad how he could recognize anyone with those sheets on. He'd say, "I know their shoes and how they walk." Back to my playmate. After the riot she was passing out packs of spearmint chewing gum to all the neighborhood children. She had cartons and cartons of the gum. I asked her where she got all that gum and she said, "Daddy got it over in Niggertown." That gum was loot from the Tulsa Race Riot of 1921! I was just an eight-year-old child then. Even though I had "done my duty" in shooting the guards with my B-B gun for mistreating the blacks, I succumbed to the lure of that spearmint gum. I chewed it!

My older brother was an eyewitness to riot activities and the aftermath of the riot. He said that he saw indiscriminate shootings of black people. They were just shot like jack rabbits! They were slaughtered like cattle. He saw bodies stacked up like cords of wood. He said many of the bodies were taken to Newblock Park which was located on the road to Sand Springs and burned in the city of Sand Springs' incinerator. Many blacks lost members of their families and never knew what happened to them. Some bodies were burned, others were buried in mass graves in the cemetery at 11th and Peoria Streets, and others dumped into the Arkansas River according to eyewitnesses.

— **Interview with Philip Rhees, age 83, June 20, 1996**

MARY JO TAYLOR
Tulsa, Oklahoma, Age 80

My Dad, Ernest Roop, was a druggist for Pat Cohen in the old Brady Hotel in downtown Tulsa. My mother, Marcella Roop, started Tulsa's first band. We lived at 901 South Cincinnati Avenue at first. During the riot of 1921, we lived at 902 South Cincinnati. That was next door to the old Manual Arts Building and near Matt McNulty Ball Park on 11th Street. There was another park, Locust Grove Park, on Cincinnati where Boston Avenue Methodist Church is today. That was Tulsa's first ball park and it was all fenced in.

We had a black laundress named Mandy. During the riot, Mandy was missing. My brother and two other men that boarded with us, a law student from St. Louis and a young oil worker, went all over the Greenwood area looking for Mandy. They never did find her. But later when things cooled down she came back to work. She said that during the riot she and others just ran and ran and ran to get out of town. She said they were just scared to death. James Butler, our colored yard man, said he ran too. I will never forget that awful riot. The smell of burning flesh is what left such a deep impression on my mind. Oh, that riot was a terrible thing.

There was so much race hatred then. I once actually saw a Ku Klux Klan crossburning. My sister Irene was courting a young man named Paul Burton (who had two brothers, Hugh and Clair). Mr. Burton was an oil man and he owned a Dodge turtleback car. Well he wanted to take Irene for a car ride and my Dad said yes, but he sent my sister and me along as chaperones. While we were out driving we came upon lines and lines of traffic that had stopped and the people were watching something. When we got close enough, we could see that it was a crossburning. You could see that big cross just burning red. I watched a while, but then I got impatient and wanted to move on. Finally, I fell asleep in the car.

I knew a lot of Tulsa pioneers then — some of the Perryman family (the founders of Tulsa) lived on the corner of Sixth and Boulder across from the old Medical Building; Prier Price and his sons, Lee, Harvey, and Jim lived near us and the boys played with my brothers. There were Jewish merchants in the area, too. I remember a Mr. Green and his tall son, whom I nicknamed "Tiny" who had specially prepared meat. I can still smell the food in that store! There were lots of fancy houses in the area with servants quarters, and barns for buggies, horses, and stables.

Yes, Tulsa has an interesting history. One of the saddest events in its history without doubt was the Tulsa Race Riot of 1921.

— **Interview with Mary Jo Taylor,**
age 80, January, 1996

$\mathcal{A}$ $\mathcal{L}ook$ $\mathcal{B}ack$

Conclusions, Statistics and a Look Toward the Future

SOME FACTS ON THE TULSA RACE RIOT OF 1921

According to Dr. Crane Brinton, considered the foremost expert on riots and revolution in the world during his tenure as history professor at Harvard University, all the revolutions, reactions, riots, and reformation movements in the history of mankind have had their roots in a common cause — upheaval due to deep-seated, long-range, long-simmering political, economic, and social imbalances (injustices) in society. Those conditions were certainly present in Tulsa, Oklahoma on May 31, 1921.

Just as sporadic, rumbling volcanoes, and submerged icebergs are often ignored, or down-played by nations until they erupt with fury to wreak havoc and destruction upon hapless populations, so was Tulsa's volatile racial climate ignored until a catalyst ignited an inferno the night of May 31st.

The seething, simmering, explosive racial climate was fueled by the worst instincts in mankind — racism, sexism, classism, greed, jealousy, vengeance, corruption, and downright violent, criminal, pathological behavior, especially at the hands of the Ku Klux Klan which had permeated all strata of society including local and state government. The state of Oklahoma had been pre-occupied with race even before statehood. It was only after President Theodore

Roosevelt threatened to block the statehood movement if racial segregation clauses were included in the Oklahoma Constitution, that leaders reluctantly drew up a "race-neutral" constitution. But immediately after Oklahoma became the 46th state in 1907, one of the first acts of its new legislature was to pass Jim Crow (racial segregation, grandfather clause) acts. In addition to the legal segregation laws which created a separate and unequal society for black people in Oklahoma, customs, mores, and illegal acts, especially "spiritual and physical intimidation" by the Klan, fueled the hostile racial climate in Oklahoma at that time. That this kind of treatment against blacks could exist, unchecked, reflects the mental atmosphere of the nation at that time, and especially the "Southern mindset" which promoted the policy of white superiority and black inferiority. There were few champions of black people at that time, and few advocates for political, economic, and social change that would have included the black population in the total fabric of society. (The few whites who tried to promote equality were ostracized by their peers; therefore little proactive racial progress was made at this time.) There was a basic lack of respect for black people and their status as second class citizens in the state was mainly accepted by all as "the natural order of things."

Yet a paradox existed in Tulsa, Oklahoma. For right in the midst of this kind of climate, North Tulsa prospered; this prosperity caused Greenwood Avenue to earn the nickname of "Black Wall Street of America." It was this prosperity that also caused white railroad men, businessmen, real estate men, as well as average working class whites to envy the blacks. Their covetousness of the Greenwood region was one of the underlying causes of the Tulsa Race Riot of 1921. Some of the acts of white mobsters during the riot clearly showed the influence of jealousy, envy, and covetousness upon the rioters. The riot was really a confrontation over possessions and power. The "Southern mindset" of that time could not accept that black people should have so much economic control!

According to Dr. Brinton, discontent over societal imbalances may simmer for long periods of time, even for centuries, until some seemingly insignificant catalyst sets off an explosion. The catalyst for the Tulsa Race Riot of 1921 was a seemingly minor incident in an elevator in the Drexel Building in downtown Tulsa. Dick Rowland, a 19-year-old bootblack, supposedly stumbled as he entered the elevator (either to deliver a package or to use the rest room on the fourth floor, the only rest room that black workers in downtown Tulsa could use at that time) and either bumped into or stepped on the foot of the 17-year old elevator operator, Sarah Page, an orphan who was attending a local business college and working part-time as an elevator operator. In a *Tulsa World* article, June 1, 1921, Page is quoted as saying that Rowland "entered the elevator without provocation and attacked her." She said she screamed for help and a clerk in the Renberg store ran to her assistance. But later, after the riot, Rowland was released from jail because Page would not press charges against him. Some friends of Dick Rowland and of his father, "Dad" Rowland who owned a lot of real estate in the Greenwood area, and some of the black pioneers featured in this book, said that there was a "relationship" between Rowland and the Page girl. There are rumors that after the riot, "Dad" Rowland sent young Dick to live in Kansas City and that Sarah Page followed him and that they lived together. Some say that they married. This has never been verified. Someday I will do more research and try to uncover the truth about Dick Rowland and Sarah Page.

There was believed to be at least one eyewitness to the elevator incident, a man who some black pioneers said later corroborated Rowland's account of the incident. But other pioneers say that this eyewitness was the very one who spread the false rumors of sexual assault. Mitchell Lane has interviewed a man who says that as a ten-year-old, he witnessed the elevator incident. Some of the black pioneers featured in the book said that there was much anger in the white Tulsa community because a white man had been lynched just a short time earlier. The man whose last name was Owens had killed a Tulsa policeman named Snyder. A lynch mob had gone downtown and took the man from his cell to Red Fork Road where he was lynched. So in a twisted, perverted way some whites felt that to lynch Rowland would somehow even the score for that white man's lynching. As whites sat around talking about the lynching of the white man and about the elevator incident emotions soared and soon the elevator incident became "a full-fledged sexual assault" in the eyes of some whites. The exact nature of the elevator incident may never be known, but some kind of altercation did occur. One newspaper account states that Sarah Page hit Rowland so hard with her purse that she broke the plastic handles. Whatever the specific details, the incident inflamed Tulsa. And some white men vowed to go down to the jail, get Rowland

and lynch him. When blacks heard of the plot, they began to arm themselves. Blacks feared that a lynching was probable because just one year earlier, in 1920, a 20-year-old black man, Roy Belton, had been lynched after being taken by a mob as he walked down the courthouse steps after he had been released from charges of killing a taxi driver. According to black pioneers who were interviewed, the first two blacks to arm themselves and to go downtown to protect Dick Rowland were Obie Mann and Mr. Strassner, owner of the Strassner Hotel on Greenwood Avenue. Soon other blacks followed suit. The collision between the lynch-prone mob and the armed blacks who were trying to protect Rowland was inevitable. The first shot was fired the night of May 31, 1921 and the full-fledged riot was on! (See Appendix for chronological charts relating to the riot.)

This riot in Tulsa earned the reputation as the worst race riot in the history of the nation. That a seemingly minor elevator incident could turn into such a holocaust is an indictment of the society at that time — a society that benignly accepted prejudice, discrimination, and racism, if not actually promoting it through legal means (segregation laws) or through de facto means (customs, mores, traditions). It is especially an indictment of the government — local and state — for the government failed to uphold one of the basic tenets of American democracy, the principle of majority rule/minority rights. That principle, in which the government protects numerical minorities (and other types of minorities, such as "status" minorities) because they can not do so themselves, was blatantly violated in Tulsa, Oklahoma during the three day riot in 1921. Not only did the government not monitor and referee the dispute according to constitutional law, black pioneers say that the first militia group, those sent in by local officials, openly sided with the whites and that their actions gave white mobsters the time that they needed to loot, pillage, burn, and destroy Greenwood Avenue. Various written and eye-witness accounts of mob activity during the riot mention that some of the Home Guards actively participated in the looting. The riot represented a low period in Tulsa history, and a wide gap between Tulsa's professed high spiritual and democratic principles! There are blatant examples of despicable, corrupt, inexcusable behavior at the hands of Tulsa's political leaders, professional businessmen, as well as that of the average, every-day white mobster.

When the riot was over there were numerous casualties, human and material, theoretical and philosophical. Documents regarding the riot generally describe the actions of the mobs as "fiendish looting, robbing, and pillaging at the hands of a small percentage of 'thugs.' " There can be no accurate account of the dead since bodies were disposed of quickly without careful recordkeeping, or most often without any recordkeeping. Maurice Willows, Director of the American Red Cross efforts in Tulsa, wrote in his December 31, 1921 report that "The number of dead was and still is a matter of conjecture. Some estimated the number killed as high as three hundred while others estimated it below fifty-five. Many bodies were hurriedly rushed to burial without records being made." Proper burial of the black dead was a major problem since Samuel Jackson's black funeral home had been burned. White funeral homes that took care of the few black dead who were embalmed and buried properly were the Stanley-McCune Funeral Home and the Mowbray Morgue. Mr. Jackson was hired by Stanley-McCune to embalm black bodies at a fee of $25.00 per body. Mrs. Eunice Jackson says that Mr. Jackson stayed in the servants quarters at the funeral home for about five days. Her husband told her of the condition of some of the black bodies that he embalmed — excessively riddled with bullet holes, or containing excessive stab wounds. Some had been bludgeoned to death with bricks, bats, or any other blunt object that a mobster could get his (or her) hands on. It has been noted that white women participated in mob activity, too. Press articles describe the women's shrill voices crying out to "kill the niggers!" Oaklawn Cemetery at 11th and Peoria received the most black bodies, though it is known that some bodies were unceremoniously dumped into the Arkansas River, and some eyewitnesses saw black bodies incinerated in Sand Springs' town incinerator. Casualties ran the gamut from ordinary "ruffian" blacks to some of Tulsa's most prominent black citizens such as Dr. A.C. Jackson whom Mayo Clinic officials in Minnesota called "one of the finest surgeons in the nation." Mr. Jackson, the undertaker who embalmed Jackson's body, told his wife that Dr. Jackson's body was just full of gunshot wounds.

The actual number of wounded is a matter of conjecture also. Willows wrote of speeding ambulances, crowded hospitals, drugstores, churches, and first aid stations where the wounded sought treatment. His records show that 763 wounded sought treatment, but this figure does not include the wounded found on all roads leading out of Tulsa, or of whites who reluctantly sought help for their wounds. (They didn't want to be identified as "mobster participants" in the riot, but suffering drove some of them to the treatment centers.) (Maurice Willows' Red Cross Report, December 31, 1921).

The physical destruction was easier to document. Greenwood Avenue looked like a war zone. Some black pioneers say it *was* a war zone and that militia, and other white officials, fired from airplanes and from trains upon North Tulsans wreaking havoc upon the helpless people, totally devastating their community. Out-of-state newspapers verify this. Figures vary slightly on the actual extent of the riot destruction. Thirty-five (or thirty-six) city blocks were looted, pillaged, and burned. Over 1,000 homes were destroyed, along with twenty-three churches, and virtually all of the prominent black businesses on Greenwood Avenue. Maurice Willows wrote in his Red Cross Report that "All that fire, rifles, revolvers, shotguns, and organized human passion could do with thirty-five blocks with its 12,000 Negro population, was done." Property loss was estimated as high as $5 million.

Another factor that contributed to the decimation of the black community during the riot, in addition to the ineptitude of the government, the racial superiority mindset of whites at that time, and the Klan-fanned mob hysteria, was the inflammatory press in Tulsa at the time, especially the *Tulsa Tribune*. The *Tulsa World* referred to North Tulsa and the black community as "Little Africa." The *Tulsa Tribune's* favorite euphemism was "Old Nigger Town." Inflammatory *Tulsa Tribune* articles, including the headline in the infamous "Bull dog" edition that called for the lynching of Dick Rowland, fanned the flames of fanaticism on May 31, 1921. (This newspaper has mysteriously disappeared from library and newspaper archives.) A scathing editorial in the June 4, 1921 *Tulsa Tribune* praised the destruction of "Old Nigger Town."

Maurice Willows was incensed by the local press articles blaming blacks for the riot. He wrote,

> "Many conflicting stories were told as to HOW the fires were started on the night of May 31st, but during the night the whole negro district had been pillaged first and burned afterwards. The method of destruction was first to pile bedding, furniture, and other burnable materials together, then apply the

"Cap" Breeding, friend and worker with Sand Springs oil millionaire Charles Page. He coordinated Page's riot refugee activities.

— Sand Springs Leader.

matches. The negroes fled, men and women carrying their children with them, with no time to take any of their belongings with them. This was NOT a RIOT, as some of the town papers called it in their screaming headlines of the next day. It was a well-planned, diabolical ouster of the innocent negroes from their stamping grounds. The planners were key persons in both races, in and with the knowledge of the police, and even reaching into officialdom in the city hall. If you can see copies of the Tulsa papers for the month of June 1921, you will see pictures of armed men on the downtown street corners, chasing every negro in sight. OH! YES! They had their ALIBI! A negro boy was supposed to have attempted an assault on a white woman in a downtown elevator, and the enraged whites had an excuse for their manufactured rage. The negro was jailed for weeks but was released after no truthful evidence was produced against him."

(Willows' Red Cross Report, December 31, 1921).

From the Maurice Willows Red Cross Report, December 31, 1921, from other records and accounts of the riot by historians, journalists, and other researchers, and from the poignant, first-hand accounts of the survivors, themselves, ineptitude of government officials and complicity of Tulsa's business and professional leaders before, during, and after the Tulsa Race Riot of 1921, can be easily documented. Out-of-town media and press organizations unflinchingly covered this aspect of the riot in which the local press, in its "rush to judgment," blamed the riot on the black people themselves. A *Chicago Defender* article published (probably) on a Saturday in October, 1921 bore the following caption: *"Ex-Police Officer Bares Plot of Tulsans: Officer of Law Tells Who Ordered Aeroplanes to Destroy Homes."* (Van Hurley was the ex-police officer who gave information to the press. He identified Capt. George Blaine as the Tulsa officer of the law who ordered the assaults from the sky and as one who had actually ridden in planes that hovered over North Tulsa, sending death and destruction down upon hapless blacks.) A *Kansas City Star* article published in June of 1921 read, *"Press Scolds Tulsa; Editors Blame Police"* (Willows Collection). In startling contrast to those articles, a *Tulsa Tribune* article, June 6, 1921, carried a story entitled *"Kiwanis Club Lauds Whites for Fighting."* The Kiwanis *"Resolved that the Kiwanis Club of*

Tulsa commends the action of those citizens of our city who during the late emergency risked their lives in overcoming, arresting and disarming the negro ruffians who sought by force of arms to intimidate officers and citizens, and impose their will on our fair city..." (Willows' Red Cross Report, December 31, 1921).

Not everyone shared the Kiwanis view of the actions of whites during the riot. In fact, there was such a lack of confidence in city government leaders that a Citizens Committee, composed of prominent city leaders, was formed. City officials during the riot included Mayor Evans, Chief of Police John Gustafson, Police/Fire Commissioner J.M. Adkison, Judge Cole, City Attorney Duncan, and Policeman Meacham. Citizens Committee members, or advisors to them, included prominent white citizens and businessmen such as Loyal J. Martin, former mayor of Tulsa, 1910-1911, Doc Kennedy, Jim McBirney, Jack Crosby, Alf Heggem, Grant McCullough, and Tom Latta.

Maurice Willows, director of the Red Cross Relief Effort in Tulsa, was assisted by A.L. Farmer, Tulsa Chapter, American Red Cross, and James L. Fieser, manager, Southwestern Division, the American Red Cross. Willows was skeptical of some of the committee's members and was downright critical of several. Later after a grand jury in Tulsa cited some of the city officials, he wrote in his Red Cross Report in December, 1921:

"Tate Brady, a political henchman who was a leader among the trouble makers, committed suicide. Buck Lewis (a real estate man with greedy intentions) met a violent death. Another had to leave Tulsa, and others had family breakups." The evidence seemed to support what out-of-town newspapers, and impartial people like Maurice Willows, said about graft, corruption, greed, racism, and collusion before and during the riot.

A grand jury was convened in Tulsa on June 9, 1921 and a probe of the riot began. The jury was instructed to get to the bottom of any law violations and to place the blame for the race war impartially upon those responsible. Most of the blame was placed upon blacks "protecting their crime-ridden area," and also upon outside agitation from their national leaders such as W.E.B. DuBois, who gave a talk in Tulsa in March of 1921, and Walter White of the national NAACP who was in Tulsa when the riot activities began. But the jury also found the political leaders negligent in not paying proper attention to the racial atmosphere in Tulsa before the riot and in not exercising proper control at the beginning of the mob activities. After the grand jury hearings, Mayor Evans was fired, Police Chief Gustafson dismissed, and according to the black pioneers featured in this book, "other heads rolled, too!" Even so, most of the blame for the riot was placed upon the blacks. The *Tulsa Daily World,* June 6, 1921 reported that the causes of the riot had been discussed in pulpits all over Tulsa Sunday June 5, 1921. Again most of the blame was placed upon lawless, armed negroes and an indifference of the higher, more moral citizens of Tulsa. But it was the Saturday June 4, 1921 *Tulsa Tribune* which gave the most scathing indictment of the black community with that infamous *"Niggertown"* editorial!

During and after the riot there was a mass exodus of blacks from the city of Tulsa. Trains and trolley cars were packed and all the roads leading out of Tulsa — in all directions — were clogged with fleeing black refugees. They flocked to Turley, Collinsville, and Bartlesville, to Sand Springs and Sapulpa, to Muskogee and Vinita, and even as far away as Kansas City. Sometimes mobs and Klansmen turned them back, even shooting, wounding, and killing some would-be refugees. Some white Samaritans were unduly kind, such as certain Sand Springs trolley conductors and pullmen who jammed their trolleys full of fleeing blacks.

For those who stayed to rebuild, it would be a tough process. But Maurice Willows and other Red Cross officials, who were called "Angels of Mercy" by grateful blacks, helped in the healing and rebuilding process.

According to Mr. Willows, one unexpected result of the riot was a surge in marriages. Sociologists explained that with their homes burned, their jobs, property, and capital gone, many women, who might have been "picky" before, now accepted marriage proposals that they would have ordinarily turned down. Necessity, and not necessarily Cupid, seemed to be the catalyst in a lot of these post-riot marriages.

Temporary tent shelters sprang up in the riot-devastated region of North Tulsa, becoming first aid centers, food supply stores, sewing rooms (with bolts of Red Cross-supplied material), carpentry tents with nails, lumber, etc., and any thing else that was required to supply the needs of the refugees. One tent even became the "law office" of P.P. Chappelle, I.H. Spears, and B.C. Franklin who went to work immediately to ensure that riot victims got proper compensation for their losses.

It became evident that despite their great losses, pioneer North Tulsans were not going to let the "Greenwood spirit" die. They set out immediately to rebuild. It would not be an easy task. They would face a concerted effort on the part of whites to thwart their building efforts — a city government scheme to deny them proper compensation for their material losses, lack of supply of building materials from local vendors, and other obvious race-impelled obstacles. But they kept on rebuilding. The "Building Latimer Brothers" got their supplies from Kansas, Arkansas, and other places. Within ten years Greenwood was "bigger and better than ever." It was now "mostly brick" so that it could withstand an inferno if necessary. In fact North Tulsa's rebuilding had been so complete that in 1925 Tulsa hosted the National Negro Business League meeting! On my living room wall is a framed, long photograph of those business men including many whose businesses had been destroyed in the riot.

The resurgence of Greenwood after the race riot is a tribute to the resiliency of those black pioneers of long ago. The black pioneers of Tulsa are adamant that the community never forgets the tragedy of the Tulsa Race Riot of 1921, but they also want people to remember the good that occurred right in the midst of that tragedy. There were acts of love, kindness, and charity on the parts of people of all races, religions, and social and economic classes during the riot. For instance, Charles Edward Arnold, a Christian Science practitioner who had an office downtown, was one of the first whites to become aware of the riot. He began at once to pray for the city and for all its citizens. Later he and a brother went out, picked up wounded and dead blacks and took them to emergency shelters or to temporary morgues. Other good Samaritans opened up their homes and hearts to fleeing black refugees, earning themselves the nickname of "hosting heroes." The W. E. Brown family opened their home, Huntleigh House, at 1030 East 18th Street to fleeing black refugees and hid twenty-five of them in their basement.

The Tulsa pioneers warn of the dangers of letting prejudice, discrimination, racism, classism, sexism, or any other divisive factor go unchallenged. They warn that such acts need to be bridled, for that riot taught that there is nothing more harmful or destructive to both perpetrator and victim than unbridled hatred.

One of the most beloved persons in Tulsa during the riot and the post-riot period was Maurice Willows who helped during the healing and rebuilding process more than any other human being. When he left Tulsa the grateful black community gave him a farewell party and a beautiful resolution written by Dimple Bush, a former Oklahoma City school teacher, which captured the sentiments of grateful black Tulsans.

Resolutions:

On the 31st night in May, 1921, the fiercest race war known in American history broke out, lasting until the next morning, June 1st., 1921. As a result of the regrettable occurrence, many human lives were lost and millions of dollars worth of property was stolen and burned. Hundreds of innocent Negroes suffered as a result of this calamity — suffered in loss of lives, injury from gun-shot wounds, and loss of property. Many of us were left helpless and almost hopeless. We sat among the wrack and ruin of our former homes and peered listlessly into space. It was at this time and under such conditions that the American Red Cross — that Angel of love and mercy — came to our assistance. This great organization found us bruised and bleeding, and like the good Samaritan, she washed our wounds, and administered unto us. Constantly, in season and out, since this regrettable occurrence, this great organization, headed by that high class Christian gentleman, Maurice Willows, has heard our every cry in this our dark hour and has extended to us practical sympathy, as best she could, with food and medication and shelter she has furnished us. And to this great Christian organization our heartfelt gratitude is extended.

Therefore be it resolved that we, representing the entire colored citizenship of the city of Tulsa, Oklahoma, take this means of extending to the American Red Cross, through Mr. Willows, our heartfelt thanks for the work it has done and is continuing to do for us in this our great hour of need.

Resolved further that a copy of these resolutions be sent to the American Red Cross Headquarters, a copy be mailed to Mr. Willows and to co-workers.

(From First Baptist Church of North Tulsa Archives)

Closure

The healing of the traumatic after-effects of the Tulsa Race Riot of 1921 has begun at last, after a 75-year conspiracy of silence about the riot. The beginning of the healing process so long overdue was made possible because of a series of events in Tulsa, Oklahoma during the 75th anniversary commemoration of the riot and the dedication of a permanent memorial at the Greenwood Cultural Center in North Tulsa.

The beautiful commemorative activities during late May and culminating in a June 1, 1996 commemoration service held, appropriately, in Mt. Zion Baptist Church which had been burned to its foundation during the riot, opened the way for the healing to begin. Over 1,200 people of all races and religions from all over the city, state, and nation, filled the church to capacity and later marched from the church to the memorial dedication. Reverend Benjamin Hooks, former director of the national office of the NAACP was the keynote speaker while other dignitaries, including University of Oklahoma President, and former U.S. Senator from Oklahoma, David Boren, gave stirring testimonials to the significance of the occasion. Rep. Don Ross, noting that no public official in Oklahoma had ever given an official apology for the riot, gave an official apology in his capacity as "a public official," an act overwhelmingly approved of by the jubilant crowd. The healing had begun! Stately, teary-eyed black riot survivors, including LaVerne Davis, Robert Fairchild, and George Monroe were deeply touched by this event.

This commemoration, this closure of the riot hurts, angers, frustrations, and the seventy-five-year conspiracy of silence needed to happen. This does not mean that the riot will ever be forgotten. It happened, it is history, and it will never be forgotten. But it can now be placed "in the memories of the heart," and the riot wounds can heal at last. The eighty-eight-year-old riot survivor Julius Williams, who has been a member of Mt. Zion Baptist Church since he was eleven years old, and who was thirteen when the rioters destroyed his church, torched his home, and destroyed everything near and dear to him, captured the significance of the memorial dedication and flame-lighting ceremony when he said:

> I have no hatred in my heart about what happened long ago in the riot. But I want people to take a good, hard look at that, a

good hard look; I want people to realize that we have achieved so much the last seventy-five years. (NOTE: Mr. Williams was referring to the black granite memorial listing the names of the Black Wall Street businesses that were destroyed during the riot, many of which were rebuilt after the riot.)

What Mr. Williams said is what historians, philosophers, sociologists, and other experts have said all along, and what ordinary people, especially minorities, feel in their hearts — that is that all people have a deep yearning to be listened to, to be recognized, understood, respected, and validated as human beings with all the rights of other human beings on the planet earth. They need to have others respect their experiences in history and to use the cause-effect relationships of the past to explain and clarify their positions in the present, and help them sort out their expectations for the future. That had never been given to the black community of Tulsa because of the conspiracy of silence regarding the race riot. This failure of the white community of Tulsa to fully and collectively acknowledge the race riot, and its failure to apply universal democratic and spiritual principles in regard to complicity in criminal behavior and other culpability issues relating to the riot are particularly galling to black Tulsans, especially to those who were survivors of the riot. Not one person was ever punished by the courts for the fire and brimstone reigned down on Tulsa that three days in 1921. The only person convicted of any charge in relation to the riot was Garfield Thompson, a black man sentenced to thirty days in jail for carrying a weapon. This is especially hard for blacks to bear since as a group, they have documented proof, and acknowledgement from those who exert political, economic, and social power in our nation, that their group is targeted harder by the judicial system at every level — from excessive "suspicious cause" scrutiny by overzealous policemen, through the entire court system from jury selection, jury exclusions, conviction, sentencing, and to the implementation of the death penalty.

Alan Dershowitz, in his fascinating and impeccably researched book, *Chutzpah*, thoroughly analyzes this phenomena and explains how Jews all over the world chafe at always being exposed to the ambiguity of double standard treatment and stereotypical comparisons. Just as Jews cannot experience closure of the Holocaust because of a lack of universal support of targeted Jews during the

Holocaust, a lack of universal acknowledgement of the unparalleled destructiveness of the Holocaust on Jewish people, and most of all a failure of the world to adequately punish Holocaust perpetrators and their sympathizers/collaborators, black Tulsans couldn't "let go of the Tulsa Race Riot of 1921," until Saturday June 1, 1996. Rep. Don Ross' apology on behalf of government officials began the closure process. Blacks hope that a lesson will be learned about the dangers of silence. Even when the causes of silence are known — shame and guilt, awkwardness, not knowing what to say or do, like awkwardness after a death, there is no excuse for silence! People must communicate. They must be sincere, honest, and vigilant and they must never stand by silently while wrong attitudes and behaviors reign supreme. When in doubt about what to say or do, reliance upon spiritual values and tried and tested democratic principles should be their guide. Short, sensitive, honest remarks are always appropriate. Appropriate remarks were made June 1, 1996 at the commemoration ceremony and repentance, forgiveness, and healing took place. By the way, I do not mean to imply that blacks want preferential treatment. Just like the Jews, we don't mind contextual, comparative analyses with other individuals and groups; we do however tire of being held to a double standard, and of stereotypical comparisons that seem to never end!

The Tulsa Race Riot of 1921 commemoration activities received positive local, state, national, and international media attention including the following:

Print Media Articles: Washington Post, May 30, 1996.
New York Times, May 31, 1996.
Jet Magazine, Johnson Publishing Company, Chicago, June 17, 1996, a Paris, France newspaper article.

Electronic Media: All local television stations, and Oklahoma City stations, covered week-long commemoration activities extensively. Featured in many of the stories were riot survivors Laverne Davis, Robert Fairchild, Ernestine Gibbs, Eunice Jackson, and George Monroe, and historians of riot research including this author. Bryant Gumbel of the *Today* Show, NBC, New York featured a Tulsa Race Riot of 1921 segment on May 31, 1996 which featured riot survivors, Davis, Fairchild, Gibbs, and Monroe.

Black Wall Street Memorial — listing of former black businesses destroyed during the riot.

One of the most tragic experiences of the Tulsa Race Riot of 1921 was what happened to a black man named J. B. Stradford. The son of a Kentucky slave, Stradford had worked himself up by his bootstraps, graduating from Oberlin College in Ohio and from Indiana University Law School. In 1899 like countless others drawn by the magnet of "a Promised Land," he came to Tulsa to seek his fame and fortune; he found it. Not only was he a prominent lawyer, but a successful business man as well. According to a newspaper article, at the time of the Tulsa riot he had assets of about $125,000 including a 65-room hotel, the Stradford, at 301 North Greenwood Avenue. During the infamous riot, his famous hotel was burned to the ground, and all his other assets were lost forever. The worst was still to come. A good Samaritan act of Stradford's during the heat of pre-riot activities led to his arrest on charges of inciting a riot. The deeply religious, highly respected Stradford, a skilled and sensitive lawyer, felt that he could perhaps defuse the volatile situation at the courthouse in downtown Tulsa where an angry mob was gathered to dispense "justice" to young Dick Rowland. So he went there to do just that. Little did he know that this well-meant Samaritan act would have such long-range, detrimental ramifications on his life as well as upon the lives of his offspring. Not only was Stradford's well-meant motivation and behavior unappreciated, it was suspect! After his arrest, a grown son of Stradford's, C. Francis Stradford, a Columbia University Law School graduate, then a practicing attorney in Chicago, gained his father's release from jail. Fearful for his life based on Tulsa's race history, almost certain that justice would *not* be dispensed toward him, J. B. Stradford slipped from Tulsa in the night and became a fugitive. Never would he set foot in Tulsa again. Neither would any of his offspring, until October 18, 1996. That act would haunt him until his death in 1935. Being a fugitive, even on unjust, trumped up charges, was a disturbing reality for this man who lived, breathed, and loved the law. In his 480-page memoir, written perhaps to ease his conscience, Stradford spoke of the tremendous pain that he continually suffered in his "fugitive state."

So on October 18, 1996, at a Greenwood Gala Event, the record was set straight at last. Before twenty-one of his descendants, who came from all over the U.S. and even from as far away as Europe, the charges of inciting a riot were dropped against J.B. Stradford. In the case of the *State of Oklahoma v. Will Robinson, et al,* June 15, 1921, one of the cases initiated by a grand jury empaneled to investigate the riot, Governor Frank Keating issued an executive pardon for J.B. Stradford (and technically charges against sixty-two other blacks listed in the June 15, 1921 grand jury indictment). The governor also proclaimed October 18, 1996 J.B. Stradford Day.

Tulsa District Attorney William LaFortune and Judge Jesse Harris officially dropped all charges on behalf of the City of Tulsa. Posthumously, Stradford's name will be added to those permitted to practice law in Oklahoma. It was a bitter sweet moment for Stradford's descendants, now among Chicago's first families, icons of that enterprising spirit exemplified by the family patriarch. J.B. Stradford's descendants include a former U.S. Representative to the United Nations, a U.S. Ambassador, lawyers, judges, teachers, college professors, government officials, television personalities, corporate executives, military officers, physicians, and entrepreneurs.

Among those attending were Ambassador Jewel Lafontant-Mankarious, granddaughter, John W. Rogers, Jr., grandson, Emma Toole Monroe, granddaughter, John Toole, grandson, Judge Cornelius E. Toole, great-grandson, Dr. Theron C. Toole, great-grandson.

Sources of Riot Information

Interviews: Black Tulsa pioneers and their relatives, friends, and acquaintances regarding prejudice, discrimination, and racism, in general, and the Tulsa Race Riot of 1921, specifically. Interviews with white eyewitnesses, some of whom had relatives or acquaintances, who were Ku Klux Klan members.

Newspapers, Magazines, Articles and Books:
The Chicago Defender, Chicago, Illinois, probably a Saturday in October, 1921.

Impact Magazine, June-July issue, Tulsa, Oklahoma, 1971.

The Kansas City Star, Kansas City, Missouri, 1921, 1922.

National Urban League, A Study of The Social and Economic Conditions of the Negro Population of Tulsa, Oklahoma, New York, 1945.

Oklahoma Bureau of Vital Statistics, Oklahoma City, Oklahoma, 1921

Oklahoma City *Daily Oklahoman*, June 1, 1921.

Oklahoma City *Black Dispatch*, June 3, 1921.

Oklahoma Historical Society Archives, Oklahoma City, Oklahoma

The Pittsburgh Courier, Pittsburgh, Pennsylvania, June, 1921.

Tulsa Historical Society Archives, Tulsa, Oklahoma.

The Tulsa Oklahoma Sun Newspaper, August 21, 1921; August 28, 1921.

The Tulsa World, Tulsa, Oklahoma, June-December, 1921.

The Tulsa Tribune, Tulsa, Oklahoma, June-December, 1921.

James Vance, "Hope is the Last Thing to Die," a monograph written in connection with *"Climbing Jacob's Ladder: The Rise of Black Churches in Eastern Cities, 1740-1877,"* and *"Oklahoma: Where East Meets West, The Role of Black Churches in the Development of Oklahoma,"* Tulsa Junior College, Smithsonian Institution Traveling Exhibition Service (SITES), and the Anacostia Museum, 1992.

Walter F. White, *"Tulsa Stabbed in the Back,"* New York Evening Post, June 11, 1921. Printed with permission in *The Tulsa World*, July 10, 1921.

The Maurice Willows Collection of Papers Regarding the Tulsa Race Riot and the Role of the International Red Cross, Tulsa, Oklahoma, June-December, 1921.

The Event of the Tulsa Disaster, Mary Elizabeth Jones Parrish, Tulsa, Oklahoma, 1921.

Death in the Promised Land, Scott Ellsworth, Louisiana University Press, Baton Rouge, Louisiana, 1982.

SOME STATISTICS ON THE BLACK PIONEERS

Number: Forty-five black Tulsa pioneers gave poignant interviews which provided much first-hand information about the pioneer experience; Fifteen pioneers are featured in the Memorial segment of the book, 13 men and two women. The five Latimer brothers were grouped as one entity — The Latimer legacy).

Race: All 45 pioneers featured in the Living Testimony segment were black; in the Memorial segment, there were 14 black pioneers featured and one honorary white.

Gender: 23 men and 22 women are featured in the testimony segment of the book.

Age: 14 participants were in their 90s, including three who were born in the 1800s;

14 were in their 80s

13 were in their 70s

 4 were in their 60s

Geographic Origins: 21 born in Oklahoma

12 born in Texas

 2 born in Arkansas

 2 born in Georgia

 1 born in each of the following states — Alabama, Illinois, Kansas, Kentucky, Louisiana, Mississippi, and Tennessee.

Eras of Migration: Most of the migration of Black pioneers occurred between 1877-1930.

Reasons for Migration: Most of the black pioneers came to Oklahoma because it had a reputation for fairness and most of these people were leaving states noted for their oppression of blacks. Some pioneers had witnessed Klan violence, lynchings, riots, and other unbearable conditions. They set out for Oklahoma hoping that it would indeed be a Promised Land for them.

Families: The strongest, most enduring, purest thing in the lives of these black pioneers were their families which included not only the nuclear family of mother, father, and their children (most of the time, lots of children), but extended families as well, grandparents, aunts, uncles, cousins who were often the children of deceased relatives, of relatives who were "having a hard time," and sometimes children who were no kin at all but who needed someone to nurture, care, and love them. Through these family units, children learned the work ethic, values, customs and mores. They were taught to be team players, to do things not only for self but for the collective good of the entire community. And at appropriate times, there was good, wholesome fun! Non-minorities are often surprised to find abundant examples of joy in the lives of people who were excluded from full political, economic, and social equality in the American society. But despite poverty, racism, and tragedies, black people then knew how to have fun (and they still do!). They did not obsess twenty-four hours a day on their plight in life. Their fashions and beauty notions, their feasts and festivals were welcomed outlets. Most of these fun-filled events were usually connected with church and school activities. Others were recreational and leisure activities in their beloved Greenwood Avenue area of North Tulsa.

Religious Institutions: Religion was as much a part of the lives of black pioneers as breathing. Their faith, deep and abiding, was a warm blanket thrown around their shoulders to ward off the chills of adversity that plagued them persistently in an unjust, unequal American society. Whatever calamities they faced — so-called Acts of God, personal tragedies, violence caused by prejudice, discrimination, and racism, or any other difficulty — they relied on their religion "to see them through."

Through all the tragedies, these pioneers relied on their God to console, sustain, and guide them. Bullet-dodging, stream-fording, circuit-riding preachers were a part of Oklahoma's rich and colorful religious history. Long before statehood in 1907, these ministers had brought the word of God to this territory which was sometimes referred to as a wild and reckless God-forsaken No Man's Land! The first churches of the black pioneers were often rooms in the simple frame homes of faithful brethren and sisters in North Tulsa. But due to dogged determination, and successful fund-raisers, beautiful religious edifices sprung up in North Tulsa, including Mt. Zion Baptist Church, Vernon AME Church, First Baptist Church, Morning Star Baptist Church and other churches.

Educational Institutions: No other people in history have seemed to yearn more for education than this group of black pioneers and their ancestors. From the cradle to the grave, they were driven by an intense desire for learning, both formal and informal. Coupled with this desire was a love-based discipline designed to whip out (no pun intended) any obstacle that might impede the revered process of learning.

The pioneers spoke with great pride, love, and appreciation for black teachers who faced the formidable task of educating black children in inferior facilities, with cast-off books and materials, in a society that did not value them equally with other citizens, and which often treated them with hostility. Right in the midst of those conditions in that type of atmosphere, strong black teachers were able to help their students remain physically, psychologically, and spiritually intact! It is no wonder that teachers are among the most respected people in society in the black culture.

These black pioneers spoke of meeting great national educators like Booker T. Washington and George Washington Carver when they came to Oklahoma in the early 1900s and 1929 respectively. They also spoke with great pride of their own educators some of whom are featured in this book.

Other Societal Institutions: These black pioneers spoke of other institutions in the black subculture that had provided a safety net for them. They spoke lovingly of community health workers who ministered to the ailing in the community, of lawyers who took up their legal causes, of county agents and home demonstration agents, librarians, scout leaders, Y leaders, ladies who worked organizations that taught girls etiquette and culture, and others who helped little black boys and girls up the road to literacy and success. They said that long before Newt Gingrich and present politicians advocated "self-help," black people were doing just that! They "took care of their own" as well as helping widows, orphans, the disabled, and even the town drunks.

Schooling/Occupations: Schooling for the pioneers ranged from a few grades of elementary school to completion of medical school and law school. Pioneers worked at jobs that ran the gamut from barbers and bakers to bankers, surgeons, and lawmakers. Most of the women had been employed in the nursing or teaching profession. Some of the participants are award-winning musicians, artists, and writers. All were extremely creative and talented in a variety of ways.

Dwellings/Lifestyles: In the past some of the pioneers lived in and under covered wagons, in caves, in temporary "homes" consisting of quilts thrown over sapling trees, sod houses, and various other makeshift "homes." Today their dwellings range from government-subsidized housing to exquisite condominiums in all regions of the city, to elegant homes in North and West Tulsa that used to belong to oil barons in the old days, to sleek, modern state-of-the-art homes of today.

Some of the participants drive old cars, jeeps, and pickup trucks; others drive Mercedes, Cadillacs, and Jaguars. Some don't drive at all. (They've long given up the car keys or had them taken away by cautious relatives.) Some pioneers buy their clothes at Wal Mart and K-Mart; others shop at Miss Jackson's and other fancy stores that once catered to the "oil women" of Tulsa. A treat for some of the pioneers is an occasional Big Mac from the North Peoria restaurant (built during Mayor Terry Young's tenure. Young, a former McDonald employee, lived on Reservoir Hill in North Tulsa and didn't want to have to drive south for a hamburger). Other pioneers dine at fancy restaurants all over Tulsa. Some even belong to the Southern Hills Country Club where in the past their "kind" could have been on the premises only as servants!

Marital Status/ Familial Relationships: Most of the pioneers featured in this book were married in their younger days, but most are presently widows or widowers. One couple — Henry and Ima Wilson Johnson — were featured in the living pioneers section of the book. Four widows were featured in this section also while their husbands were featured in the deceased memorial segment — Elizabeth Chappelle, Jeanne Goodwin, Fannie Ezelle Hill, and Thelma Whitlow. Two father-son sets were included — Major Sylvester Latimer and Caesar Latimer, and Buck Colbert (B.C.) Franklin and Dr. John Hope Franklin.

Physical Characteristics: One of the difficulties of research for a book such as this dealing with elders is that natural attrition limits the subject pool. That is why it is so urgent for writers, historians, artists, photographers, etc. to document history while subjects are still available, and in good enough health to recount it. Many Tulsans who participated in the development of the city have passed on. Thankfully there are always those people who are blessed with good longevity genes, who maintain good physical and mental health, and who are active and productive in their later years. Such was the case of the majority of the pioneers. Physically most of them enjoyed reasonably good health. Some were amazingly agile, even robust, and did not allow age to put any limitations upon them! A few were downright frail and I fretted, fussed, and worried over them like a mother hen. I am sure that I violated some Journalism 101 principle such as "Thou shalt not bond with the subjects interviewed," but I just couldn't help it. These wise, loving, elderly people allowed me into their homes and hearts; they became family to me and I love them. Physically they were just beautiful. Spirituality and goodness were reflected in their faces, faces that ranged in color from as black as the darkest African to so white that they could "pass" for white if they wanted to and hair texture from thick and "coarse" to "fly-away white." Physical size also ran the gamut from the imposing figures of 6 foot 6 inch tall Rev. B.S. Roberts, and the ample, still athletic-looking frame of Henry Johnson who used to play football at Tuskegee Institute in the 1930s, to feather-light, diminutive Anita Hairston and Maxine Johnson.

Mental Characteristics: Most of the participants had minds like steel traps and could recall incidents of fifty, sixty, seventy, and eighty years ago with clarity. Some admitted to slowing down mentally. Temperaments ranged from gentle and placid (Tomissa Chatman was a symphony in seriousness) to volatile/firebrands such as Maxine Johnson, Rev. Andrew Phillips, and that old irascible cowboy Wesley Young!

Most of the participants were surprisingly without rancor, despite having weathered much racism and tragedy in their lives, including the Tulsa Race Riot of 1921 for some of them. Most were spirited and had a wonderful zest for living.

Tragedies: Many of the participants had suffered tragedies such as childlessness, miscarriages, stillbirths, deaths of children of various ages ranging from infancy to middle age plus. One lost a middle-aged son, a professional who was shot to death in a random street killing in a large American city. They had grappled with (and mostly overcome) race-based injustice and poverty. Some survived so-called "Acts of God" such as the tornado of 1911, and acts of cruelty and oppression by humankind such as the Okmulgee Shootout in 1908, beatings, lynchings, near-lynchings, and the most catastrophic event that ever occurred in the history of this city, the Tulsa Race Riot of 1921.

Humor, Wit, Wisdom: Despite plenty of man-made troubles, and "Acts of God" to deal with, Tulsa's black pioneers were not ashes-and-sackcloth doomsayers; they were (and still are) remarkably wise, witty, and innovative people. Through all of their experiences — the tender moments or the violent episodes — they maintained a keen sense of humor, and a balance in life that enabled them to defy the odds, thumb their noses at adversity, and survive! Those survival instincts had been honed in slavery by their ancestors and passed on to their children and grandchildren. It was an art learned by trial and error during slave days (and the oppressive years following) and mastery of such skills was often a matter of life and death. Thus black people were experts at "getting by," "getting over" (circumventing adversity), and no people were better at making something out of nothing whether it was food, clothing, or shelter!

History: All of the pioneers were lay historians. In their own words, they have documented their experiences and those of their ancestors. Their tools were not tomes of brittle paper, replete with statistics, but "living history" like the fourteen flat irons that belonged to Tennessee Perryman's mother, irons that she heated over an open fire, wiped the smut off, and ironed clothes for white people. Other Tulsa pioneers showed off their artifacts too. The women, their faces glowing with pride, showed their old sewing baskets and pedal sewing machines, quilt pieces and patterns centuries old, and, of course, their "pretty things" like Alice Andrews' plate collection hanging on the walls in her apartment, and Amos T. Hall's nieces, Jean McGill and Carolyn Tolliver, showing the Hall glassware that was over a hundred years old. The men showed their guns, knives, swords, and war uniforms. George Monroe generously lent me two of his prized artifacts to photograph — a handful of coins that his father kept in a mailbox in 1921 (they melted into a heap the first night of the Tulsa Race Riot), and the land deed to his grandfather's farm in Perry, Oklahoma which was signed by President Theodore Roosevelt in 1908.

Culture: All of the black pioneers featured in this book took great pride in black culture. In their interviews they spoke in glowing terms of the families, churches, schools, community institutions, foods, festivals, fashions, furnishings, customs, traditions, ideals, language, art, literature, music, dance, and other factors that comprised their culture, a subculture born out of necessity due to the exclusion of black people from the mainstream society at that time. Two strong unifying themes of these people was their love of music, and their love for the Greenwood area (Greenwood Avenue was named for a white land agent who worked with Indians in early Tulsa). Though Greenwood will never be "The Black Wall Street of America" again, these pioneers still view the street as the central core, the heart and soul of the black North Tulsa community. Gone is the pulsating, vibrant, dynamic self-contained Greenwood of the past. Gone are the segregation days that created the region and the era. It is good that black Tulsans today have access to all geographic quadrants of the city. But it also good that blacks still have Greenwood! The Greenwood Cultural Center, the churches in the area, and the businesses there comprise a soothing, healing balm to black Tulsans, especially to those elderly pioneers who remember the old Greenwood.

The North Tulsa community is very proud of its Greenwood Cultural Center located in the heart of what was known as "Deep Greenwood" in the old days. Key figures in the founding and maintenance of the magnificent center are:

Senator Maxine Cissel Horner, Oklahoma Senate, District 11, Tulsa: Life-long Tulsan, community activist, and a major procurer of state funds for the development and expansion of the Greenwood Cultural Center, Inc.;

Representative Don Ross, Oklahoma House of Representatives, District 73, Tulsa: Tulsa-born community activist, civil rights leader, businessman, and a major procurer of state funds for the development and expansion of the Greenwood Cultural Center, Inc.

Dr. Lawrence A. Reed, prominent Tulsa surgeon (native of Okmulgee), community leader, and director of the Greenwood Cultural Center, Inc.

Black North Tulsans treasure their legacy. They have learned and loved from all kinds of people, from leaders such as those described earlier in the book and from those who were not leaders but who taught lessons as well. Evon Rollerson speaks eloquently of her childhood on Greenwood and the lessons that she learned from "Penny Annie."

Interview with Evon Rollerson, Business Management Student, The University Center of Tulsa (Langston University), Tulsa, April 4, 1995. Ms. Rollerson was born April 14, 1949 at Moton Hospital at the end of Greenwood (on Pine Street).

"Growing Up on Greenwood: From a Child's Point of View,"
Evon Rollerson.

My parents, Dr. Lloyd Reed Rollerson and Myrtle Fagin Rollerson, owned Meharry's Drug Store on North Greenwood. My father named the store "Meharry" because he graduated from Meharry Medical School in Memphis, Tennessee. Later, Dad moved his store to a new location on Greenwood. My father was twenty years older than my mother. My mother, married with four children, went to college. She took Leon, Willa, and me with her to Langston. Eric stayed in Tulsa to go to school and to help Dad with the drug store. When my mother got her degree, she couldn't find a teaching job in Tulsa. The all-black schools already had all the teachers they needed. So she took us kids with her and went to teach at a little two room country school in her hometown of Chandler, Oklahoma. (She taught grades 1-5 and the other teacher taught grades 6-12. And students of all ages taught the students who were younger than them!)

I would like to have a reunion with all the kids who grew up on Greenwood. I'd like to see what they remember and compare it with what I remember. I remember so much about Greenwood then — the good times, the feeling of security, of being loved and protected by the entire Greenwood community.

Some of the things I remember about Greenwood are the pie lady on Greenwood who sold great pies (my favorite was raisin pie); all the restaurants and businesses on the Strip; and the entertainment and recreation buildings on The Strip. The favorite entertainment of us Greenwood Strip kids was going to the Rex Theatre which had a ten cents admission charge. I don't know why we bothered to go inside the theater; we didn't pay a bit of attention to the film that was showing. We giggled, talked, and walked around. We did everything but watch the movie! It's a wonder we didn't get thrown out!

Even though we liked the Rex, we were more fascinated by another entertainment place, a dark smoky place called "The Blue Something-or-Other." We would watch the sharply dressed adults going in and out of there. Sometimes we'd even run up and peek in, but we didn't dare go in because someone in the neighborhood would surely see us and tell our parents. Then we'd be in serious trouble!

The children of Greenwood entrepreneurs ran together. We were a close-knit group, almost like family (like the "army brats," the children of military personnel). My best friends were Susan Arkle who was raised by the Kennebrews who owned a grocery store and the daughter of the family that owned Johnson's Photography. We were like sisters! They loved to come visit me at the drug store (my home was the quarters over the store). They genuinely liked me for myself, but it didn't hurt that when they came to see me were there also other things such as sodas, gum, candy, peanuts, cookies, and comic books to devour! We also had the first television on the Strip — a small black and white set. All the people in the neighborhood would come and watch that little television screen. Fight nights were very popular. I believe the fights came on Tuesday nights. In "the old days," listening to boxing on the radio was perhaps the favorite of all entertainment for black men and boys in Oklahoma and across the nation. Women and girls liked the boxing matches too and used the occasions to provide tasty, homemade treats for those boxing nights. These were more than just athletic events; they were great social occasions and one of the few occasions where black men in the ring could prevail over other races of men. Joe Louis was the all-time favorite.

I took music lessons at the Latimer School of Music. Julia Latimer Warren was my piano teacher. She was a great teacher. I believe she graduated from the Julliard School of Music in New York. I walked to my lessons from the Deep Greenwood area all the way up to Pine Street. It was really quite a long walk. I always felt safe in the Greenwood area. Everybody looked after each other. I knew all these Strip people — the professional business people and their families, the skilled and semi-skilled people and their families, and "the characters" that hung out on Greenwood. I liked them all. And I trusted them all. I had absolutely no fear — no fear of traffic, no fear of the people, no fear of anything. I knew my boundaries and I knew that the whole community loved me and was looking after me. I could hear people say, "That's Doc Rollerson's daughter." They genuinely cared about children in those days. It just made us feel warm and protected inside. I was always an obedient child so the community didn't have to tell my parents about what I had done wrong. (Greenwood adhered to the old African philosophy that it took the whole community to raise a child.) But my brothers were another story. They weren't really bad. They were just mischievous and got into the usual "boy things." But the Greenwood boys didn't get too far out of line. They knew that the whole community was watching them and if they did something too wrong, their parents would be told and they would surely be in trouble.

About those "characters" on Greenwood in those days, there were beggars like Penny Annie, numbers runners, drunks, and prostitutes. But even those "shady" characters were nice to us kids. They respected our parents and they knew that we were being

Joe Louis, heavyweight boxer, a favorite of black Americans during the 1930s, 40s, and 50s.

"raised right." So in their own way, they tried to help in our rearing. If they saw any of us going where we shouldn't, or doing what we shouldn't be doing, they told our parents. You see everyone on the Strip took an interest in children and tried to help guide them in the right direction.

Penny Annie was something else. She would come into the drug store and pretend to be engaging in a serious conversation, but she always got around to begging for pennies! There was a man called "Crazy Red" because he was always drumming — in his head, on tables, on chairs, just drumming everywhere. The man drummed all the time. I will never forget my growing up days on North Greenwood and all the wonderful people who loved me and helped to mold me into a good, decent, loving human being.

Foibles, Fallacies, and Failures: Lest I be accused of undue (favorable) bias toward the North Tulsa pioneers or to black people in general, and of not using all the evidence or of covering up or worse, let the record show that I am aware of the humanness of the participants described in this book, as well as of the humanness of all North Tulsans, and of the weaknesses and foibles that accompany and beset the human experience in general. It is a fact that in all populations, in all cultures, some group members succumb to weaknesses and some even resort to unacceptable, and sometimes, illegal levels of behavior, for which they are punished according to the customs, mores, and laws of their culture. Some North Tulsans fell into that category. At least one black Tulsa author is writing a book about that aspect of Tulsa. Leon Davis says that his book, *Corn Whiskey, Gambling, Choc Beer, Crack Cocaine in Black Wall Street, 1836-1994,* will cover the "shady" side of North Tulsa — the borderline activities like bootlegging and numbers running, plus the "dirt" on downright, hard-core criminality that existed in the area. Just as there are warts in the overall history of the whole nation (the founding of the classic democracy in the midst of slavery and the exploitation of Indians), there are warts in North Tulsa's history. But these warts do not nullify the good and positive achievements of the people and the nation. Neither will the warts of North Tulsa history dilute or diminish the achievements and accomplishments of the early pioneers in the face of stupendous odds. Davis promises that his book will be a "bombshell and an eye-opener." It probably will be, for there were North Tulsans with feet of clay. Some were disbarred, imprisoned, or murdered because of their underground, shady, or illegal, criminal activities. But most black Tulsans were decent, law-abiding citizens who tried to take advantage of opportunities, who tried to dilute or minimize barriers and obstacles, and tried to be "the best that they could be." Most of them succeeded.

SUMMARY: Significance of the Testimonies of Tulsa Pioneers

And so this book is now completed after a year of intensive and extensive work. Sometimes it seemed as if I would never see fruitage from my efforts, but it is here at last! Now that the story of those black pioneers has been told, what conclusions can be drawn? What predictions can be made? How can we use this information from the wise, elderly black pioneers to make Tulsa, and the world, a better place? Exactly what is the significance of their legacy?

In my opinion the major contribution of the pioneers' stories is that they validate and empower a long-neglected segment of the city (and of American society, in general) — the aged and minorities, especially blacks. This validation, via a tremendous pool of eyewitness testimonies (similar to Holocaust survivors' eyewitness accounts of World War II history,) corroborated by traditional, empirical research is vibrant and compelling, and enriches and empowers like no other forms of historical research can do.

This eyewitness history is like a limb of black history that has been grafted back onto the tree of American history. The limb was always there; it was just obscured and cut off by prejudice and racism. Newly uncovered knowledge such as this leads to a better understanding of the past. It promotes the development of respect, understanding, and appreciation between diverse groups — groups often divided by race, religion, gender, geographic, and class differences. Information is power and can be used to insulate people from mistakes of the past, and can prevent the perpetuation of mistakes into the future. There are powerful object lessons in this pioneer history for all generations of Tulsans.

This pioneer history is timely. Until three decades ago, there was little validation of black history, black culture, black people. While much information about "The Black Experience" emerged in the 1960s and 1970s, much of it was hastily put together and of limited value. There is still a void in the telling of the true and complete story of black people in history. It is hoped that this pioneer history will help somewhat to fill the void about the history of black people in Oklahoma. It is hoped that this information can help all people to: Recognize the legacy of the past; utilize time-honored, time-tested and proven legacies from the past to help them to live more productively in the present; and look toward the future, armed with faith, hope, and vital lessons learned from the past.

I hope that the legacy of this book won't end with a one-time reading. I hope that there will be an on-going process whereby each reader will draw upon the wisdom and the advice offered by the wonderful pioneers whose stories are told. The information and knowledge that the elderly black pioneers of Tulsa, and white eye-witnesses to the era in history have shared with us needs to be infused into our lives day-by-day, hour-by-hour, minute-by-minute. All of us need these lessons of history — the elderly while they are still with us, the middle-aged who are the core of society (the working wheels), the youth undergoing rites-of-passage to adulthood, and those yet unborn who will need these lessons if they are to survive and thrive.

Like the rest of the nation, Tulsa has had problems with some of its youth, especially black youth. Feeling disconnected from society, yearning for the strong, tight, loving bonds of family, some have turned to gangs. Black pioneers of Tulsa hope that this information, this knowledge of black Tulsa history, will help bring alienated groups of black Tulsa teens *"back into the fold"* where they can reconnect with their pioneer ancestors and will feel, like the pioneers featured in this book feel, the loving bonds of family and community, nurturing, protecting, upholding, and guiding them.

These wise elders have left the Tulsa community a rich legacy. They want us to learn the lessons of the past so we won't keep repeating the same mistakes over and over. The terrible tragedy in Oklahoma City (the bombing of the Alfred E. Murrah Federal Building on April 19, 1995 which killed 168 people including 19 children) caused the pioneers to reflect on the dangers of unbridled hatred and the need for love, compassion, and tenderness between all mankind. One of the traits of the black pioneers that most impressed me was their love and compassion for everyone, their total lack of bitterness despite all the hardships they had suffered including prejudice, discrimination, and, for some of them, the terrible 1921 Tulsa Race

Riot, an event that the white Tulsa community has ignored with a 75-year conspiracy of silence. Not until June 1, 1996 did a public apology come for that terrible event and it came from a black politician. Still Tulsans are pleased that the healing has begun.

The black pioneers who survived the terrible race riot of 1921 caution us to be vigilant regarding our state of thought, for thoughts lead to actions. They warn us to avoid prejudiced, hate-filled thoughts for such thinking leads to the downfall of both perpetrator and victim. Some of the worst events in the history of mankind (wars, riots, holocausts, etc.) had their beginnings in hate-filled thoughts. Their advice was that we look at what is in the hearts of our fellow man and not at the color of his skin or at his political, economic, or social status. Regarding injustice they advised to leave the recompensing to God, the great equalizer, the supreme dispenser of justice, mercy, and retribution. Tulsans, are you listening? Not only should Tulsans listen. This advice is universal in nature and, if followed, will bless the whole human race.

All Americans must keep the vision before them, the vision of equality, opportunity, freedom and justice that can be the reality in the United States. Not only is it the desire of black Tulsa pioneers that this book will enrich, unify, and bless the Tulsa community, but that it can serve as a model for the entire nation because of its universality. It can provide a peaceful, healing lesson for all mankind that inhabit and share the planet earth. It is the nature of mankind to dream, to reach for something higher than the material, secular world can offer. Let us all — Americans of all races, religions, creeds, geographic locations, political, economic, or social status — keep the dream alive. We must keep this vision, this dream, ever before us. *"Where there is no vision, the people perish."* Keep the vision before you. Let not the people perish!

I expect to hear from the community that some prominent and valuable black Tulsa pioneers, who surely ought to have been included, were left out of this book! It is true that there are many other eminently qualified Tulsans who have contributed much to the Tulsa community and who could have been included in this book, but all could not be included due to time and space constraints. Those names are still out there and can and should be utilized in future writings about Tulsa's culturally rich history. Some names have even been listed in the appendix of this book. The three categories are broad, generic ones based loosely on time and quality of service to the North Tulsa community. If anyone is offended by an "inappropriate age classification," just mentally remove yourself to an "age-appropriate" category! There are historians, journalists, and others "out there" right now, perhaps, getting ready to write about Tulsa's wonderful pioneers. There are plenty of them to write about!

It has been my privilege, and my joy, to share with the reader these poignant experiences of black Tulsa pioneers. In the words of the prophet Joel:

> *And it shall come to pass afterward, that I will pour out my spirit upon all flesh; and your sons shall prophecy, your old men shall dream dreams, your young men shall see visions.*
>
> **Joel 2:28**

May this book help all generations — past and present — to dream the same dream and to see the same visions of universal love.

Supplemental Interviews:

Cartwright, Roscoe C., Jr. "What It Was Like Growing Up a Military Brat," Tulsa, Oklahoma, September 29, 1994.

Childers, Mark Allen. "My Grandfather, Charles Edward Arnold, Christian Science Practitioner: Burying the Black Riot Dead, The 1921 Tulsa Race Riot," Tulsa, Oklahoma, October 11, 1994.

Clark, Vivian Dr.,University Center of Tulsa, November 3, 1994.

Cox, Jayme. Director, Leadership Tulsa, October 11, 1994.

Crowell, Samuel D. "Black Pioneer Farmers in Perry, Oklahoma, Late 1800s, Early 1900s," September 30, 1994.

Driver, Cleta. Principal, Carver Middle School, Tulsa, Oklahoma, October 25, 1994.

Faubion, Wayne. "Cowboys and Ranchers: The Big V Ranch, the 101 Ranch and How I Met and Worked With Black Cowboy Bill Pickett," October 29, 1994.

Lyon, Frank. "Setting Up Indian Stores: The Dakotas, Nebraska, Kansas, and Oklahoma," November 4, 1994.

Madison, Tava. Multicultural education teacher, Roosevelt Elementary School, Tulsa, Oklahoma, October 25, 1994.

Mason, Archie. Director, Indian Pupil Education, Tulsa Public Schools, November 3, 1994.

Petit, Vivian Minter. "The Black Farm Wife in Oklahoma, 1920s-1950," December 16, 1994.

Randolph, Dr. Henry. "Black Farmers and Livestock Breed Choices," Knoxville, Tennessee, Telephone Interview, December 17, 1994. (Dr. Randolph, a Veterinarian, is a native of Okmulgee, Oklahoma.)

Randolph, Mattie Mae Minter. "Occupations for Blacks in Okmulgee, Oklahoma, 1920-1950: Farming, Day Work, and The Glass Plant," Tulsa, Oklahoma, December 18, 1994.

Wilson's Family Store. Tulsa, Oklahoma, December 15, 1994.

Sober, Gerald. "Growing Up in Ponca City, Oklahoma: Cowboys and Ranchers That I Have Known," Ponca City, Oklahoma, October 29, 1994.

Sober, Nancy Hope. "Cherokee Indian History and The Black Freedmen," Ponca City, Oklahoma, October 29, 1994.

Stephens, Donald. "Black Cowboys and Other Blacks in Western (American) History," Tulsa, Oklahoma, December 13, 1994.

Walton, John and Margaret. Owners of The William G. Skelly Mansion, Tulsa, Oklahoma, October 24, 1994.

Willis, Ida Dennie. Owner, The Ida Dennie Willis Museum of Miniatures, Dolls, and Toys, Tulsa, Oklahoma, Tulsa, Oklahoma, October 27, 1994.

Wilson, J. B. Owner, Wilson's Barbecue, Tulsa, Oklahoma, December 15, 1994.

Appendices

Appendix 1 —List for the Future
Tulsans Who Have Made a Difference

I. Wise Elders:

Primus Wade, Dimple Baldwin, and H.O. Vaden; The Spann, Hanson, Birmingham, Johnson, Monday, Thompson and Williams families; Seymour Williams, A.G.W. Sango, Scipio Sango, Katie Duckery, Wyonia Bailey, Mabel Little, Verna Kemp, Eugene Guy, Mary Barber, Dorothy Weaver, Viola West, Lulu Williams, Barney Cleaver, Dr. Norvell Coots, Andrew Thompson (Greenwood Drug Store), Smith, (owner of Welcome Grocery on North Greenwood, a relative of Della Sewall), Ernest Crenshaw; also Joe McDowell, Leonard and Elizabeth Holman, Dr. and Mrs. Rollerson and many, many others...

II. The Middle Generation:

J. Homer Johnson, Shirlee Johnson, Maxine Horner, Don Ross, Drs. Charles and Anita Christopher, Julius and Wennette Pegues, Mable Rice, Josie Vann, Rev. Melvin Bailey, Rev. Bertram Bailey, LaVerne Hill, Ida Dennie Willis, Dyanne Mason, Maybelle Wallace, Millard House, Dr. Lawrence A. Reed, Joe Robinson; also Jack Henderson, Ruford Henderson, Eddie Evans, Marvin Blades and many, many others...

NOTE: Some of the wise elders told me to include Don Thompson and Eddie Faye Gates in this category. As one who was raised to be respectful of elders, I do humbly add those two names.

III. The Rising Young Generation:

Joe Williams, Derek Wayne Gates, Mitchell Lane, Stephanie Chappelle, Kevin Matthews, Leon Rollerson, Edward Guess, Keenan Meadors, Hannibal Johnson, and many, many others...

NOTE: To be added to this list, in the future, will be young people who are now still in high school and college, but who have have already expressed a love for the North Tulsa community and who have begun to work for its preservation through such organizations as the African-Male Coalition, and various school, fraternity, sorority, and other community organizations. (Some fine young people that I know through their work at the Greenwood Cultural Center are Tone Jones, Jabar Shumate, Keisha Harding, and Ferris Vickers. There are hundreds of others in the community just like them with great potential to help the community; we need only tap into that potential and channel it toward positive activities on behalf of the city.)

Appendix 2 —A Simplified, Chronological, Annotated Listing of Significant People, Places, & Events Relating to the Tulsa Race Riot of 1921

General Statistics, Tulsa, 1921:

White Population	70,000
Black Population	11,000
Blacks Detained During Riot	6,000

People: Local
Political Figures:

Mayor	T.D. Evans
Police Chief, Tulsa County Jail	William McCullough
Police Chief, City of Tulsa Jail	John A.Gustafson
Police Commissioner, City of Tulsa	J.M. Adkison

Judge Biddison — presided over Grand Jury hearings of the Tulsa Race Riot of 1921 which began June 9, 1921.

Van B. Hurley — former Tulsa policeman who gave detailed descriptions, to national media, about the dropping of nitroglycerin bombs from aeroplanes under Tulsa police instructions.

Capt. George Blaine — Tulsa policeman said by Van B. Hurley to have ridden in one of the aeroplanes that hovered over the city during the riot.

People: State
Political Figures:

Governor	J.B.A. Robertson
Commander of Oklahoma National Guard	Adjutant Gen. Charles F. Barrett

(Seven companies of armed Oklahoma National Guards from eastern Oklahoma, and two companies of regular troops from Ft. Sill regained control of Tulsa after the worst rioting of May 31st and June 1st, 1921).

Recent Lynch Victims: Tulsa, 1921

Roy Belton — a 20-year old black Tulsa man was jailed in 1920 on charges of killing a taxi driver. He was acquitted months later, but as he walked down the Court House steps after being released, he was abducted by a white mob, taken to a "hanging tree" in Sand Springs and lynched. White policemen directed traffic to the area where a festive atmosphere prevailed as sightseers witnessed the hanging.

White man named Owens — had been abducted and hanged in Red Fork. He had been accused of killing a policeman.

Attempted Peacemakers:

Barney Cleaver, black deputy sheriff, tried to calm 300-500 armed black men at County Courthouse on Boulder May 31, 1921.

Andy Brown, prominent black businessman, stepped right up to white mob and tried to reason with them in the courthouse/Boulder area. Was shot dead at point blank range.

A.J. Smitherman, a black Tulsa policeman known for his reasonableness and rationality. He could not reason with the Klansmen who took him to the top of Standpipe Hill, bit off half his ear, and tried to make him eat it!

J.B. Stradford, Prominant Tulsa businessman/lawyer who fled Tulsa after he was charged with inciting a riot.

Rabblerousers, Troublemakers, and the Ku Klux Klan:

FIRST LIST: Contained the elite upper and middle class Klan members including local political leaders, business and professional people, including the following:

Grant McCulloch, bank president and owner of Drexel Building and other Tulsa real estate. Blacks understand him to be a member of the Klan.

Washington Elias Hudson, was a prominent Klan leader, and an Oklahoma legislator. Lake Hudson in East Tulsa is named for him.

There was a bitter U.S. Senate race between Gene Lorton and Senator Pine, who was a well-known Klansman.

Tulsa County Sheriff William McCullough was said to be a former Klansman.

SECOND LIST: Included large numbers of average, working class Klan members; and large numbers of taxi drivers, musicians, and artists.

NOTE: The duties of Klan members ran the gamut from recruiting members, record keeping, holding marches and meetings, to tarring, feathering, maiming, and killing "enemies." Eyewitnesses of the riot mayhem have identified prommient political, business, and professional men as drivers of the "Mob Patrol Cars" and as pilots of the aeroplanes (described as between 6 and 12) that dropped bombs on black refugees.

Good White Samaritans:

W.R. Holway, owner of Holway Engineering Company, a road builder, dam builder (brought water to Tulsa via Spavinaw Dam), and prominent Tulsa businessman. Was a permanent enemy of the

KKK. He refused the Klan's order to fire 13 Catholics who worked for his firm. Was a man noted for his integrity. He once walked out of a meeting with prominent Tulsa businessmen when he was asked how much of the money they were donating to his road building projects would be kicked back to them. Despite repeated attempts of the Ku Klux Klan to influence Mr. Holway via bribes, interference with his loan applications, building permits, etc., Mr. Holway never waivered. He stuck to his high principles and was a prosperous and respected Tulsa businessman. He is now deceased but the Holway firm still exists as a prominent business in Tulsa and is operated by Mr. Holway's two sons Donal K. Holway and W.N. Holway. (Information from an interview with a Holway engineer, July 21, 1996)

Charles Edward Arnold - see Chapter 6.

W.E. Brown Family - see Chapter 6.

People: National

George Washington Carver — respected black leader who visited Carver Junior High School in 1929.

W.E.B. DuBois — visited Tulsa in March, 1921.

Booker T. Washington — who once visisted Muskogee.

Walter White, Director, the national NAACP — was in Tulsa just before the race riot began.

Appendix 3 —Places — Locations of Key Tulsa Buildings and Riot Sites

Drexel Building — between Boston and Main on Second Street, near Renbergs Clothiers.

Tulsa City Jail — Fourth Street and Elgin Avenue.

Tulsa County Jail — Sixth Street and Boulder (now the location of Boatman's Bank, formerly BANK IV).

Ku Klux Klan Building (BENO Hall — Be No Nigger, Be No Catholic, Be No Jew!) — North Main Street and Easton Avenue.

Dixie Theater on Greenwood Avenue — where black Booker T. Washington High School graduating students were rehearsing the night of May 31, 1921.

Sand Springs Amusement Park — where white Central High School graduating students were attending the annual POW the night of May 31, 1921.

Paradise Baptist Church, just off of North Greenwood Avenue — where some black Tulsans, soon-to-be-refugees, were attending a Baptist Youth Program the night of May 31, 1921.

Holy Family Catholic Church, downtown Tulsa — where seven-year-old Ruth Sigler (now historian/author Ruth Sigler Avery) had just finished reciting a poem and holding up her doll, Rosemary, for the delighted audience to see. (The program was cut short because of the gathering mobs in the downtown area.)

Six-year-old Opal Long (later Tulsa community leader Opal Long Dargan), suffering with a case of measles, was trying to get to sleep in her home which would soon be looted later that night of May 31, 1921.

Boundaries of Black Tulsa Settlements, 1921:

> North - Midland Valley Railroad tracks north to Pine Street;
> South - Frisco Railroad tracts, First Street just off of Archer;
> East - Lansing Street
> West - Cincinnati Avenue beginning at Archer and extending to Elgin

(Locations from interview with Robert Fairchild, July 24, 1996)

Internment Centers:

1. Convention Center — Boulder Avenue and Brady Street where first black detainees were taken.
2. McNulty Ball Park/Old Fairgrounds Area — Independence Street and Lewis Avenue area; 11th Street and Harvard Avenue (now the University of Tulsa Skelly Stadium area).
3. Booker T. Washington High School, Greenwood Avenue/Easton Street (present Rogers University, formerly UCT New Conference Center Buildings).

Cemeteries and Burial Places:

> Oaklawn Cemetery — 11th Street and Peoria Avenue where most of the black riot dead were buried in Potter's Field.
> Rose Hill Cemetery — By the old Rose Hill Church on Richmond Avenue (near the present Rose Hill Church at Admiral Boulevard and Yale Avenue). Before the race riot, the Ku Klux Klan used to hold cross burning on the south side of Rose Hill Church.
> Newblock Park on the road to Sand Springs — Black bodies were incinerated in the Sand Springs incinerator here.

(Information from an interview with John Bullock, July, 1996; verified by further research.)

Railroads:

> Frisco —- Headquarters located at First Street in downtown Tulsa. This railroad track was the dividing line between South (white) Tulsa and North (black) Tulsa;
> Katy — Between First and Second streets in downtown Tulsa, one block from Elgin Street. On the Muskogee route;
> Midland Valley — tracks ran directly behind Vernon A.M.E. Church (east of the church), just off Greenwood Avenue and Archer Street;
> Santa Fe — To the north and east of the downtown area. Crossed

Lansing, then went straight northeast to Mohawk Boulevard, then due north to Owasso, Collinsville, etc.

(Railroad information courtesy of Robert Fairchild.)

Trolley Cars:
Northern Route: Trolleys ran down Archer Street. Just before Greenwood, the trolley turned left, then went by Vernon A.M.E. church, then north to Haskell and Greenwood, then on to the northeast.

Western Route: The trolley ran from near the Frisco railroad tracks on First Street, then it ran southwest. Then it went due west to Sand Springs.

On June 19th each year, Tulsa blacks filled the trolley cars on their way to the Charles Page Park in Sand Springs. It was the official celebration of the day that blacks in Texas were notified of the Emancipation Proclamation of Abraham Lincoln.

On August 4th each year, trolleys would again be filled with black people on their way to the Sand Springs Park. August 4th was the anniversary of the date that Oklahoma blacks learned of the Emancipation.

(Robert Fairchild.)

Appendix 4 — A Chronology of Riot Activities and Destructions

1. May 30, 1921 Event:
The Drexel Building Elevator Incident between Dick Rowland and Sarah Page, 9:00 or 9:30 A.M. Dick Rowland fled.

2. May 31, 1921 Events:
Tulsa Tribune published inflammatory Bulldog edition of its newspaper. "To Lynch a Nigger Tonight" headline, 3:00 P.M., May 31, 1921.

Dick Rowland arrested and taken to Tulsa city jail.

Dick Rowland moved to a more secure jail area at the Tulsa County Court House 4th floor, at Sixth Street and Boulder Avenue. Ironically, Rowland occupied the same cell that Roy Belton, a black lynch victim in 1920, had occupied.

Three Strangers Incident, 4:00 P.M. Three strange white men went to the County Court House and demanded that Sheriff McCullough hand Rowland over to them for a lynching party that night.

Peacemakers attempt to soothe the increasing white mob crowds. (Andy Brown, Barney Cleaver, Sheriff McCullough, et al).

Failures of the political officials; failures of the peacemakers.

Escalating mobs of whites: About 5,000 lightly-armed whites.

Escalating response of blacks: Began with about 50 heavily-armed blacks (which later swelled up to 500-1,000 according to some estimates).

9:00 P.M., May 31st, a white man attempted to take a gun from an armed black man (identity of the wounded black man is in question. Robert Fairchild says that it was Simon Berry's very big and tall brother who was a World War I veteran; Historian Scott Ellsworth says that it was a WWI veteran but does not identify the veteran).

10:00 P.M., a full fledged Race Riot was now on!

Riot Activities and Destruction Locations May 31, 1921:

10:00 P.M., Boulder/Court House Area, Main Avenue, and Boston Avenue Area — part of the white mob began driving blacks toward their own area.

Court House Boulder Area — part of white mob remained here; Armed blacks from North Tulsa proceeded to this area. When the two groups met, there was gunfire and casualties. And pawn shops and hardware stores in the area were broken into and looted by both blacks and whites according to some of the pioneers interviewed by this author, pioneers who had first-hand knowledge of the incidents.

Frisco Railroad Area — blacks forced back across the Frisco Railroad tracks where they had tried to take a stand to protect their community.

10:30 P.M., May 31st, Greenwood to Pine Area — white, surging, looting mobs began destroying the heart of the black community in Tulsa, the Greenwood area. Eventually, 36 blocks were reduced to rubble and ashes. One white mobster was quoted as saying (while he looted): "These damned niggers have better things here than lots of white people have!" Even women looted. They filled shopping bags with stolen goods. Indiscriminate shooting of innocent black men, women, and children.

3. June 1, 1921: Beginning about 12:30 A.M.

(Witnesses describe the May 31st activities as a race war between armed whites and blacks; they describe the June 1st activities as a military war assault on black Tulsa and black Tulsans.)

Brickyard Hill — North on Greenwood Avenue, past Vernon A.M.E. Church (present location of New Conference Center buildings, Rogers University, formerly UCT). Much riot destruction in this area. See Houston photographs. Old black man pushing a cart was shot dead becoming Brickyard Hill's first casualty according to some black eyewitnesses.

Standpipe Hill — one block east of North Cincinnati, and approximately two blocks west of Greenwood Avenue where, on June 1, 1921, a machine gun was mounted and white mobs reigned gunfire on fleeing black refugees. (Presently located on this site is the Pioneer Plaza Senior Citizens Complex.) The Cincinnati Avenue/Latimer Street area was the northernmost region of black settlement in 1921 and contained the largest concentration of blacks in Tulsa at this time.

1:00 A.M., Gov. J.B.A. Robertson, in Oklahoma City, received a request for assistance from Tulsa officials.

Shortly after Gov. Robertson received the request for help, sent via a Sand Springs, Oklahoma telegraph, first national guardsmen were sent to Tulsa.

9:00 A.M., June 1st, martial law declared by Adjutant Gen. Charles F. Barrett. The guards took control of the city and rounded up blacks who were taken to three internment centers. Green Cards were issued and blacks without such cards were automatically detained.

4. Officials Regain Control of the City of Tulsa:

June 2, 1921 — organizations were formed to assist riot victims (see Organizations which follow).

June 3, 1921 — Gov. Robertson called for a Grand Jury investigation.

June 9, 1921 — Grand Jury sworn in

Appendix 5 — Organizations

White:

The Citizens Committee — Prominent white business and professional citizens comprised this committee which was formed in protest against the inept local and county officials who had let the race riot get out of hand. Members included: Loyal J. Martin, Chair of the Committee, former mayor of Tulsa, Jim McBirney, Jack Crosby, Alf Heggem, Pat Hurley, Grant McCullough, Doc Kennedy...

Medical Welfare Committee Formed — See Willows Red Cross Report, December 31, 1921.

Black:

Colored Citizens Relief Committee, First Baptist Church of North Tulsa (the oldest black church in Tulsa) was created mainly to deal with the new City of Tulsa Fire Ordinance which was a major impediment for black riot claims.

Appendix 6 — Ironies During the Riot

1. Random shootings of innocent men, women, and children.
2. Mistaken identity killings: Several are sadly recounted by riot eyewitnesses.
   a. a young white clerk stepped out of the Hotel Tulsa on South Cincinnati to look at riot activities and was shot in the back.
   b. a white man stumbled into a crowd of armed black men north of the Frisco railroad depot and was beaten severely.
   c. White mobsters mistook a white man for a black man in the Frisco railroad "war zone." The poor man was shot so many times that he couldn't be identified.

3. White ignorance of black geographic boundaries caused some black edifices to be spared. Buildings such as First Baptist Church of North Tulsa were left standing because white mobs thought they were white-owned buildings!
4. Amidst looted and burned buildings, right in the midst of ashes and debris, the *Oklahoma Eagle* newspaper building was left standing.

Appendix 7 — Humorous Incidents During the Riot

1. The Paris, France silk blouse incident: Mrs. Alice Andrews recalled the story of a black North Tulsa woman who had bought an exquisite silk blouse in Paris (which was stolen by looters during the race riot). After the riot, a black maid in South Tulsa saw a white woman wearing that blouse! To make a long story short, the persistent owner of that blouse got it back after the riot!

2. The suit-with-the-name-in-label incident: Another story had a similar ending. A North Tulsa man recognized his expensive suit (which was being worn by a white man after the riot). The suit-wearing white man denied that the suit was riot loot. But when a sympathetic policeman made the man show the name inside the lapel label, the black man's ownership was established and he got his suit back (after the white man was allowed to find himself some alternative clothes!).

Appendix 8 —Despicable Behavior Incidents Remembered by Riot Victims

1. Black male refugees having to keep their hands raised at all times.
2. Jeering, laughing, hate-filled white mobsters and on-lookers.
3. Police complicity with mobsters. In one incidence, the police, in response to a false rumor that heavily armed blacks were en route from Muskogee to aid besieged North Tulsa blacks, a Tulsa police-owned machine gun was mounted on a flatbed truck and turned over to white men to keep blacks from entering or leaving Tulsa. The machine gun was fired, indiscriminately, at innocent black men, women, and children.
4. Massive, full-scale looting by mobsters, and by some Home Guard militia members. Big trucks were brought in to take away pianos, organs, victrolas, and other large items. Jewelry, curtains, small rugs, etc. were stuffed in shopping bags, or carried on the arms of greedy looters.
5. The added, hate-filled gesture of burning down everything after the looting was completed.

Appendix 9 — Post Riot Events

1. Seething frustration, anger of blacks at inadequate response of the city (except for the Red Cross) to the plight of black refugees.
2. Punitive City Ordinances/Black Counter Lawsuits
3. Rebuilding despite lack of support from the Tulsa business and political communities

Appendix 10 — Black History and Culture

See Chapter 1.

Appendix 11 — The 75-Year Conspiracy of Silence by Tulsa Regarding the Tulsa Race Riot of 1921

Sarah Page would not file charges against Dick Rowland. Charges dropped by the City of Tulsa on September 28, 1921.

There was the Grand Jury investigation which was held in June of 1921, but even there, punishment was mild — the loss of political seats and patronage. There was no real sense of closure, no punishment commensurable for the massive destruction caused by the race riot. There was a total lack of applying the standard principles of retribution and punishment for complicity in criminal behavior. The issue of culpability simply was not addressed in Tulsa. Not only was there no justice, there was no acknowledgement of the immediate and long range ramification of the riot and there was a deliberate cover-up regarding the riot, a conspiracy of silence that lasted seventy-five years.

There was the massive "loss" of key documents and statistics, of, newspaper articles, and other pertinent records pertaining to the riot. Historians have found that there was blatant destruction of relevant materials and fraudulent, corrupt behavior on the part of political, business, and professional people who should have acted better! Some examples of cover-ups are as follows:

1. Misfiled police documents, discovered later, which confirm early accounts of riot destruction and deaths (deaths were listed at 305, rather than the official city listing of 66).
2. Untrue Oklahoma Vital Statistics Bureau listings. Only 40 deaths were listed in Tulsa county during the week of the riot. The death rate had to be more than that as it was more than that during normal times!
3. The Adjutant General of the State of Oklahoma had no records of National Guard activities during the race riot period (May-July, 1921) though extensive records exist for all other periods from the late 1800s to the present.
4. The Final Home Edition, the Bulldog edition, of the May 31, 1921 *Tulsa Tribune* newspaper was either cut from newspaper, or the total newspaper was destroyed.
5. Even the local newspaper morgue files, of the NPC, nor the Microfilms Section of the Tulsa City County Library System, nor the archives of the

University of Tulsa, nor the archives of the Tulsa Historical Society, nor the archives of the Oklahoma Historical Society have copies of that infamous newspaper. Yet, it is known that the paper surely did exist.

6. Oklahoma law requires that state editions of local papers — The *Tulsa World*, The *Tulsa Tribune*, et al — be filed in the permanent records of archives at the Oklahoma Historical Society. Yet, that paper is not there.

Appendix 12 — Lessons Learned — Riot Causes, Effects, Methods of Promoting Racial Harmony in the Future

Underlying Causes of the Riot:

Political: Lack of political balance in the American nation at the time of the 1921 race riot. Blacks were second class citizens who did not enjoy full political rights and protections at that time.

Economic:

1. There was a post World War I recession in the nation at the time of the riot. There were many white job losses in Tulsa.
2. Most blacks held lower wage jobs and this working class population did not suffer as much unemployment as whites did.
3. There was a black, affluent middle class in the Greenwood area and whites were jealous and bitter over this phenomena.

Social: According to the social dynamics of the time period of the race riot, all over the United States, black people were on the lowest rung of the social class ladder. They were expected to stay in "their place." The paradox of Greenwood upset that "normal" balance in Tulsa society.

Dangers of Inaction in a Nation:

The poignant words of Martin Niemoeller of Germany bear remembering: *"When they came for the Gypsies, I said nothing because I wasn't a Gypsy. When they came for the Catholics, I said nothing because I wasn't a Catholic. When they came for the Jews, I said nothing because I wasn't a Jew. When they came for me, there was no one left to speak up for me!"*

Appendix 13 — Key Riot Sources & Interviews

See Chapter 7.

Bibliography

(P=Primary Source; S=Secondary Source; A=Article)

Introduction — Race

Doyle, Bertram W. *The Etiquette of Race Relations in the South: A Study in Social Control.* Chicago, 1937. (S)

Franklin, Dr. John Hope. *From Slavery to Freedom: A History of American Negroes.* New York, Alfred A. Knopf, 1956. (S)

———. *The Militant South, 1800-1861.* Cambridge, MA, Cambridge University Press, 1956. (S)

———. *History of Racial Segregation in the United States.* American Academy of Political and Social Science, Annals, CCCIV (March 1956). (A)

———. *Racial Equality in America.* Chicago, University of Chicago Press, 1976. (S)

———. *Race and History: Selected Essays.* Louisiana State University Press, Baton Rouge, 1989. (S)

Gates, Eddie Faye. "Black Literature in the Secondary Schools: A Look at Race and History," unpublished paper delivered at The National Conference of English Teachers Convention, Kansas City, Missouri, 1978. Revised and reprinted, 1991. (A)

———. "African-Americans: Historical Perspective," unpublished manuscript delivered at The National Council for the Social Studies Convention, Detroit, Michigan, 1981. (A)

Hall, Dr. Ronald, Russell, Kathy, and Wilson, Midge. *Color Complex, The Politics of Skin Color Among African-Americans.* Anchor Books, Doubleday, 1992. (S)

Korngold, Ralph. *Thaddeus Stevens: A Being Darkly Wise and Rudely Great,* (about Stevens' housekeeper) Westport, Conn., Greenwood Press, 1970, reprint of 1955 ed. (S)

———. *Thaddeus Stevens: Scourge of the South* (about the influence of Stevens' racial views on the defining and shaping of U.S. post-Reconstruction racial policies). Westport, Conn., 1970, reprint of 1959 ed. (S)

Logan, Rayford W. *The Negro in American Life and Thought: The Nadir, 1877-1901.*New York, 1954. (S)

Quarles, Benjamin. *The Negro in the American Revolution*. University of North Carolina Press, 1961, reprint of 1953 ed.(S)

Southern Literary Messenger. "The Difference of Race Between the Northern and Southern People." Volume XXX, June, 1860. (A)

Tocqueville, Alexis de. *Democracy in America*. Alfred A. Knopf, New York, 1972 (1945). (P)

United Nations Economic and Social Council (UNESCO), UNESCO STAFF, et al. "Scientific Findings on Race," Paris, France, July, 1950. (P)

West, Dr. Cornel. *Race Matters*. Beacon Press, Boston, MA, 1993. (S)

Chapter 1 — Africa; African Heritage

Africanus, Leo. *The History and Description of Africa*. New York, (n.d.). (P)

Bennett, Lerone, Jr. *Before the Mayflower: A History of Black America*. Johnson Publishing, Chicago, 1959. (S)

Birmingham, D. *Central Africa and the Atlantic Slave Trade*. Roland Oliver, Oxford University Press, England, 1968. (S)

Boahen, A.A. *Topics in West African History*. Cambridge University Press, New York, 1969. (S)

Bohannen, Paul. *Africa and Africans*. Natural History Press, New York, 1964. (S)

Chu, E. and Skinner, E. *A Glorious Africa*. Doubleday-Zenith, Garden City, New York, 1965. (S)

Clark, Leon. *Through African Eyes: Cultures in Change*. Praeger Press, New York, 1969. (S)

Davidson, Basil. *The African Slave Trade*. Atlantic-Little Brown, Boston, 1961. (S)

———. *The African Genius*. Atlantic-Little Brown, Boston, 1969. (S)

Dobler, L. and Brown, W.A. *Great Rulers of the African Past*. Doubleday-Zenith, Garden City, New York, 1965. (S)

Fage, J.D. *A History of West Africa*. Cambridge University Press, New York, 1969. (S)

Gibbs, James L. *Peoples of Africa*. Holt, Rinehart, and Winston, New York, 1965. (S)

Hughes, Langston, Meltzer, Milton, and Lincoln, C. Eric. *African-American History*. Scholastic, New York, 1970. (S)

July, Robert. *A History of the African People*. Praeger Press, New York, Scribners, 1986. (S)

Kimble, George H.T. *Tropical Africa: Land and Livelihood*. Volume I, and "Society and Polity," Volume II, Twentieth Century Fund, New York, 1960. (S)

Kolevzon, Edward. *The Afro-Asian World*. Allyn & Bacon, Inc., Boston, 1972. (S)

Marquand, Leo. *The Peoples and Policies of South Africa*. Oxford University Press, New York, 1969. (S)

Oliver, Roland. *The Middle Age of African History*. Oxford University Press, London, 1967. (S)

———. *The Dawn of African History*. Oxford University Press, New York, 1968. (S)

Ottenburg, Simon and Phoebe. *Cultures and Societies in Africa*. Random House, New York, 1960. (S)

Rich, E. and Wallerstein, I. *Africa: Tradition and Change*. Random House, New York, 1973. (S)

Rodney, W. *West Africa and the Atlantic Slave Trade*. Northwestern University, Chicago, 1967. (S)

Toppin, Edgar. *The Black Man in the United States*. Allyn & Bacon, 1973. (S)

Turnbull, Colin. *The Lonely African*. Anchor Press, New York, 1963. (S)

Ward, Baldwin H. *Pictorial History of the Black American*. Year, 1973. (S)

Zell, Hans and Silver, Helene. *A Reader's Guide to African Literature*. African Publishing Corporation, New York, Holmes and Meier, 1983.

Chapter 2 — Blacks in America — Revolution Era, Slavery, The Civil War, Reconstruction

Allen, Richard. "The Life, Experience, and Gospel Labors of the Rt. Rev. Richard Allen." Philadelphia, 1887. (P)

Aptheker, Herbert. *American Negro Slave Revolts*. New York, International Publishing Co., 1993. (S)

Baker, T. Lindsay and Julie P. Baker. *The WPA Oklahoma Narratives*. University of Oklahoma Press, Norman, 1996.

Bancroft, George. *History of the United States from the Discovery of the American Continent*. (8 vols), BCLI, U.S. History Service, 1970 reprint of 1858 ed. (S)

Baylor University Archives. "Slave Narratives: WPA Project," 1930's. Waco, Texas. (P)

Blassingame, John W. *The Slave Community, Plantation Life in the Antebellum South*. Oxford University Press, 1979 (1940). (S)

Brown, Henry Box. "Narrative of Henry Box Brown." Boston, 1851. (P)

Brown, John. *Slave Life in Georgia*. London, 1855. (P)

Brown, William Wells. "Narrative of William W. Brown, A Fugitive Slave." Boston, 1847. (P)

Catteral, Helen T. "Judicial Cases Concerning American Slavery and the Negro," Washington, 1929. (S)

Curtin, Philip D. *The Atlantic Slave Trade: A Census*. University of Wisconsin, Madison, 1969. (S)

Delaney, Lucy Ann. "From the Darkness Cometh the Light: Or Struggles for Freedom." St. Louis, n.d. (P)

Douglass, Frederick. "My Bondage and My Freedom." New York, 1855. (P)

Elkins, Stanley. *Slavery: A Problem in American Institutional and Intellectual Life*.Chicago, 1959. (S)

Fisher, Miles Mark. "Negro Slave Songs in the United States." South Carolina, The Citadel Press, 1978 reprint of 1953 ed. (P)

Fogel, Robert W. and Engerman, Stanley. *Time on the Cross: The Economics of American Negro Slavery*. 2 vols,. New York, W.W. Norton Company, 1995 reprint of 1974 ed. (S)

Franklin, Dr. John Hope. *From Slavery to Freedom: A History of American Negroes*.New York, Alfred A. Knopf, 1956. (S)

Frazier, E. Franklin. *The Negro in the United States*. New York, Free Press, 1965 reprint of 1949 ed. (S)

Genovese, Eugene D. *The Political Economy of Slavery*. New York, Random House, 1965. (S)

———. *Roll, Jordan, Roll: The World the Slaves Made*. New York, Random House, 1974. (S)

Gutman, Herbert. *The Black Family in Slavery and Freedom, 1750-1925*. New York, 1976. (S)

Hart, Albert Bushnell. *Social and Economic Forces in American History*.Chautauqua Home Reading Series, Harper & Brothers, 1915. (S)

Henson, Josiah. *The Life of Josiah Henson*. Boston, 1849. (P)

Korn, Bertram W. "Jews and Negro Slavery in the Old South." Elkins Park, Pa., American Jewish History, 1961. (S)

Hurston, Zora Neale. "Cudjo's Own Story of the Last African Slaver," *Journal of Negro History*, XII, October 1927. (P)

Langston, John Mercer. *From Virginia Plantation to the National Capital*. Hartford, 1894. (P)

McKitrick, Eric L. *Slavery Defended: The Views of the Old South*. Prentice-Hall, Englewood Cliffs, N.J., 1963. (S)

National Archives, Washington, D.C. "Records of Freedmen and Abandoned Lands" Record Group 105. (P)

Oklahoma Historical Society. "Slave Narratives: WPA Project, 1930s." Oklahoma City, Oklahoma. (P)

Olmsted, Frederick Law. *A Journey in the Seaboard Slave States*. New York, 1856. (S)

Phillips, Ulrich Bonnell. *American Negro Slavery*. New York, 1918. (S)

———. *Life and Labor in the Old South*. Boston, 1929. (S)

Rawick, George P., ed. "The American Slave: A Composite Autobiography." 31 vols. (WPA Interviews, 1930s), 1978 (1972). (P)

Savit, Todd L. *Medicine and Slavery*. Urbana, Illinois, 1978. (S)

Sharp, William F. *Slavery on the Spanish Frontier: The Colombian Choco, 1680-1810*. Norman, Oklahoma, 1976. (S)

Stampp, Dr. Kenneth. "The Historian and Southern Negro Slavery." *American Historical Review*, LVII, April, 1952. (A)

———. *The Peculiar Institution*. Random House, New York, 1956. (S)

Still, William. *The Underground Railroad*. Philadelphia, 1872. (P)

Vassa, Gustavas (Olaudah Equiano). "The Interesting Narrative of the Life of Olaudah Equiano or Gustavas Vassa, the African." London, 1794. (P)

Washington, Booker T. *Up From Slavery*. Cambridge, 1928. (P)

Woodson, Carter G. *Education of the Negro Prior to 1860*. Washington, D.C., 1919. (S)

Chapter 3 — Reconstruction; The Freedmen Era

Billington, Ray Allen. *Westward Expansion: A History of the American Frontier*. Macmillan, New York, 1974. (S)

Coulter, E. Merton. *The South During Reconstruction, 1865-1877*. Louisiana State University Press, Baton Rouge, 1947. (S)

Du Bois, W.E.B. "The Freedmen's Bureau." *Atlantic Monthly*, LXXXVII, 1901. (A)

———. "Black Reconstruction: An Essay toward a History of the Part Which

Black Folk Played in the Attempt to Reconstruct America, 1860-1880." New York, 1935. (S)

————. *The Souls of Black Folk*. New York, Amereon, Ltd., 1976 reprint.

Dunning, William Archibald. *Reconstruction: Political and Economic*. Essay Index Reprint Service, 1977 reprint of 1907 ed. (S)

Fleming, Walter Lynwood. *Documentary History of Reconstruction*, BCLI - U.S. History Service, 1993 reprint of 1907 ed. (S)

————. (ed). *Documentary History of Reconstruction: Political, Military, Social, Religious, Educational, Industrial, 1865-1906*. New York, 1966. (S)

Franklin, Dr. John Hope. *Reconstruction After the Civil War*. University of Chicago Press, 1961. (S)

————. *Reminiscences of an Active Life: The Autobiography of John Roy Lynch*.University of Chicago Press, 1970. (P)

Leckie, William. *The Buffalo Soldiers*. The University of Oklahoma Press, Norman, 1975. (S)

Micheaux, Oscar. *The Conquest: The Story of a Negro Pioneer*. University of Nebraska Press, Lincoln, Nebraska. Reprinted 1994 from original 1913 ed. by Woodruff Press, Lincoln, Nebraska.

————. *The Homesteader: A Novel*. University of Nebraska Press, Lincoln, Nebraska. Reprinted from 1917 ed. published by the Western Book Supply Company, Sioux City, Iowa.

Perman, Michael. *Reunion without Compromise: The South and Reconstruction, 1865-1868*. Boston, Cambridge University Press, 1973.(S)

Pierce, Paul S. *The Freedmen's Bureau*. Iowa City, 1904. (S)

Simpkins, Francis B. "New Viewpoints of Southern Reconstruction" *American Historical Review*, XLV, 1939-1940. (A)

Taylor, A.A. "Historians of the Reconstruction." *Journal of Negro History*, XXIII, 1938. (A)

Quarles, Benjamin. *The Negro in the Civil War*. University of North Carolina Press, 1961. (S)

————. *The Negro in the American Revolution*. Duke University, Chapel Hill, North Carolina, 1961. (S)

Stuart, Charles Allen. *RFD*. New York, W.W. Norton and Company, 1938. (P)

Wilson, Elinor. *Jim Beckwourth*. (Black Frontiersman). University of Oklahoma Press, Norman, 1980. (S)

Woodward, C. Vann. *Origins of the New South, 1877-1913*. Louisiana State University Press, Baton Rouge, 1951. (S)

Chapter 3 — Expansion; Migration; Oklahoma; Tulsa

Beers, Fred. *Shoeing and Blacksmithing, The First Generation: A Half Century of Pioneering in Perry, Oklahoma*. The Charles Machine Works, Inc. (Ditch Witch), Ponca City, Oklahoma, 1991. (P)

Berkhofer, Robert F., Jr. *The White Man's Indian: Images of the American Indian from Columbus to the Present*. New York, Random House, 1978. (S)

Clarke, Milton and Lewis. "Narratives of the Sufferings of Lewis and Milton Clarke." Boston, 1846. (P)

Collings, Ellsworth, and England, Alma Miller. *The 101 Ranch.* University of Oklahoma Press, Norman, 1937, 1971.

Debo, Dr. Angie. *Prairie City.* Council Oak Books, Tulsa, Oklahoma, 1985 from book originally published by Alfred A. Knopf, Inc., 1944. (S)

Dershowitz, Alan. *Chutzpah.* Little, Brown, and Company, Boston, 1991. (P)

Dunn, Nina Lane. *Tulsa's Magic Roots.* Oklahoma Book Publishing Company, 1979. (S)

Easter, Eric, Cheers, D. Michael, and Brooks, Dudley. *Songs of My People: African Americans: A Self-Portrait.* Little, Brown and Company, Boston, 1992. (P)

Ellsworth, Scott. *Death in the Promised Land.* Baton Rouge, Louisiana University Press, 1982. (S)

Halliburton, Dr. Rudy. *Red Over Black, Black Slavery Among the Cherokee Indians.* Greenwood Press, Westport, Connecticut, 1977. (S)

Impact Magazine. "The Disaster of the 1921 Race Riot." Tulsa, Oklahoma, June-July Issue, 1971.

Ketchum, Richard M. *Will Rogers: His Life and Times.* American History Publishing Company (Distributed by McGraw Hill), New York, 1973. (S)

Lanker, Brian. *I Dream A World: Portraits of Black Women Who Changed America.* Stewart, Tabori, & Chang, New York, 1989. (P)

Littlefield, Dr. Daniel. *The Cherokee Freedmen.* Westport, Connecticut, Greenwood Press, 1978. (S)

"Oklahoma Eagle" Newspaper. "Second Annual Greenwood Jazz Celebration," Tulsa, Oklahoma, August, 1989. (A)

Oklahoma Historical Society Archives, Oklahoma City, Oklahoma.

Oklahoma Tourism and Recreation Department, "Oklahoma Today" Magazine, July-August. Oklahoma City, Oklahoma, 1992, pp. 30-37. (A)

Parrish, Mary Elizabeth Jones. *The Event of the Tulsa Disaster: The Race Riot of 1921.* Tulsa, 1921. (Privately Published). (P)

Sober, Nancy Hope. *The Intruders, The Illegal Residents of the Cherokee Nation.* Ponca City, OK, Cherokee Books, 1991. (S)

Stanton, Elizabeth Cady, et al (eds). "History of Woman Suffrage," 1881-1992, 6 vols. (S)

Tulsa Historical Society Archives, Tulsa, Oklahoma.

Tulsa Junior College. "Climbing Jacob's Ladder: Oklahoma: Where East Meets West, The Role of Black Churches in the Development of Oklahoma." Printing by Sun Oil Company, Tulsa, Oklahoma, 1992. (S)

White, Walter. *The Nation* Magazine. National NAACP, New York, 1921. (A)

Willows, Maurice. *The American Red Cross Report.* Tulsa, Oklahoma, December 1921.

Miscellaneous:

Kimball, Yeffe and Anderson, Jean. *The Art of American Indian Cooking.* Simon & Schuster, Inc., New York, 1965.

Kraus, Barbara. *The Cookbook of the United Nations: 350 Recipes from Member Nations.* Simon & Schuster, Inc., New York, 1970.

Odarty (Odaatey), Bill. *A Safari of African Cooking.* Visas Choice International, Flushing, New York, 1992.

Index